# LOCAL JUSTICE
# IN AMERICA

# LOCAL JUSTICE
# IN AMERICA

---

*Jon Elster*
*EDITOR*

*Russell Sage Foundation* • *New York*

## The Russell Sage Foundation

The Russell Sage Foundation, one of the oldest of America's general purpose foundations, was established in 1907 by Mrs. Margaret Olivia Sage for "the improvement of social and living conditions in the United States." The Foundation seeks to fulfill this mandate by fostering the development and dissemination of knowledge about the country's political, social, and economic problems. While the Foundation endeavors to assure the accuracy and objectivity of each book it publishes, the conclusions and interpretations in Russell Sage Foundation publications are those of the authors and not of the Foundation, its Trustees, or its staff. Publication by Russell Sage, therefore, does not imply Foundation endorsement.

**Library of Congress Cataloging-in-Publication Data**

Local justice in America / Jon Elster, editor.
    p.  cm
    Includes bibliographical references (p.    ) and index.
    ISBN 0-87154-233-1
    1. Social justice—Case studies.  2. Social choice—United States—Case studies.  3. Distributive justice—Case studies.  4. United States—Social conditions—Case studies.  I. Elster, Jon, 1940–
HM216.L63  1995
303.3'72—dc20                               94-39623
                                                   CIP

The paper used in this publication meets the minimum requirements of American National Standard for Information Sciences—Permanence of Paper for Printed Library Materials. ANSI Z39.48-1992.

Text design by Marilyn Marcus.

RUSSELL SAGE FOUNDATION
112 East 64th Street, New York, New York 10021

10 9 8 7 6 5 4 3 2 1

# Contents

# Contributors

**Jon Elster** is Robert K. Merton Professor of Social Science at Columbia University.

**Patricia Conley** is assistant professor of political science at Northwestern University.

**J. Michael Dennis** is a consultant with ABT Associates in Chicago.

**Gerry Mackie** is a graduate student in the department of political science at the University of Chicago.

**Stuart Romm** works as a computer analyst in Chicago.

# Preface and Acknowledgments

## *Jon Elster*

T HIS VOLUME is the third book-length publication from the "local justice" projects that have been underway in the United States, France, Norway, Germany, and Brazil since 1987. The first was my book, *Local Justice* (1992), which outlined a general conceptual and explanatory framework for the study of in-kind allocations of scarce goods and necessary burdens. Because that volume covered allocative systems for a number of goods and in a number of countries, it was necessarily somewhat sketchy with regard to empirical detail. The second volume, *Éthique des choix médicaux* (1992), edited by Nicolas Herpin and myself, was a more narrowly focused analysis of the allocation of kidneys for transplantation in the United States, France, and Norway.[1] That volume also contains a study by Herpin of the French system of allocating sperm for artificial insemination. The present volume also aims at achieving more depth at the expense of breadth, by close-up studies of allocative processes in one country—the United States.

The American local justice project was originally planned to cover three arenas: health, education, and work. It was and remains my belief that the allocation of scarce goods in these domains is a crucial determinant of the life chances of individuals. When the project was nearing completion, however, I decided that the allocation of citizenship through immigration and naturalization also belonged among these fundamental processes, especially in a country with high rates of immigration such as the United States. The timing had consequences for the methodology. The chapters below on college admission, kidney transplantation, and worker layoffs build on extensive original research, in the form of interviews, participant observation, and surveys. Because there was not time to carry out a similar analysis of the immigration process, the chapter devoted to that issue is based on secondary sources only.

Today, I wish that I had had the occasion to include a further set of questions: those related to children, parenting, and old age. The issues of child custody, child placement, adoption (where the scarce good can be either the child or the parent), admission to nursery schools (which can be a scarce good either for the child or the parent), and admission to nursing homes (which can be a scarce good either for the old people concerned or for their relatives) are pervasive sources of misery and conflict, and they provide some of the most striking illustrations of the dilemmas of allocation. The reader is referred to other publications for local justice analyses of child custody, of nursery schools (in Norway), and of adoption (in the United States).[2] Herpin's study of artificial insemination in France is also relevant here.

This volume is intended to be relatively self-contained. In the Introduction, therefore, I lay out some of the main organizing principles that are discussed at greater length in *Local Justice*. The following chapters offer detailed analyses of allocative practices in the fields of education, health, work, and citizenship. They offer vivid demonstrations of the complexity and variety that seem to be features of all systems of decentralized in-kind allocation. They also show how these local processes take place in a larger context of political struggles and secular changes in the value systems of the citizens. One reviewer has remarked (*Journal of Public Policy* 12, 4) that in *Local Justice* national politics were curiously absent. I agree, but I also believe that the present volume does something to redress that imbalance. In the Conclusion, finally, I try to say something about the distinguishing features of local justice *in America*. Not surprisingly, matters of race and ethnicity are at the forefront. Other key features of American allocative systems are the fear of discretion and the emphasis on effort and merit as bases for allocation.

Acknowledgments to individuals were given in the Preface to *Local Justice*. I want to emphasize, however, the contributions of Steven Laymon to the local justice project in general and to the study of education in particular. For comments on the Introduction and Conclusion to the present volume thanks are due to Jonathan Cole, Patricia Conley, Ingrid Creppell, Michael Dawson, Gerry Mackie, David Messick, Stuart Romm, Cass Sunstein, and two anonymous reviewers. At the institutional level, the main acknowledgment is to the generous support of the Russell Sage Foundation. The chapter on education received additional support from the Spencer Foundation and the College Board.

## NOTES

1. English translation, London: Frances Pinter, 1994.

2. J. Elster, *Solomonic Judgements,* Cambridge: Cambridge University Press 1989, Chapter 3; M. Toft and D. McIntyre, "Adoption as an Issue of Local Justice," *Archives Européennes de Sociologie* 33 (1992), 83–108; B. Rasch, "Barnets Beste. Om Fordeling av Barnehageplasser" ("The Best Interest of the Child. On the Allocation of Places in Kindergarten"), Working Paper #3 1990, Institute for Social Research, Oslo.

## CHAPTER ONE

# Introduction:
# The Idea of Local Justice

## *Jon Elster*

L OCAL JUSTICE deals with decentralized in-kind allocation of scarce goods and necessary burdens. In the present volume we discuss the allocation of three goods—college admission, kidneys for transplantation, and immigration rights—and of one burden, viz., layoffs from work. In my earlier book, *Local Justice,* I also considered, albeit much more briefly, the following:

- military service in wartime
- demobilization from the army
- allocation of sperm for artificial insemination
- selection of adoptive parents
- award of child custody
- admission to kindergarten
- division of household work
- allocation of prison space
- rationing in wartime

The task of this introduction is to introduce the basic conceptual issues of local justice problems and to illustrate them with examples taken from the four case studies developed in subsequent chapters. Basically, therefore, what follows is a condensed and more narrowly focused version of Chapters Two through Five of *Local Justice.* More substantive comments on local justice in

America, as revealed by the case studies, are reserved for the conclusion.

## The Magnitude of the Problem

To assess the importance of local justice issues in the life of the citizens, one would have to take account of the full range of such questions that can arise in the lifetime of an individual, from the nursery school to the nursing home. I believe we would find that local justice decisions are no less important than the market and redistributive state policies in shaping the life-chances of the individual. This will have to stand as conjecture. It is possible, however, to be more precise about the four issues discussed in the following chapters.

To begin with, importance can be assessed from two points of view. On one hand, we can ask how many individuals are affected by a given type of allocative justice. On the other hand, we can ask how strongly it affects each of those individuals. Immigration becomes very important on both dimensions: it affects huge numbers of would-be immigrants in other countries, for each of whom immigration to the United States is intensely desirable. From a different perspective, the volume and composition of immigration are also very important for those who are already U.S. citizens, notably in an era of kin-based immigration. In quantitative terms, the Immigration Act of 1990 targets about 700,000 immigrant admissions per year.

Going to college is an important determinant of life chances. Going to a particular college is less important. Admissions officers administer a good that is sought after by very many and that may be seen as very important or relatively unimportant, depending on which of these two perspectives is chosen. In quantitative terms, nearly 1½ million students move from high school to one of nearly 3,000 colleges every year. Of these, about half are 4-year colleges that exercise some selection among applicants.

Being laid off from a job can be a very bad thing; keeping your job can be very important. It is also a problem that affects a substantial number of individuals. From 1981 to 1985, 5.1 million workers with 3 years or more of tenure on the job were displaced,

2.8 million due to plant closings, 2.3 million due to layoffs from continuing operations.

Because of the fallback option of dialysis, getting a kidney transplant is not a life-and-death issue (unlike heart and liver transplants). A transplant does, however, represent a very substantial improvement in the quality of life. Currently, over 24,000 people are waiting for cadaveric kidneys, while the available supply of cadaveric kidneys per year has varied between 6,900 and about 7,800 in recent years. In addition, about 2,000 kidneys from living donors are made available each year.

## Goods Versus Burdens

In a formal sense, the distinction between goods and burdens is inessential because exemption from a burden can always be conceptualized as a good. In a psychological sense, however, the distinction matters. To assume a burden constitutes a loss compared to the status quo, whereas getting a good represents a gain. Because people have different attitudes toward gains and losses,[1] we should expect to see different principles used in their allocation.[2] For the sake of convenience, this introduction refers only to "goods" as a shorthand for goods and burdens.

Occasionally, it may be hard to say whether a given object of allocation is a good or a bad. As Romm notes in Chapter Four, in many collective bargaining agreements, "senior workers have the right to waive their seniority and take layoff. Apparently, they often do so in the event of temporary layoffs." But in the cases discussed in the present volume, this ambiguity is marginal.

## Some Characteristics of Goods

Four major dimensions of the goods allocated in local justice systems are rigidity of supply, divisibility, homogeneity, and scarcity.

Goods are rigid in supply if there are no reliable ways of increasing the available amounts at short notice. The supply of kidneys, for instance, fluctuates for a number of reasons. Also, the government might take legislative steps in order to affect the long-term determinants of supply. But at any given time hospitals cannot promise a patient that a kidney will be forthcoming, even disregarding the question of goodness of match. The rigidity is overcome only in countries (such as Norway) that rely heavily on relatives as living donors. After kidney allocation, we can rank jobs, college places, and immigration in increasing order of flexibility. These are goods that are either divisible (jobs) or easily expandable at short notice, either at the margin (college places) or in large numbers (immigration places).

Goods can be divisible or indivisible. Because few goods are literally indivisible, indivisibility must be taken to mean that division would entail a drastic reduction or even destruction of the good's utility. To cut a child in two, as in Solomon's first judgment, would not leave anything of value. By contrast, dividing a loaf of bread in two parts entails an increase in total utility, assuming that bread has decreasing marginal utility for each consumer and that the utility functions of different consumers are roughly similar. An intermediate case is found in St. John 19:23–24: "Then the soldiers, when they had crucified Jesus, took his garments, and made four parts, to every soldier a part; and also his coat; now the coat was without seam, woven from the top throughout. They said therefore among themselves, Let us not rend it, but cast lots for it, whose it shall be." The coat would not have been rendered entirely worthless by being cut into four parts. If they had been sufficiently risk averse the soldiers might have preferred getting a quarter of the cloth with certainty over a 25 percent chance of getting the entire coat.[3]

In the local justice issues considered below, the only divisible good is that of work. In this case, work-sharing is a prominent alternative to layoffs and is currently considered in several European countries as a way of reducing double-digit unemployment figures. In general, such schemes may involve either losses or gains in productive efficiency. If there are losses, the employer may insist on lower wages. Yet even working at lower wages, employees may experience a utility gain (compared to a layoff lottery) because of the increasing marginal utility of money. And even if there is no such gain, they may prefer work-sharing because of risk aversion.

Next, the goods to be allocated can be homogeneous or heterogeneous. When nothing matters beyond the simple decision of Yes or No, as in immigration, the good is homogeneous; otherwise it is heterogeneous. Heterogeneity can matter in two ways. First, some units of the good may be of inherently higher quality, so as to be more intensely desired by all applicants. Second, some units of the goods may be superior in the eyes of some individuals, but inferior in the eyes of others. Although admission to college in itself is a homogeneous good, the coupling of admission with financial aid gives rise to the first kind of heterogeneity (unless the amount of aid is the same for all). Even with open admission (i.e., in the absence of scarcity), the allocation of financial aid would still create issues of distributive justice. Kidneys are also heterogeneous, because a given kidney may be more or less suitable for a given recipient. Getting a kidney is not all that matters: it is also important to get one with a good match. This illustrates the second kind of heterogeneity. Heterogeneity (especially of the second kind) is a reason against using an allocating mechanism that fails to differentiate among recipients, such as equal division, rotation, lotteries, or queuing. It may or may not be a decisive reason, depending on how and how much the heterogeneity matters and on the strength of other considerations.

Finally, the good can be scarce or abundant. By abundance, I mean that there is enough of the good to satiate everybody who wants or needs it. With indivisible goods, such as immigration, kidneys, or college places, abundance means that there are enough units to satisfy all applicants. With a divisible good, such as work, abundance means that everyone can work as many hours as he or she wants at the going rates. (Note that the allocation of overtime work can also be a matter of local justice.) In cases where there are both homogeneity and abundance, no issues of distributive justice can arise. Although the cases discussed below are all characterized by scarcity, with or without homogeneity, there are instances in which the distributive conflicts are due to heterogeneity under conditions of abundance. The allocation of dormitory places to students or of committee places to legislators are examples.[4] In some countries, parts of the system of higher education also function in this manner: although everyone is guaranteed a place at some university, not all universities are equally attractive or not equally attractive to all applicants. Although Conley's analysis below of college admissions considers the process only from the point of view of the individual university, one might argue that in the whole system of selective colleges almost all applicants are eventually accepted somewhere (partly, however, because of self-selection). In the terminology to be explained below, although each college uses a selection procedure, the system as a whole approaches a placement procedure.

## Selection, Admission, and Placement

Following Willem Hofstee,[5] I distinguish among selection, admission, and placement as procedures for allocating indivisible goods. A selection procedure compares individuals against each other, usually by producing a ranking list, and accepts them by starting at the top and going down the list until the good is exhausted. An admission procedure compares individuals against an absolute threshold and offers the good to all those and only those who exceed the threshold. A placement procedure regulates the allocation of nonscarce heterogeneous goods, ensuring that each individual ends up with some unit of the good.

Among the goods discussed here, college places, layoffs, and kidneys for transplantation are allocated by selection procedures. In the case of kidneys—a good with rigid supply—this could hardly be otherwise. Colleges, however, might choose to admit all those who fulfill certain criteria, which might be set so as to ensure an expected number of applicants that is compatible with the capacities and needs of the institution. Because universities can always accommodate marginal adjustments in teacher/student ratios and similar factors, small deviations from the expected number would not matter. Or one could have an admission system for one subset of applicants (e.g., in-state residents) and then use a selection system to fill up the remaining places. Because the pool of applicants is uncertain and comparisons among them are costly, such procedures might have some advantages from the institution's point of view. In the case of layoffs, however, the candidates for layoffs are known; moreover, the only way of establishing the desired cut-off point for (say) seniority is to establish each worker's seniority, which means that one might as well use a ranking list.

As Mackie explains in Chapter Five, the American immigration system has been and remains based partly on admission, partly on selection. On one hand, there is kin-based admission; on the other hand, there is selection by queuing, lotteries, and other procedures within overall quotas for different categories and regions. Because kin-based admission was adopted on the basis of its intrinsic justice rather than as a proxy for a numerical target, it has had a number of unforeseen consequences. In the terminology explained below, the use of admission here serves as a principle of first-order allocation and not—as is the case when admission is a proxy for a numerical target—as a second-order principle.

The four case studies have no examples of a full-blown placement system. The idea that college admission is an indirect placement system has already been noted. Mackie discusses proposals to organize refugee admission as a placement system, with several countries sharing the refugees among themselves.

## First-Order, Second-Order, and Third-Order Actors

Following Guido Calabresi and Philip Bobbit,[6] I distinguish between the first-order decisions that determine the amount of the scarce good that is available for distribution, and the second-order decisions that determine how that amount is to be allocated. I deviate from their usage by relying on a more inclusive concept of first-order decisions. Whereas they refer to these as decisions by "society," meaning presumably the political system, I include any decisions, by any set of actors, that are *intentionally* made for the purpose of affecting the supply of the scarce good. (Thus, a change in the speed limit that reduces the number of car accidents and thereby the supply of organs for transplantation is not a first-order determination of kidney transplants.) With regard to immigration, Congress and the president are the only first-order actors. With regard to college admissions, the first-order actors are the board of trustees or regents of the university. With regard to layoffs, first-order decisions are made by top management. With regard to kidneys, the supply is affected by legislative and financial measures and by the decisions by individuals whether to let their organs, or those of relatives, be used for transplantation purposes.

Second-order decisions about allocation are usually made by a different set of actors. The only exception is immigration: here Congress sets the criteria for admission as well as number of admittees. (In fact, as noted above, Congress has less control over the total number of immigrants than over the categories of individuals to be admitted.) In the allocation of college places, admissions officers, constrained by general university policies and (for public schools) by the legislature, are the main second-order actors. In the allocation of kidneys, transplant centers, heavily constrained by the centralized UNOS rules (see Chapter Three), make the crucial second-order decisions. In the selection of workers for layoffs, lower-level managers and personnel managers interact to produce the final list, as described in Romm's interviews. Although in most cases these managers are not directly constrained by legislation, they act to minimize the risk of litigation based on various antidiscrimination laws.

We may also introduce the concept of third-order actors: applicants for—or potential recipients of—the scarce good. In the most extended sense, this could include almost everybody. All non-Americans are potential immigrants to the United States, and everybody can get end-stage renal disease (ESRD). A more tractable idea is to define third-order actors as those who, under some set of current circumstances, would apply for the good. This includes not only actual applicants, but also those who would apply if the institutional rules were changed. Thus, some people may not apply for elite colleges because they know they cannot get in, but they would apply if those colleges switched to a lottery system. As noted above, some people may be deterred from getting on the list for transplantation because of the costly post-operative medication. The vast appeal of immigration lotteries indicates that the number of potential immigrants to the United States in this sense is large indeed.

There are a number of interaction effects among the three levels of decision. A change in the second-order rules may affect first-order decisions. Thus, as Dennis reports, for a while it was widely (but falsely) believed that allowing organs to be transplanted into foreign citizens would reduce the willingness of U.S. citizens to donate. More emphasis on seniority and less on ability in layoff procedures may cause a reduction in profits and thus a need to lay off more workers. Conversely, a change in the total amount to be allocated may affect the rules of allocation, typically (I conjecture) such that reductions lead to more emphasis on efficiency while increases give more space for equity. New second-order rules can induce new third-order decisions, as applicants modify their behavior so as to become entitled to the scarce good. The use of seniority as a layoff principle induces people to stay in the firm, just as skill-based immigration selection induces potential immigrants to acquire scarce skills, and merit-based admission criteria induce students to work hard in high school. Conversely, unforeseen and undesirable third-order adaptation may induce changes in the second-order rules, to close loopholes. If would-be applicants to a public college begin moving to the state in order to benefit from the less stringent admission criteria or lower tuition rates for residents, the college may respond by imposing a one-year residency condition.

## The Place of Money in Local Justice Systems

In *Local Justice* I defined this concept so as to exclude the allocation of money. Although many decentralized allocation processes do concern money, they are usually linked up with the global systems of transfers, subsidies, pensions, and the like. (Here and later *global* refers to the society-wide context, not to the international community.) The progressive income tax, for instance, undoes part of the inequality that is created in the labor market. By contrast, in-kind allocation is rarely subject to mechanisms of this kind. The losers are not compensated. Layoffs are an obvious exception to this statement because of the existence of unemployment benefits. Note, however, that this compensation occurs in the context of allocating a burden rather than a good. Because of the salience of the status quo, there will always be pressure to minimize negative deviations from the reference point.

I should add that in the previous paragraph I conflated two issues that really ought to be kept separate: the place of money in the allocation process and the existence of compensation for the losers. One could well imagine that those who fail in one arena received in-kind compensation in the form of goods allocated in another arena. Those who are laid off from work might get priority in the college admissions process. Although this mechanism is not in fact observed, a similar one is: Drafted war veterans—the losers in the selection for the burden of doing military service—often get priority for jobs, notably government jobs, and for college and medical treatment. (However, volunteers and career soldiers also enjoy these advantages.)

In addition to money being used to compensate the losers, it can be offered to the winners to enable them to accept the scarce good they have been offered. Colleges do not decide only whom to admit and whom to refuse; they also decide on financial aid to those who are admitted. A similar complementarity between a scarce good and financial aid exists in the arena of kidney transplantation. As Dennis observes in Chapter Three, because of the limited Medicare coverage of post-transplantation medical expenses, "prospective transplant recipients who lack private health insurance might be deterred or even screened out." This observation indicates that money, in addition to being an object of allocation, also can serve as a mechanism of allocation. If the scarce good is useless without money, then refusal to give financial aid effectively amounts to a screening process. As Conley writes in her chapter below, when Yale University wanted to keep Jews out, "financial aid was limited for Jews by limiting financial aid to poor students in general."

Money can also be used as an allocation mechanism in a much more direct way—by allowing the better-off to buy the scarce good for themselves. While common in many other times, places, and arenas, in the United States today this practice is marginal in the four arenas we are considering. Nearly all U.S. universities use "need-blind" admission, in the sense that no student is turned away on the basis of inability to meet the costs of higher education. However, some financially strapped colleges such as Brown and Smith have recently abandoned this policy. Under the current American immigration scheme, 10,000 visas a year (less than 2 percent of the total) are available for those who will invest a million dollars or more in job-creating enterprise employing at least 10 U.S. workers. The National Organ Transplantation Act of 1984 prohibits the purchase of organs for transplantation. Although one might imagine workers who are candidates for layoffs paying the firm money to keep their jobs, the idea is obviously impracticable and would certainly be illegal. Although one does observe workers taking a wage cut to avoid layoffs, this does not take the form of competition among individual employees.

Finally, income and wealth can be used as status criteria (see below). The "God committee" that allocated dialysis in Seattle (see Dennis's Chapter Three) used income and net worth as indicators of social usefulness. In this case, it was not a question of *using* one's wealth to get the scarce good: rather the mere *possession* of wealth showed that one was worthy of getting it.

## Criteria and Mechanisms of Allocation

With the exception of immigration policy, none of the arenas we are considering has a uniform allocation procedure. Private colleges essentially do what they want. With regard to public colleges, admission procedures may be uniform within a state, but can differ strongly across states. Private enterprises use widely differing layoff procedures. Although unionized firms are more likely than the nonunionized to use seniority as a main criterion, the way in which it is implemented and combined with other criteria is far from standardized. More surprisingly, perhaps, the UNOS rules for kidney allocation turn out to have a large scope for local variations (contingent on UNOS approval).

This being said, the elementary building blocks that are used in a given arena are pretty much the same. These pure principles—to be discussed in a moment—are virtually never used by themselves to the exclusion of others. Rather, we find that in the allocation of a given good a number of different criteria and mechanisms are used, in succession or in combination. Mixed principles is the virtually exceptionless rule in local justice. In cases such as immigration policy, the complexity of the mix can become Byzantine in the extreme, as the reader will glean from Mackie's Chapter Five. The other arenas do not, however, lag far behind. Local justice is like a coastline: When we move closer up, the larger-scale variations reproduce themselves in ever-finer grain.

I distinguish among four main categories of pure principles: egalitarian criteria; queuing mechanisms; status-based criteria;

and a trio of criteria based on the individual's situation and performance in, respectively, the past, the present, and the future.

*Egalitarian criteria.* Equal division is often seen as a baseline, the procedure to be used in the absence of reasons to the contrary. (See the final section of the Conclusion, however, for an argument that in matters of local justice *efficiency* is more frequently used as a baseline.) However, the principle of physically dividing the scarce good so as to give equal amounts to everybody is inapplicable in the arenas of immigration, transplantation, and college admission. Jobs can be divided, however, as witnessed by the use of work-sharing as an alternative to layoffs. Romm's case studies do not find much evidence of work-sharing in practice, however.

When physical division will not work, there is always the alternative of dividing the good probabilistically—through an equal-chance lottery.[7] Although this mechanism has occasionally been proposed for layoffs, kidneys, and college places, it has never to my knowledge been adopted in practice in any of these arenas. Many admission officers will agree that, for a subset of the applicants, the decision to accept some and reject others is for all practical purposes a random event, but they shy back from using a formal lottery. The explanation may lie in Conley's observation that the admission officers to whom she spoke "did not want to alienate guidance counselors or applicants by arbitrary or nonsensical patterns of acceptances and rejections," such as might have been produced by a lottery device. The one arena in which lotteries are extensively used is immigration. Although the visas are actually awarded by a procedure of first-come, first-served by order of mail receipt, under the circumstances (almost a million applications for a few thousand positions) it mimics the features of a fair lottery.

*Queuing.* I use this word as a general term for a number of different mechanisms that are all based on the sheer passage of time. First, there is queuing proper—standing, sitting, or lying in line for the scarce good. This procedure is not used in any of the cases studied here. Second, there is allocation according to one's place on a waiting list, a procedure that is a partial determinant of the allocation of kidneys and of immigration places. Third, there is allocation according to seniority, a procedure that is extensively observed in layoff situations. Finally, there is allocation according to age. This criterion can also be seen as a status-based principle. Note that college admission is the only arena in which no form of queuing is used.

When a queuing mechanism is used as the only principle of allocation, only the ordinal aspect of the ranking matters. As mentioned above, however, no actual processes are based on a single principle. When combined with other criteria, one can also take account of the cardinal aspect of the ranking. Romm finds that in some collective bargaining arrangements there is a quality-seniority tradeoff, in which length of seniority and not only the mere fact of seniority matters. In the early forms of the UNOS allocation system, candidates for transplantation received points for their ordinal place on the waiting list, a system that is capable of producing anomalies.[8] More recent forms, based on the number of months on the waiting list, are not vulnerable to this problem.

**Status-based criteria.** Status properties belong to the individual by virtue of biological, behavioral, or institutional determinations. (The phrase is vague and perhaps inadequate: the reader is asked to focus instead on the examples that follow.) Status properties that can matter for local justice include age; gender; race and ethnicity; bodily features, such as height, weight, and color of eyes or hair; physical and mental disabilities; literacy; sexual orientation; wealth; residence; occupation; trade union membership; religion; citizenship; marital status; and kinship. Sometimes these criteria are used because they are believed to be appropriate in their own right: American citizens ought to understand English. In other cases, they are used as observable proxies for other criteria: kin-based immigration is based on an assumption that close relatives have a need to be with each other.

The active reliance on status criteria is most prominent in immigration policy. The main status criteria used to screen immigrants have been literacy, national origin, place of birth (not—as Mackie explains—always the same as national origin), occupation, marital status, and kinship. In other arenas, status is today increasingly seen as irrelevant. Whereas earlier generations of applicants to college could be asked to send a photo or indicate their height and weight (to screen out the socially and ethnically undesirable), such practices have been discontinued. But children of alumni and staff still get preferential treatment in admission, as do in-state residents when applying to state universities.

Yet these are secondary matters compared to the overwhelming importance of race and, to a somewhat lesser extent, gender. A full discussion of the role of these criteria is postponed until the Conclusion. Here I note only that they can enter the picture in three different ways. First, there is the principle that allocation shall be status-blind: it ought to proceed as if the applicants' race or sex were unknown. Next, there is the idea that allocation shall be status-representative, in the sense that the status composition of the recipients should match that of the population at large or, more frequently, of the applicants. Third, there is the idea of affirmative action: the allocation of goods such as college places and jobs shall be status-offsetting, to improve the position of less-favored groups in society.

***Desert, need, and efficiency.*** I group these criteria together, perhaps somewhat artificially, because they can be placed on a temporal continuum. Allocation according to desert looks to what the applicants have done in the past. Allocation according to need considers their situation in the present. Allocation according to efficiency compares how well they can use the scarce good to benefit themselves or others in the future. In addition, one may combine backward-looking and forward-looking schemes in *incentive systems,* which operate by telling individuals at time $t_1$ that their reward at time $t_3$ will depend on their performance at time $t_2$.

Layoffs according to seniority is often presented as a desert-based system: workers who have devoted their life to the firm deserve to be kept on. The practice can also be seen as an incentive system: to reduce turnover, management tells the workers that they are more likely to be protected from layoffs if they stay in the firm. Basing college admission on high-school grades can also be justified in both perspectives. Thus, nearly one-third of the admission officers in Conley's survey said that they used grades as an admission criterion to set the right incentives for high-school students. There may have been an element of desert reasoning when a large number of Vietnamese who had taken part in the

American war effort were accepted as refugees. (As far as I know no Vietnamese were induced to collaborate by promises of American citizenship in case the United States lost the war.) Neither desert reasoning nor incentive reasoning is used in the allocation of kidneys for transplantation. Although one might imagine a system in which people were turned down for transplantation if they get ESRD as a predictable outcome of their life style, proposals to this effect have not (yet) had much impact.

In our case studies, the most prominent use of need as an allocative criterion is found in kin-based immigration. There are also elements of need-based reasoning in the allocation of kidneys, notably when priority is given to patients who need a kidney urgently because of failure on dialysis. In such cases, however, the same priority can be justified on the basis of forward-looking reasoning. A kidney is used more efficiently if it raises the survival chances of one patient from 0 to, say, 50 percent than if it is used to get another patient who could survive on dialysis off that treatment.[9] In current American layoff practices, need—as measured by the number of family dependents—is not a major consideration, although management will sometimes take it into account.

Efficiency considerations, in the context of local justice, must not be confused with global ideas of utilitarianism or wealth-maximization. Only in the case of immigration decisions are efficiency criteria—giving preference to workers with rare skills and to people willing to invest in jobs for Americans—interpreted in a global sense. In the context of kidney allocation, efficiency is taken to mean that the kidney should be given to the patient with the smallest probability of graft rejection. We might get quite different choices if we wanted to maximize the number of life years spent off dialysis (a criterion that would favor young patients), and different results still if the idea was to minimize the cost of treatment (a criterion that would favor those who can go back to a paid job). In the layoff context, efficiency is often taken to imply that one should retain the more able workers in order to maximize the profits of the firm. Again, we might get very different choices if we took into account the social costs of caring for workers who are unable to find a job elsewhere (assuming that the firm could afford to retain them). With regard to education, efficiency is sometimes taken to mean that admissions should maximize "social value added." In practice, this criterion cannot be implemented. To do so, an admissions officer would have to calculate the difference between the social value that would be produced by admitting a given applicant and the value that would be produced if that candidate was accepted by some other college to which he had applied—a task that is essentially impossible, especially if admissions officers at other colleges are supposed to reason in the same manner. In practice, therefore, efficiency is usually taken to imply admission of the students who will graduate with the best grades.

*Mixed principles.* In practice, as I said, all systems of allocation are mixed. The mix can take a number of different forms. Sometimes a subset of the scarce good is allocated by one pure principle, another subset by a different principle, and so on. Immigration policy is organized along these lines, as detailed in Chapter Five below. In college admissions, an analogy is Harvard's former practice of creating a "happy bottom quarter" by admitting 25 percent of each class on athletic rather than scholastic criteria. The main procedure in admissions, as well as in layoff selection and kidney allocation, is nevertheless to apply uniform but complex principles to all candidates.

A common way of combining different pure principles is by using a point system. Kidney allocation in the United States is currently regulated by a procedure of this kind, with points given for medical efficiency (likelihood of graft survival, which is based on the number of antigen matches) and time on the waiting list. Some state colleges use a point system in their admissions process, with weights assigned to high-school grades and tests according to their ability to predict future performance. Informally, some colleges also assign points for disadvantages of various kinds. As Conley explains, this process may be backward-driven, in the sense that the weights are assigned so as to get a preset number of minority applicants admitted. In Chapter Five, Mackie details the failed attempt by Edward Kennedy and Alan Simpson to introduce point systems in the immigration process. Although such systems are occasionally used to regulate layoffs in other countries, this procedure is not observed in the United States.

Criteria may also be combined lexicographically, with the secondary criterion being used to break ties. If the first criterion is very coarse-grained, ties may be very common, so that the secondary criterion becomes in fact the more important one. As Romm explains in Chapter Four, this is the case for many layoff procedures that use seniority to break ability ties. Other layoff procedures follow a different two-step sequence. First, one determines the subset of candidates with "minimal qualifications" to do the job. In the next step, seniority is used to select from within this pool. Romm also points to the use of informal tradeoffs between level of qualification and length of seniority. In the college admissions system such tradeoffs are ubiquitous, especially in smaller institutions. Interviews with admissions officers show that the tradeoffs, while informal and intuitive, also have a great deal of structure (see the grid reproduced by Conley as Figure 2.1). A salient finding is that whereas many private institutions trade nonacademic excellence off against academic merit, public institutions are more likely to set up a tradeoff between economic or cultural disadvantage and academic merit.[10]

## Further Effects of These Criteria and Mechanisms

The primary effect of an allocative scheme is to channel the good to the group of recipients defined by the criteria and mechanisms embodied in the system. In addition, there are at least two other effects. First, the scheme may have a disparate impact on groups not specifically targeted or excluded by the scheme. If the scheme tells the allocators to direct the good to members of group X, and most X's are also Y's, then a de facto consequence of the scheme is to allocate the good disproportionately to members of Y. When these *secondary effects* are in fact intended by the rule makers, legal scholars refer to them as disparate intent. If a rule maker who wants to target group Y finds himself prevented by the law or public opinion from doing this, he may achieve substantially the same goal by allocating the good to X. (To escape detection, it may then be essential that only most—rather than all—X's are Y's.) Second, an allocative system may change the behavior of first-order and third-order decision makers by virtue of the *incentive effects* created by the scheme.

The theme of secondary effects or disparate impact has an

important place in all the case studies. On its face, Yale's rule of refusing financial aid to poor applicants (see above) was racially neutral. De facto, however, it had a disproportionate (and intended) impact on Jewish applicants. Another facially neutral Yale policy from the 1920s was that of seeking geographical diversity in the incoming class, thus (intentionally) reducing the number of applicants admitted from the populous and heavily Jewish state of New York. Today, as mentioned above, some schools will target the educationally disadvantaged as an indirect way of raising the number of minority students admitted.

In the layoff arena, Romm explains in some detail how seniority systems can have a disparate impact on women and members of minority groups. Although these systems are not in themselves discriminatory, their disparate impact is a result of past discrimination, which has prevented these employees from accumulating the necessary seniority. As a result, some courts have found that seniority systems are in violation of Title VII of the Civil Rights Act of 1964. (Most court decisions, however, go the other way.) Romm's interviews also show that managers are very aware of the possibility that a layoff scheme might have a disparate impact on members of protected groups.

With regard to transplantation, Dennis shows how the facially neutral principle of allocating kidneys according to medical efficiency leads to disproportionately fewer blacks receiving transplants. This outcome comes about for three reasons: blacks have different antigen patterns than those of the white population; they are overrepresented in the population of patients; and they are underrepresented in the population of donors. By contrast, he reports that the underrepresentation of women among the recipients of kidney transplants does not seem to be a secondary effect of the allocative system.

As Mackie explains, disparate intent is rampant in immigration. The facially neutral literacy test was intended to screen out immigrants from Southern and Eastern Europe and was abandoned when literacy in this region rose. Similarly, the search for a national-origins baseline to be used in calculating immigration quotas was blatantly influenced by the ethnic biases that would be produced.

I have already mentioned that local justice schemes can be

set up for the purpose of generating certain desirable incentives among the potential recipients. Many incentive effects, however, are entirely unintended and unforeseen. Often, rule makers naively assume that applicants for the scarce good are naive, in the sense that they will act as if they were ignorant of the rules. When applicants adapt strategically to the rules, the intentions of the rule makers may be thwarted. While quite important in many other arenas—for instance, if married men or students are exempt from military service, more will marry or go to college—this problem seems to be somewhat marginal in the four arenas under consideration here, which is not to say that it is totally absent. It is plausible that layoff systems based on seniority set up a disincentive for acquiring skills, but I have no information about the magnitude of this effect. If spouses are exempt from immigration quotas, some arranged marriages may result. Applicants to college may try to manipulate residence requirements to their advantage. If kidneys are made available to foreign nationals, some patients from abroad may visit the country who wouldn't otherwise have done so.

I have also mentioned that allocative rules can set up incentive effects for the first-order actors who determine the amount of the scarce good that will be available for allocation. In the four case studies, this connection seems to be important only in the field of kidney transplantation. According to Dennis, there is not much truth in the once-popular idea that allowing transplantation to foreign nationals reduces the willingness to donate organs. He argues, however, that there is a close connection between the system of kidney allocation and the level of kidney procurement. Because the actual extraction of a kidney has to be done by a transplant surgeon, allowing him to keep one of the two kidneys for use in his own transplantation center tends to stimulate his procurement efforts.

## Explaining Local Justice

Once we have identified the mechanisms and criteria used to allocate a particular scarce good in particular time and place, we can move on to try to explain why that particular scheme was adopted.

Some writers, notably Calabresi and Bobbitt, rely heavily on functional explanation. I have discussed their view, and my disagreements with it, in *Local Justice*. In my opinion, intentional explanations are more promising. Such explanations have two main elements: the preferences of the various actors involved and the constraints that they face.

Beginning with the constraints, let me first note that these can be more on the hard side or on the soft side of the spectrum. In transplantation there are a number of absolute constraints that are not the object of choice and deliberation. Compatibility of blood type must be respected. Transplantation is doomed to fail if the recipient has preformed antibodies against the antigens of the kidney. By contrast, the importance attached to goodness of match between antigens is a matter of opinion and indeed of controversy, partly about factual matters (does goodness of match matter in the post-cyclosporine era?) and partly about normative matters (is emphasis on matching unfair to some patient groups?).

To be able to practice selective layoffs, rather than closing down altogether, a firm must survive to make a profit. In some contexts this is a hard constraint, which will rule out layoff schemes that have very generous severance payments and early retirement schemes or that emphasize seniority at the expense of ability. In other contexts, state willingness to subsidize ailing enterprises makes for "soft budget constraints." Although that phrase was originally coined by Janos Kornai to describe how firms operate under Communism, it also applies to many non-Communist societies with active industrial policies. Many U.S. firms would have to lay off more workers or go out of business completely were it not for protectionist government policies. With soft budget constraints, more generous layoff schemes become feasible. I do not mean that the subsidies are made for the purposes of supporting a particular layoff scheme. Rather, generous or costly schemes emerge because the subsidizing authorities are unable to determine the exact cause of the firm's losses and because managers do not want to confront the workers if they do not have to.

Rule makers are to some extent also constrained by public opinion. The history of local justice is filled with scandals caused by revelations that the allocating institutions practice discrimination, tolerate waste, allow for strategic manipulation by recipients, or use discretionary procedures that invite bribes, caprice, and irrelevant intrusion of personal values. The reader will notice that the history of immigration and ESRD technology, in particular, is littered by scandals that have forced radical changes in first- and second-order decisions. It is of no particular importance whether we refer to the need to avoid scandals as a constraint or a preference. (Is the manager's need to avoid bankruptcy a constraint or a preference?) What matters is that we recognize the elusive but important role of public opinion in the shaping of local justice practices.

Given the constraints, we can turn to the preferences of the relevant actors: first-order authorities, professional allocators, and potential recipients or applicants. Here the explanation must address two issues: mechanisms of preference formation and mechanisms of preference aggregation.

Consider first preference formation. As an approximate first cut we may assert that first-order authorities are moved by global efficiency concerns, second-order allocators by conceptions of local equity and local efficiency, and third-order recipients by their self-interest. These differences are largely an effect of the more-or-less inclusive scopes of the actors. To the extent that first-order authorities consider allocative matters, in addition to their constraint-setting role in fixing the total to be allocated, these authorities tend to look at all the ramifications of a rule system, including incentive effects and how allocation may benefit those other than the recipients. One would expect, for instance, Medicare administrators to have a preference for transplanting patients who will be able to go back to work. Second-order authorities tend to form their preferences with a view to choosing among applicants, partly to ensure fairness and partly to make sure that the good goes to someone who can really benefit from it. To use again the example of transplantation, doctors are partly concerned with patients who suffer from some kind of "medical bad luck" and partly with the need to ensure graft survival. Individual applicants have no systematic tendency or reason to look beyond themselves, which is not to say that they never do.

Consider next preference aggregation. The first question is whether all the actors are likely to have an impact on this process. Specifically, it might seem as if third-order actors—with the obvious exception of organized labor in the selection of layoff principles—have little influence in shaping the rules. Would-be immigrants, for example, do not even belong to the society in which the rules evolve. Their preferences are, as it were, an idling part of the machinery. As is clear from Mackie's chapter, however, U.S. citizens lobby actively for immigration rights for applicants from their country of national origin. Similarly, even though inner-city black candidates for transplantation lack the resources to promote their interests, doctors do it in their place. To some extent, those who have been accepted at a selective college also see themselves as representing the interests of future applicants. The rule seems to be, therefore, that third-order actors are represented, if at all, by proxy. Although, as I said, the role of labor unions in the determination of layoff principles is a major exception, a form of virtual representation can occur in this arena as well, when nonunionized firms adopt the seniority principle for layoffs to forestall drives for unionization.

The diversity of aggregation mechanisms in the four arenas is such as to suggest that no general theory—similar to the theories of utility maximization and profit maximization to explain the behavior of consumers and firms—will ever be available. It is nevertheless possible to identify two main types of mechanism: bargaining and coalition formation.

A paradigmatic case of bargaining is the determination of layoff principles as part of a collective bargaining agreement. It would be tempting but wrong to expect the relative importance of ability and seniority to reflect the relative bargaining power of management and labor. First, management may have its own reasons for preferring seniority. Second, and more importantly, the union may want to use its bargaining power to get its way on wages or working conditions rather than on layoff procedures. The latter point also applies to congressional logrolling over immigration. It is not simply a question of group A accepting a quota for an immigrant class favored by group B in exchange for the support of group B for a class favored by A. In addition to—or instead of—such exchanges, A might demand the support of B on some issue not related to immigration. When local justice issues are embedded in a larger context and are resolved as part of a package solution, the outcome may be very different from what it would have been if these issues had been the subject of separate negotiations. In the latter case, the bargaining powers of the parties would be directly reflected in the outcome. One might expect, for instance, to see the adoption of a point system that incorporated the criteria favored by the different parties, with weights corresponding to their bargaining power. Note, however, that point systems can also owe their origin to a consensual process, if all parties agree on the relevant criteria and their weighting.

Coalition building occurs when different parties, for different reasons, agree on some specific allocative procedure. As Mackie demonstrates, alliance formation is very common in immigration policies. Often, one group will support a given principle because of its primary consequences, whereas another will look more to the secondary consequences. Some will support literacy tests because they resonate with the idea of individual merit, and others because it will tend to exclude immigrants from certain regions of the world. Some will support kin-based immigration because it resonates with family values, and others because it has desirable geographical implications. In the arena of transplantation, some doctors will emphasize time on the waiting list because they believe in the inherent fairness of queuing, and others because they want to promote the chances of black patients. As mentioned above, employers no less than employees may agree on the regulation of layoffs by seniority.

In the most general case, we observe coalition building as well as bargaining among coalitions, both within the more-or-less hard constraints of first-order supply and public opinion. Although the case of immigration stands out in its complexity, I believe that all the case studies demonstrate that the processes that shape allocative procedures resist any attempt to reduce them to some overarching general mechanism.

## NOTES

1. See notably D. Kahneman, J. Knetsch, and R. Thaler, "Experimental Tests of the Endowment Effect and the Coase Theorem," *Journal of Political Economy* 98 (1990), 1325–1348.

2. In "Allocation by Lot," *Social Science Information* 29 (1990), 745–763, W. Hofstee shows, for instance, that people are more willing to accept the use of lotteries to allocate bads than to allocate goods.

3. Note that this possibility does not depend on the soldiers being so destitute that they could not afford to gamble: that would bring us back to the case of decreasing marginal utility. It is enough to assume that they are so conservative that they did not want to gamble.

4. See A. Hylland and R. Zeckhauser, "The Efficient Allocation of Individuals to Positions," *Journal of Political Economy* 87 (1979), 293–314.

5. Hofstee, "Allocation by Lot."

6. G. Calabresi and P. Bobbitt, *Tragic Choices*, New York: Norton, 1978, p. 19.

7. For a general discussion of the use of lotteries in allocation and decision making, see Chapter 2 of my *Solomonic Judgments*, Cambridge: Cambridge University Press, 1989.

8. H. P. Young, "Equitable Selection of Kidney Recipients," *Journal of American Medical Association* 26 (1989), 2957.

9. In *Local Justice,* pp. 92–93 I argue that in liver and heart transplantations there is a tendency for the need and efficiency criteria to diverge from one another.

10. Although point systems (linear and additive) also define tradeoffs, they are of a special kind. If we consider a two-dimensional process, a point system will assign a sum $ax + by$ to a candidate who scores $x$ and $y$ on the two criteria. The indifference curves will be straight lines. In a multiplicative tradeoff, he might be assigned a number $x^a y^{1-a}$ ($0 < a < 1$), with the indifference curves curving away from the origin. Assume that the two criteria are level of skill and number of years of seniority. If we want to express the intuition that it takes a larger difference in seniority to compensate for a given difference in skill at low-skill levels than at high-skill levels, we must use the multiplicative rather than the additive formulation. Or to take a more graphic example: We need the multiplicative expression if we believe that in a tradeoff between need and ability as determinants of layoffs it would take a greater difference in ability to offset the difference between no children and one child than to offset the difference between nine and ten children.

# CHAPTER TWO

# The Allocation of College Admissions

## Patricia Conley

T HE STUDY of the procedures and criteria employed in the college admissions process has great normative implications, given the importance of education in contemporary American life. Access to higher education significantly shapes an individual's life chances; competition for admission to the university is competition for professional success and social position.[1] Because admission is an indivisible good that cannot be divided among several individuals, hard choices must be made. Increasingly, the choices must also be justified to the public and to the applicants. As the admissions process is becoming more open, admissions officers are forced to be more explicit and consistent. At the same time, many admissions officers jealously guard their discretionary prerogatives, arguing that the exercise of trained judgment is indispensable if universities are to fulfill their social and intellectual functions.

This chapter describes and explains the mechanics of college admissions at public and private universities in the United States. Local justice in the study of college admissions is defined by the problem of allocating a given number of university positions to a given number of applicants. Admission to college is often discussed normatively, as though there were a single operative principle, academic merit, on which all applicants should be ranked and judged for admission. Yet, as I will show, both history and current practice reveal several compelling objectives on the part of institutional decision makers as well as difficult choices about the operationalization of these objectives.

I focus exclusively on the perspective of the institutional officers making undergraduate admissions decisions at four-year public and private institutions.[2] Variation in the process of college admissions is found in both substance and procedure. On the substantive side, there is much variation in the extent to which academic merit is weighed against factors such as athletic ability, race, leadership potential, or relationship to an alumnus. On the procedural side, some colleges use highly discretionary procedures, whereas others tend to use mechanical formulae that allow little scope for discretion.

Controversy about college admissions revolves around the relative weight given to the objectives of a selection policy, the measurement of those objectives, and the representation of groups. Because we live in a society where college applicants have had access to vastly different educational resources, and because administrators believe that college life is more than what takes place in the classroom, admissions officers have a difficult job. They know that the tradeoffs they make and the qualities they seek at the individual level add up to the inclusion or exclusion of different groups of applicants. Academic merit has always been the major criterion for college admissions, but it is rarely the only one.

In order to describe and explain the allocation of college admissions, I rely upon several sources of data. I use information from three national surveys, personal interviews, university documents, and applicant files. The American Association of Collegiate Registrars and Admission Officers (AACRAO) and the College Board conducted national surveys of admissions practices in 1979 and 1985.[3] Both surveys received responses from at least 1,000 four-year public and private institutions out of a population of roughly 1,700 accredited four-year institutions. My own survey was mailed in November of 1989 to a national sample of 500 directors of admissions. The sample was randomly selected from the four-year public and private universities and liberal arts colleges listed in the *1988–89 College Handbook* compiled by the College Board. Almost 55 percent (274) of the original sample of admissions officers responded.[4]

I conducted hour-long personal interviews with fifteen admissions officers at thirteen selective institutions.[5] The ratio of applicants to places at these institutions ranged from 3 : 1 to 10 : 1. Most had six times as many applicants as places. I spoke with either the director (dean) of admissions or an associate director since these individuals know about the mechanics of the admissions process in addition to official university policies and constraints.[6] The officers that I interviewed had several years of experience in college admissions, and they were often very familiar with the mechanics of the process at other selective institutions.

There is a great deal of information about the admissions process that is publicly accessible. Along with the standard materials sent out with application forms, most institutions have university reports or documents that describe the admissions process in great detail. In addition, at one university, I gained access to the applicant files right after the final admissions decisions had been made. I read a random sample of 302 applicant files, coding the characteristics of the applicants along with the evaluations of the admissions officers.

I begin the chapter with a brief history of college admissions in the United States. In this century, admission to the nation's most prestigious institutions has changed from an open-door policy to a mixture of admission and selection procedures.[7] Considerations beyond academic merit were first introduced in order to exclude groups of applicants (such as Jews, women, and minorities); today these same considerations are used to include groups historically excluded. Next, I outline the major objectives and criteria that shape college admissions today, utilizing data from the surveys, interviews, and university documents. I describe a variety of implementation procedures with attention to debates over the use of quotas in the admissions process. Finally, I address the consistency and accountability of decisions made by admissions officers.

Like other issues of local justice, the allocation of college admission blends multiple principles. Desert, equity, and efficiency are all compelling objectives in the selection process. Admissions policies reward applicants for past academic achievement and select for those who are best able to benefit from a college education. Admissions policies also compensate disadvantaged applicants, with the goal of equitably distributing educational resources across various groups in our society. As in other arenas of local justice, facially neutral procedures are scrutinized for their disparate impact on cultural, religious, and racial groups. In addition, the allocation of admission according to any one objective leads to an abundance of possible implementation criteria and procedures.

## The History of College Admissions in the United States

### College Admissions Before World War II[8]

In the nineteenth century colleges were small, catered to local communities, and were characterized by a strong religious ethos on campus.[9] College life at selective institutions was more focused on gaining social status than on pursuing intellectual excellence for its own sake.[10] College admission was localized. Young men, mostly of the upper classes of society, would study with a private tutor or at an academy. They would go to the college of their choice in the fall and take an oral entrance exam with faculty members. Exams were particular to each institution and covered Latin, Greek, and mathematics. Some colleges even offered their own "college prep" programs since secondary schools were not universally available.

University presidents in the mid- to late-1800s promoted the idea of an educational system, a unified set of training beginning in the common school and reaching its pinnacle in university training. Public secondary schools were developed, and colleges changed from denominational to lay control. Entrance exams became written exams, and more subjects were added. Reform controversies centered around the proper substance of a college education in an industrial democracy. The screening mechanism for college admission was simple. College applicants were determined by the self-selection of upper-middle and upper-class young men. Secondary school teachers and principals were relied upon to encourage only those students best suited to a college education and leadership positions in society. Most public school curriculums were not aimed toward college; since they did not teach Latin, few of their graduates were equipped to survive college entrance exams.

In the late 1800s some colleges pushed selection of students on to secondary schools even further by means of "certification." In 1870, for example, the University of Michigan began the practice of waiving entrance exams for students from "accredited" high schools. High school principals had the responsibility of issuing certificates to young men which assured them automatic admittance to the university. High schools were accredited by having proper resources and college prep course offerings. Regional associations were formed for accrediting high schools, though this admissions practice was slow to catch on in the Mid-Atlantic states and at Ivy League institutions.[11]

Land grant colleges and state universities grew in the late 1800s in order to deal with problems posed by the Industrial Revolution and mass immigration. The Morrill Act of 1862 increased revenues for state colleges teaching "such branches of learning as are related to agriculture and the mechanic arts."[12] Land revenues from the Morrill Act had most effect when added to previously existing state university endowments. These institutions were not selective, and since they tended to be vocationally oriented, public high school graduates were prepared for entry.

At the turn of the century, new disciplines such as history, chemistry, and physics were accepted as viable courses of study, and for the first time college students were able to choose one of many available courses of study. Some top educators, notably President Nicholas Murray Butler of Columbia University, urged uniform subject entrance requirements and uniform entrance examinations. The College Entrance Examination Board (CEEB) was founded in 1900 and administered its first exams in 1901. Member colleges were not obliged to abandon their own exams or admit students at particular levels of achievement, and they could pick the specific subject exams necessary for admission. Slowly the tests gained legitimacy. Uniform testing and requirements made inter-institutional comparisons possible, and debates about admission policy lost some of their local character.

Some institutions required so many tests that secondary schools were put in an impossible position in the task of preparing their students. Most students couldn't pass tests in every area. For a time, colleges admitted students with deficiencies in a particular area on the "condition" that they study and pass the exam once admitted. When this system failed to work, colleges began to make a tradeoff between the exams and high school grades. A student with good grades, for example, might have to pass only four exams, in areas of his choice. The use of high school grades also let institutions make allowances for students who for some reason had a bad day at exam time.

Most institutions in the early part of this century did not have the luxury of turning students away. In 1920, only thirteen of the forty most renowned colleges turned down any applicants.[13] A small number of liberal arts institutions tried to increase the quality of their applicant pools by limiting enrollment, recruiting widely, and raising tuition.[14] Apparently, administrators thought that even the appearance of selectivity would increase the number of applications. The top institutions competed with each other for many of the same students, following the lead of the few institutions that were already practicing selective admissions procedures. Two early examples are worth mentioning.

Columbia's President Butler requested an investigation of the declining number of applicants from a local and prestigious high school. The report was presented in 1908, and it recommended that "only such students should be admitted as are susceptible of education and as may be of benefit to the student body."[15] The underlying message of the report was that East European Jews were not "of benefit to the student body"; the parents of the students at the prestigious high school didn't want their children to go to college with Jews. Columbia could not, however, simply supplement exams with a question about religious affiliation in order to limit the number of Jews. Quotas would have been unacceptable to significant numbers of faculty members and to interest groups outside of the university. Instead, Butler established an Office of Undergraduate Admissions that began using a variety of admissions criteria beyond entrance examinations. Applicants' grades and the quality of their high school would be considered. Recruitment activities were heightened for "desirable" students, and Jews were encouraged to attend City College.

Later, nonacademic criteria and an application form were employed to help screen out the socially undesirable. Butler also introduced an "honors" system to recognize two tracks of students—

those who were serious intellectuals and those who were serious socializers. In his 1919 Annual Report he wrote:

> We need at Columbia more men, not fewer, who pursue a college course with no vocational aim in view, but who wish to furnish the mind for enjoyments, for happiness, and for worth in later years.[16]

Jews were not likely to have the wealth and security necessary to have "no vocational aim"; they were also not viewed as socially desirable mixers for white Anglo-Saxon Protestant students. Columbia's reliance on psychological testing and character evaluations cut the proportion of Jews on campus in half.[17]

Dartmouth is a second example of early attempts at a selective admissions policy. Like other institutions, Dartmouth had traditionally taken all qualified applicants. In 1919, Dartmouth rejected 100 applicants on a "first-come, first-served" basis. Applications continued to rise, and Dartmouth President Ernest Hopkins instituted a comprehensive selective admissions process. In 1922, he outlined the nine principles of the process:

1. Exceptional Scholarship, which shall be considered sufficient basis for selection.
2. High Scholarship, which shall be considered prima facie evidence in favor of selection.
3. Personal Ratings by school officers and others acquainted with the applicant and distinctive abilities evidenced by School Activities submitted by the latter.
4. Priority of Application.
5. The Principle of Occupational Distribution.
6. The Principle of Geographic Distribution.
7. All properly qualified Sons of Dartmouth Alumni and Dartmouth College Officers.
8. Low Scholarship shall be presumptive evidence of unfitness for selection.
9. The entire class will be selected on the basis of qualifications and no one allowed to enter because he has secured rooming accommodations.[18]

These kinds of criteria are still used today. At the time, the quest for occupational or geographic diversity was new. While Hopkins desired an "aristocracy of brains" based on academic excellence, his critics charged that his plan was a subterfuge for the favoring of alumni children and athletes over others, particularly Jews.[19]

The subject of quotas limiting the number of Jews was one of the most prominent controversies at selective institutions when they first began limiting enrollment numbers. Yale's dean of freshmen stated a popular view among some administrators when he said that, although Jews are among the most talented intellectually, they are "more or less in the nature of a foreign body in the class organism."[20] Controversy over limiting the enrollment of Jews fundamentally shaped newly selective admissions criteria in two important ways. First, overt quotas came to be viewed as taboo. Harvard's President Lowell (1909–1933) created a public relations disaster for his institution when he openly advocated quotas on the number of Jewish students.[21] Jewish intellectuals, the American Federation of Labor, and the governor of Massachusetts, among others, were swift to condemn the practice of quotas, and Harvard was forced to make a public report condemning religious discrimination by the use of enrollment ceilings.

Second, psychological tests and "character" and geographic diversity were employed and justified as legitimate selection criteria. After Harvard's experience, administrators had to proceed cautiously. Yale is one of the most notorious examples, using four methods to control the number of Jews.[22] First, applicant character would be considered and judged by the Board of Admissions. Second, relatives of alumni would be given preference over other applicants.[23] Third, financial aid was limited for Jews by limiting financial aid to poor students in general.[24] Fourth, the administration refused admission to applicants from high schools in the Yale vicinity, which supplied 75 percent of the Jews already attending Yale.

When other institutions became selective, the criteria used by Yale and Columbia would be considered legitimate to employ whether or not there was an intention to discriminate against Jews or anyone else. I have discussed discrimination against Jews because administrators felt this would be publicly unacceptable if revealed, and they were forced to devise subtle ways to deal with their bias. Discrimination against women and minorities in college admissions was accepted and not as controversial and therefore did not have the same impact on admissions early in this century.

In the 1920s and 1930s most admissions officers, where they existed, were salesmen.[25] During the Depression, in particular, colleges were under intense financial pressure to find students who could pay tuition. The vast majority of institutions had "open door" policies in which all qualified students were accepted. The college registrar made the admissions decisions, which were fairly straightforward. Individual applicants independently passed a pre-established academic threshold; they were not compared or ranked.[26] For private schools, the threshold was based upon exams and completion of a certain pattern of high school coursework. For public institutions, the threshold was the attainment of a high school degree at a state-accredited secondary school.[27]

An extensive system of two-year "junior colleges" was built in the 1920s; these serviced mostly individuals from lower socioeconomic groups. The junior colleges were originally intended as extra preparation before attending four-year college, but they eventually offered terminal semiprofessional training. During the Depression, enrollment in public institutions and junior colleges surpassed enrollment in private institutions for the first time. Though most public and private institutions were not selective, higher education was still viewed as a privilege for the wealthier segments of society.

### College Admissions Since World War II

In 1900 only 4 percent of all 18- to 21-year-olds attended college. By 1947, 16 percent of all 18- to 21-year-olds were enrolled, in addition to one million veterans.[28] The "G.I. Bill," or Serviceman's Readjustment Act of 1944 guaranteed a college education and job training for all servicemen who had served at least 90 days. Most campuses found a way to deal with the overwhelming number of servicemen entering college.[29] Veterans briefly changed the atmosphere on campus by breaking down racial and religious barriers and intensely focusing on academic success. The experience of the veterans encouraged more kinds of students to consider a college education. It was only after the departure of veteran students that most institutions, private and public alike, had to limit enrollment for logistical reasons.

In the late 1940s a series of major reports was released on the state of higher education in America.[30] In 1947 the Truman Commission on Higher Education presented a report that criticized the college system for a lack of equal opportunity, especially for the poor. The report also lashed out against the practice of setting quotas to limit the numbers of blacks and Jews. The report stated that "The quota, or *numerus clausus,* is certainly un-American. It is European in origin and application, and we have lately witnessed on that continent the horrors to which, in its logical extension, it can lead. . . . The quota system cannot be justified on any grounds compatible with democratic principles."[31] Junior colleges were renamed *community colleges,* and it was recommended that at least two years of post-secondary school training be free for all citizens. The "democratic creed" demanded that an individual have "an equal chance with all others to make the most of their native abilities."[32]

A college education came to be viewed as the ticket to social mobility. In the 1950s and 1960s the self-selection of applicants was the main focus of reform efforts. Educators took issue with the notion that the self-selection of applicants naturally brought out the best talent.[33] Before the war, little attention was given to the question of exactly who should attend college. Little attention was given to the fact that the self-selection of applicants might result in the talented yet poor segments of society being underrepresented.

Educators no longer believed that the main obstacle to a higher education was financial. Instead, they believed that "most of the real screening has all along been done by the accident of socioeconomic origins, early environment, and the various levels of aspiration habitually characterizing particular groups and subcultures."[34] Colleges heightened recruitment in the belief that they were charged with "finding and developing potential talent, [with] less emphasis on simply rewarding talent already developed."[35]

Old policies had used quotas to exclude specific segments of society; new policies would use quotas to include those who had historically been excluded. After the war, distinctions on the basis of race would become more relevant than distinctions on the basis of religion.

In addition, the influx of war veterans in college strengthened the claims of reformers who argued that intelligence and motivation were more important to college success than the mastery of specific subjects in high school.[36] Academic success in college was found to be best predicted by general aptitude tests and class rank, not by knowledge of specific subjects. Throughout the 1960s, high attrition rates were frowned upon and admissions standards were raised.[37] Many public institutions abandoned open admissions policies that required only a high school diploma.

College admissions offices became more and more bureaucratized in the 1960s and 1970s. Selective institutions made decisions in a manner not too different from the criteria and procedures that exist today. However, increasingly the demand for equality for previously excluded groups meant that educators would face the choice between continuing to exclude minorities and changing admissions criteria. The 1978 Supreme Court decision in *Regents of the University of California* v. *Bakke* has shaped recent admissions policies in important ways and deserves special mention.[38]

The plaintiff, Alan Bakke, was a white veteran in his early thirties who applied to medical school at the University of California at Davis in both 1973 and 1974. Bakke was denied admission to UC-Davis medical school and all other medical schools to which he had applied. At the University of California at Davis, there were over 2,500 applicants each year for 100 slots. Sixteen of those available places were part of a special program for the disadvantaged, which had different standards of admission. Bakke claimed that the minority applicants accepted under this special program were less qualified than he and alleged that he was a victim of racial discrimination in violation of the equal protection clause of the Fourteenth Amendment to the U.S. Constitution.[39]

The university argued that its mission to serve the needs of all of the people in the state was the source of its voluntarily implemented two-track system. The state's responsibility to foster equality outweighed a particular individual's right to equal treatment. Moreover, the medical school was creating minority role models who would later provide care in underserved minority communities. In addition, the university argued that their preference for minorities was meritorious; minority capabilities simply could not be fairly judged against the white majority of applicants. Equal opportunity meant fair competition and open doors, but this would not be possible without further action to remedy past wrongs.

In a 5 to 4 decision in June of 1978, the Supreme Court ruled that the special admission program was unlawful under the Fourteenth Amendment and that Bakke should be admitted to medical school. A different majority ruled that, although separate tracks and quotas could not be used, race could be considered a factor in the admissions process. Race may not be used as the sole criterion for college admission, but it is a legitimate criterion when used with other factors. The admissions process should treat each applicant as an individual, to be compared with all other candidates for all available positions. Standards must apply evenly to all and quotas may not be established.[40]

### College Admissions Today

Nearly one and a half million students move from high school to one of nearly 3,000 colleges every year.[41] A slight majority of these are four-year, as opposed to two-year, public and private institutions.[42] Ten percent of four-year public institutions and 15 percent of four-year private institutions report open-door admissions policies, in which all high school graduates are admitted. Around 73 percent of all four-year institutions report that the "majority of individuals who meet some specified level of academic achievement or other qualifications above and beyond high school graduation are admitted." Only 12 percent of four-year public institutions and 15 percent of four-year private institutions report that they accept only a "limited number" of individuals with qualifications beyond a high-school diploma.

The directors of admissions offices are themselves mostly white men with college backgrounds in education, the social sciences, and the humanities.[43] A slight majority have master's degrees and most never attended the institution where they work. About a third worked in college admissions at a different institution before their current job. Many, particularly at public institutions, worked in another university office, such as the office of the registrar. Almost 50 percent have worked in college admissions for less than five years. Overall, the admissions profession is characterized by extremely high turnover for those in their first three years.[44] On average, the public institution admissions directors have been in the profession longer than their private institution counterparts.

## Major Objectives of College Admissions

### *Academic Merit*

Academic excellence is the traditional and most commonly recognized goal of higher education and the most celebrated qualification among college applicants. Many believe that the university should be, above all, devoted to the extension, preservation, and communication of knowledge.[45] According to this point of view, the university's chief contribution to society—and the reason society insists on its preservation as an institution—rests on its capacity to cultivate intellectual excellence among young scholars. The implication for the admissions process is that those applicants who demonstrate the greatest potential for excellence are chosen for admission.[46]

However, most of the applicants to selective institutions pass a high threshold of intellectual achievement. How does one choose the best class of 1,000 students when faced with over 1,500 applicants who are valedictorians, over 5,500 applicants with math SAT scores over 700, and over 2,500 applicants with a 4.0 grade point average?[47] In addition to academic excellence, admissions officers consider the value added by the education for the student's life, the student's contribution to the university community, the societal context of their decisions, and the incentive effects of various admissions policies. Administrators also face two major constraints: the financial health of the institution and pressure from groups outside the university. These objectives and constraints shape both the substantive criteria used to make student selection decisions and implementation procedures.

### Value Added

A standard line in college brochures reads as follows: "Ultimately, we offer admission to those students who, in our judgment, will best take advantage of the educational opportunities at the university." Those who "best take advantage of" the opportunities available at the university could be one of two distinct types. On the one hand, they could be students who will receive the largest *increment* of benefit from their education. For example, this could be the talented poor, who will get most benefit because they start out with the least amount of background. Or they could be members of minority groups that have previously been denied educational opportunities. On the other hand, it could be students who, as one admissions director put it, are " 'A' going in and 'A' going out." The best-prepared students going in will probably be at the highest *level* of preparation going out.

Those who will best take advantage of educational opportunities might also be those for whom the education leads to the largest contribution to society in the future. "Value added" refers to the difference between the social contributions of students who did not receive the college education and the social contributions of identical students who did receive that college education.[48] The best selection mechanism may be defined as one that maximizes the value added of admitted students, where value added could be academic or social. It could be defined as changes in attitudes or behavior, or as an increase in future earnings.

While value added arguments shape admissions decisions, they are usually qualified. If society is biased or unfair, using social value added may reinforce existing injustices. If ability at the end of high school is a function of earlier social inequalities, then selecting students who will reach the highest levels of academic achievement means selecting those who are already most advantaged.[49] If we wish to maximize the future earnings of those selected for admission, and we know the job market is biased against certain types of individuals (on the basis of race, religion, or level of social skills), then in order to maximize value added we would have to introduce those same biases in the admissions process.[50]

### Contribution to Community

Among admissions officers, another consideration is the applicant's potential contribution to the university community. First, a student contributes to the university community if he or she advances the intellectual excellence of others. As noted previously, Dartmouth's first dean of admissions advocated the development of a student body composed of individuals drawn from diverse geographic and economic backgrounds in order to promote intellectual excellence.[51] University officials today still promote the view that, in order to develop intellectually and socially, students need exposure to the wide variety of experiences that a diverse student body provides. This is one argument for different types of racial, cultural, and socioeconomic diversity.[52]

Second, students contribute to the university by tuition and by supporting their alma mater as they enter their professional lives. Children of alumni are favored since it is hoped that the family will come to see the school as an extension of their lives, as important as church or local community organizations. Finally, the contribution to community includes those students who "mix well" or display those qualities most appropriate to the special flavor of the institution as a whole.[53] In 1985, for instance, 47 percent of all four-year private institutions and 12 percent of all public institutions reported that the "compatibility" between student and institution was an important factor in admissions.[54] Universities need students who will participate in extracurricular activities.

A curious twist on this last theme is the notion of the "happy bottom quarter," whose student member is not chosen because he or she best promotes academic excellence. Robert Klitgaard quotes a dean of admissions who says:

> Twenty-five percent of the entering students would end up in the bottom quarter of the class. If they were former academic stars they would be unhappy . . . so intentionally admitting less academically able students as "the bottom quarter," who were strong in sports or social life or the arts and would therefore not care so much about

their academic standing, would make everyone's educational experience happier.[55]

Historically, the notion has its precedent, for example, in Columbia University's admissions policy earlier this century. One of the admissions directors I interviewed put it this way:

> They keep everybody else sane. They'll probably move things around here, get involved. But on sheer academic credentials you'd have a hard time justifying it. Not that you're worried they can't do the work. But you're just so conscious of how many others with better credentials you have to turn down.

College life is about a community broadly defined, and those who would contribute to dorm life, the school paper, or volunteer activities are valuable.

### Societal Context

Admissions officers at selective institutions communicate their institution's selective nature to prospective applicants through the literature and application forms that they send out. In general, most Americans are familiar with the names of Ivy League and other prestigious and selective institutions. Therefore the application process is marked by a large amount of self-selection. Applicants tend to be very good about not applying to too many schools with standards far above their own high school and test performances.[56]

Admissions officers recognize that certain types of applicants do not represent themselves as well as they might. Usually, these applicants are the first generation in their family to attend college or they come from an environment in which information about college is limited. Most high schools place students on separate tracks depending upon whether or not they plan to go on to college. Admissions officers are familiar with the tremendous variation in high school preparation throughout the country.

The social context of the student, even if not explicitly introduced in the selection process, conditions evaluations of applicants. Educational and economic disadvantage are considered for four main reasons. First is the belief that applicants should be compensated for disadvantage which is effectively beyond their control. Applicants should not be penalized for lack of resources and information. Second is the belief that it would be unfair to compare the disadvantaged with other students on admissions indicators without taking the disadvantage into account. On average, SAT scores are lower for the economically disadvantaged, even when controlling for race and gender.[57] Third, in a situation where two applicants are identical based upon indicators of academic ability, the applicant who has overcome obstacles is more valuable. Either the disadvantaged person worked harder and should be rewarded for effort or overcoming obstacles is evidence of a desirable personality trait, such as motivation. Finally, some admissions officers believe that the economic diversity of the incoming class is as important as racial and geographic diversity. Economic diversity promotes intellectual excellence and also fulfills the university's obligation to improve the lives of individuals in groups previously denied opportunity.

Admissions officers also pay attention to the consequences of their decisions for communities and groups of applicants. For example, a director of admissions describes his concern about community leadership:

> When we have someone who is the first applicant from some little rural school in 15 years and finally have a really serious academician as a model to everyone in the community, we really think twice about turning them down. They're not as strong as a lot of our applicants but what kind of signal are you sending to this community by turning down the best kid they've had in 15 years? We may still turn them down but at least we feel bad about it. In some cases we feel so bad we decide to admit them.

A different director of admissions describes one of the goals of the admissions process as achieving a "campus student population in parity with the ethnic composition of the state, and really of the nation, anticipating how rapidly the nation is changing, that because we are a public institution we have a responsibility to educate all the different constituent groups and prepare them for the 21st century." Like other admissions officers, he is aware that one side effect of his individual decision may be discrimination against groups.

In practice, ostensibly neutral admissions criteria have the potential of rewarding or punishing groups. Admissions officers know that if they use standardized test scores as the major criterion for admission to math and engineering programs, women will be at a distinct disadvantage in gaining admission.[58] They are aware that preference for the children of alumni disadvantages members of different ethnic groups.[59] One admissions officer described how, at his institution,

> What they did was say "We will no longer give special preference to lower-income students." That is a neutral standard but 80 percent of the students in question were Asian. From my vantage point they could've easily said we're gonna eliminate short students or students with black hair. They knew what the effect was going to be in racial terms.

Admissions officers shape criteria and procedures by anticipating the impact on groups of applicants. Historically, intentions have been both discriminatory and inclusive.

### Incentive Effects

Admissions officers also care about the incentive effects of the admissions process on both accepted and rejected applicants. With respect to accepted applicants, part of the "secrecy" in college admissions is undertaken to protect the self-esteem of some groups of applicants once they arrive on campus. The average test scores of football players, minority students, women, or any other easily identifiable groups are usually not made public. One director said that his office started using a crude rating index in the admissions process rather than an index based upon studies of the prediction of performance because the more sophisticated index "took on a life of its own." Faculty members labeled students according to their index scores. Some directors argue that economic disadvantage should be used instead of underrepresented minority status, partly because this would not stigmatize students once they reach campus.

With respect to rejected applicants, most colleges check the consistency of decisions within high schools at the end of the process. Admissions officers do not want to alienate guidance counselors or applicants by arbitrary or nonsensical patterns of acceptances and rejections. A different dilemma in admissions at selective institutions is that the admissions officers do not know any individual applicant's rank order preferences over all institutions to which the applicant has applied. When applicants look the same, they cannot make decisions based upon knowledge of which applicant prefers their institution more.[60] Therefore they may reject a large portion of those applicants who wanted them most.[61]

Admissions criteria produce incentives for both applicants and high-school administrators. If test scores are perceived to be most important, high-school students who want to go to college will focus most of their efforts on preparing for the tests. If the nature of high-school coursework is very important, high-school administrators will have an incentive to spend resources on college prep and advanced placement courses. One director of admissions bemoaned the fact that "too many kids are being stampeded into posturing to gain admission." The goal, he said, should "not be for a candidate to shape a life to fit the college, but to find a college compatible with and validating the style developed naturally."

### Other Constraints

Admissions officers must consider the financial welfare of their institution. A selection procedure may be costly to administer. Also, while admissions officers generally do not cite the ability to pay tuition as an important factor in the admissions process, tuition revenues are undeniably important. A small number of colleges, such as Brown and Smith, have moved away from "need-blind" admissions.[62] At Smith, for example, applicants are ranked and a budgeted amount of financial aid is distributed starting with the top-ranked students and moving to lower-ranked students. Once the budget is exhausted, those qualified lower-ranked applicants who can pay for their education are preferred over those qualified lower-ranked applicants who need financial aid.

Admissions officers are not the only actors involved in the admissions process. The broad guidelines for admissions policy are often set by the university board of trustees, council of deans, or chief executive officer, in cooperation with the office of admissions. Faculty members may also have a prominent role. Athletic and performing arts departments will make demands for particular students. State institutions are constrained by rules set down by the state legislature.

## Implementation Criteria and Procedures

The major objectives of college admissions—merit, value added, contribution to community, and societal context—are widely shared across institutions. In this section I describe how the major goals of admissions policy are operationalized. I describe the specific criteria, or pieces of information about applicants, and actual selection procedures.

### Criteria

The individual criteria used to make college admissions decisions may be divided into five categories: administrative prerequisites, academic merit, personal qualities, individual welfare, and background characteristics. A particular criterion may be assessed using more than one indicator or attribute. For example, academic merit may be evaluated on the basis of test scores, high school class rank, writing samples, and depth of high school coursework.

Admissions criteria serve as traits, proxies, or mediating variables.[63] Personal qualities and background characteristics are traits in their own right. Other factors are indicators of or proxies for an underlying trait. For example, high school grade point average is a proxy for intellectual ability. Finally, some criteria are not traits or proxies but are mediating variables that condition the interpretation of other criteria. Indicators of educational disadvantage, for example, might condition the interpretation of test scores or patterns of coursework.

Administrative prerequisites include the requirements that are absolutely necessary for admission to any institution. Almost all four-year public and private institutions require that the applicant have a high school diploma.[64] In addition, the majority of four-year institutions require or highly recommend that applicants complete a particular high school course program.[65] An additional basic requirement is that the applicant must have taken either the ACT or SAT test, whether or not the score makes a difference in the decision-making process.[66] Finally, the applicant must fill out the application and any relevant applications for financial aid.

In my 1989 survey, respondents were asked to rate the importance of various indicators in the admissions process on a scale ranging from one (do not consider) to five (single most important factor). I asked about all categories of admissions criteria except for administrative prerequisites. Specifically, respondents were asked "Once a student has met all obligatory requirements, how important is each of the following factors?" The average importance of indicators is presented in Table 2.1 for the full sample and for public and private institutions separately. For the sake of clarity, the factors have been grouped into five categories, though some factors would obviously fit into more than one category.[67]

Indicators of academic merit are the most important factors in admission decisions for both public and private institutions. High school GPA is rated as the most important factor in admissions, a result consonant with previous admissions surveys.[68] Test scores, class rank, and the depth and breadth of high school coursework are the next three most important factors. Officers at public institutions clearly do not consider as many factors; after the indicators of merit, only applicant race and motivation appear, on average, to be of even minor importance. Private university admissions officers, on the other hand, tend to use more indicators of academic merit, such as letters of recommendation or essays. They also consider personal qualities and the fit between the applicant and the institution. The least important indicators for both groups of admissions officers were socioeconomic status, parental occupation, financial need, age, and religion.[69]

Interviews are more important for private institutions. Many admissions directors eliminated interviews for the same reason that they eliminated required photographs with applications, namely that interviewers or file readers might unconsciously indulge in stereotyping. The admissions processes that still conduct interviews tend to do so for three reasons. First and foremost, alumni are happy when they are involved. Alumni interviews

## *Table 2.1*
### AVERAGE IMPORTANCE OF ADMISSIONS FACTORS

|  | Public | Private | All Institutions |
|---|---|---|---|
| **Academic Merit** |  |  |  |
| High school GPA | 3.8 | 4.1 | 4.0 |
| SAT/ACT | 3.7 | 3.6 | 3.6 |
| Achievement test scores | 1.7 | 2.4 | 2.1 |
| High school rank | 3.1 | 3.5 | 3.3 |
| High school coursework | 3.7 | 4.0 | 3.9 |
| Essays | 1.7 | 2.9 | 2.4 |
| Letters of recommendation | 1.9 | 3.1 | 2.5 |
| Interviews | 1.7 | 2.8 | 2.3 |
| High school reputation | 1.9 | 2.5 | 2.2 |
| **Personal Qualities** |  |  |  |
| Sense of social responsibility | 1.4 | 2.5 | 2.0 |
| Leadership ability | 1.9 | 2.8 | 2.4 |
| Motivation or initiative | 2.0 | 3.3 | 2.7 |
| Extracurricular activities | 1.8 | 2.5 | 2.2 |
| **Background Characteristics** |  |  |  |
| Age | 1.3 | 1.4 | 1.4 |
| Race | 2.1 | 2.1 | 2.1 |
| Religion | 1.0 | 1.3 | 1.2 |
| Intended major | 1.9 | 1.8 | 1.8 |
| Relative of alumni | 1.5 | 2.2 | 1.9 |
| **Individual Welfare** |  |  |  |
| Socioeconomic status | 1.3 | 1.5 | 1.4 |
| Parental occupation | 1.1 | 1.2 | 1.1 |
| Financial need | 1.1 | 1.2 | 1.2 |
| **Individual and Institution** |  |  |  |
| Diversity of accepted class | 1.8 | 2.4 | 2.2 |
| Compatibility of student/instit. | 1.5 | 2.8 | 2.2 |
| Athletic/special skills | 1.9 | 2.1 | 2.0 |
| $N =$ | 123 | 151 | 274 |

1 = Do not consider

2 = Minor factor

3 = Moderately important factor

4 = Very important factor

5 = Single most important factor

**46**

are a public relations mechanism that get alumni participating for the institution. Second, interviews are used to provide information to applicants and to help them understand the kinds of information that would be most useful in the admissions process. As one director of admissions noted, "it is most important with the least sophisticated applicant," who needs to learn how to best present his or her background. Third, some institutions use interviews as a sort of character evaluation, included with other letters of recommendation in the applicant's file. This is the most questionable practice, since interviews have not been shown to predict future success.[70]

Table 2.2 presents the frequency of responses to the question concerning the importance of admissions indicators. One quarter of the sample selected grade point average as the "single most important factor" in the admissions process, with substantial numbers choosing either class rank or coursework. Only 5 percent selected test scores as the single most important factor in making admission decisions. The differences between public and private institution respondents outlined previously are evident in this table as well. For several groups of factors—in particular, indicators of academic merit, personal qualities, and individual/institutional fit—private institution responses are much more evenly distributed.

To discover why admissions officers consider some factors more important than others, I offered survey respondents the ten alternatives presented in Table 2.3.[71] By far the most frequently cited reason for the use of a particular configuration of admissions factors was that these factors would best predict the academic success of students at the institution. Almost one-third of the sample cited the creation of positive incentives for high school students or the expectation that selection on certain factors would channel quality applicants to the university in the future. More of the private university sample seemed concerned with the latter. Public university officers were much more likely to cite state or federal government standards and much less likely to cite prediction of the later professional success of students.

Table 2.4 shows that many institutions make routine exceptions to formal academic requirements.[72] Public and private university responses are different, as one might expect. In general,

*Table 2.2*

## IMPORTANCE OF ADMISSIONS FACTORS: DISTRIBUTION OF RESPONSES

| | Public | | | | | Private | | | | | All | | | | |
|---|---|---|---|---|---|---|---|---|---|---|---|---|---|---|---|
| | 5 | 4 | 3 | 2 | 1 | 5 | 4 | 3 | 2 | 1 | 5 | 4 | 3 | 2 | 1 |
| GPA | 25.2 | 46.3 | 16.3 | 2.4 | 8.1 | 25.8 | 64.2 | 7.9 | .7 | .7 | 25.5 | 56.2 | 11.7 | 1.5 | 4.0 |
| SAT/ACT | 5.7 | 65.9 | 18.7 | 4.1 | 4.1 | 4.6 | 58.9 | 29.1 | 4.0 | 2.0 | 5.1 | 62.0 | 24.5 | 4.0 | 2.9 |
| Ach. Test | .8 | 4.1 | 12.2 | 23.6 | 54.5 | .7 | 17.2 | 22.5 | 28.5 | 24.5 | .7 | 11.3 | 17.9 | 26.3 | 38.0 |
| Class Rank | 15.4 | 35.0 | 13.0 | 8.9 | 23.6 | 9.9 | 46.4 | 31.1 | 9.3 | 2.0 | 12.4 | 41.2 | 23.0 | 9.1 | 11.7 |
| Coursework | 17.9 | 56.1 | 10.6 | 4.1 | 8.1 | 23.8 | 58.3 | 12.6 | 2.0 | 1.3 | 21.2 | 57.3 | 11.7 | 2.9 | 4.4 |
| Essays | 0 | 4.9 | 17.9 | 19.5 | 53.7 | 2.0 | 31.1 | 37.7 | 12.6 | 15.2 | 1.1 | 19.3 | 28.8 | 15.7 | 32.5 |
| Letters | 0 | 3.3 | 18.7 | 40.7 | 35.8 | 1.3 | 27.2 | 51.0 | 15.9 | 3.3 | .7 | 16.4 | 36.5 | 27.0 | 17.9 |
| Interviews | .8 | 2.4 | 16.3 | 24.4 | 54.5 | 0 | 21.9 | 41.1 | 25.2 | 10.6 | .4 | 13.1 | 29.9 | 24.8 | 30.3 |
| HS Reput. | 0 | 5.7 | 21.1 | 24.4 | 47.2 | 0 | 4.6 | 49.7 | 29.8 | 14.6 | 0 | 5.1 | 36.9 | 27.4 | 29.2 |
| Soc. Resp. | 0 | 1.6 | 10.6 | 16.3 | 69.9 | 0 | 13.2 | 35.1 | 29.1 | 18.5 | 0 | 8.0 | 24.1 | 23.4 | 41.6 |
| Leadership | 0 | 4.1 | 24.4 | 26.0 | 43.9 | 0 | 15.9 | 58.3 | 17.2 | 7.3 | 0 | 10.6 | 43.1 | 21.2 | 23.7 |
| Motivation | .8 | 10.6 | 21.1 | 22.8 | 42.3 | 2.0 | 41.7 | 35.8 | 13.2 | 4.0 | 1.5 | 27.7 | 29.2 | 17.5 | 21.2 |
| Extracurr. | 0 | 1.6 | 19.5 | 31.7 | 45.5 | 0 | 11.3 | 43.7 | 31.1 | 12.6 | 0 | 6.9 | 32.8 | 31.4 | 27.4 |

*Institutions (Public and Private columns grouped)*

| | 5 | 4 | 3 | 2 | 1 | 5 | 4 | 3 | 2 | 1 | 5 | 4 | 3 | 2 | 1 |
|---|---|---|---|---|---|---|---|---|---|---|---|---|---|---|---|
| Age | 0 | 0 | 11.4 | 10.6 | 76.4 | 0 | 2.0 | 2.0 | 27.2 | 67.5 | 0 | 1.1 | 6.2 | 19.7 | 71.5 |
| Race | .8 | 16.3 | 25.2 | 8.1 | 48.0 | 0 | 15.2 | 22.5 | 11.9 | 47.0 | .4 | 15.7 | 23.7 | 10.2 | 47.4 |
| Religion | 0 | 0 | .8 | .8 | 96.7 | 1.3 | 1.3 | 6.0 | 6.6 | 82.8 | .7 | .7 | 3.6 | 4.0 | 89.1 |
| Major | 0 | 8.9 | 20.3 | 20.3 | 48.8 | 0 | 6.6 | 11.3 | 35.8 | 45.0 | 0 | 7.7 | 15.3 | 28.8 | 46.7 |
| Alumni Rel. | 0 | 0 | 11.4 | 26.8 | 59.3 | 0 | 3.3 | 31.1 | 42.4 | 19.9 | 0 | 1.8 | 22.3 | 35.4 | 37.6 |
| Ses | 0 | 1.6 | 5.7 | 11.4 | 78.9 | 0 | 5.3 | 9.3 | 13.9 | 70.2 | 0 | 3.6 | 7.7 | 12.8 | 74.1 |
| Par. Occup. | 0 | 0 | 0 | 4.9 | 93.5 | 0 | 0 | 2.0 | 14.6 | 82.1 | 0 | 0 | 1.1 | 10.2 | 87.2 |
| Need | 0 | .8 | 0 | 5.7 | 91.9 | .7 | 1.3 | 2.6 | 8.6 | 84.8 | .4 | 1.1 | 1.5 | 7.3 | 88.0 |
| Diversity | 0 | 10.6 | 16.3 | 17.9 | 53.7 | .7 | 15.9 | 33.8 | 23.2 | 24.5 | .4 | 13.5 | 25.9 | 20.8 | 37.6 |
| Compatib. | 0 | 4.1 | 12.2 | 15.4 | 66.7 | .7 | 23.8 | 33.8 | 30.5 | 9.3 | .4 | 15.0 | 24.1 | 23.7 | 35.0 |
| Skills | 0 | 1.6 | 32.5 | 22.0 | 42.3 | 0 | 3.3 | 31.8 | 36.4 | 25.8 | 0 | 2.6 | 32.1 | 29.9 | 33.2 |
| N = | 123 | | | | | 151 | | | | | 274 | | | | |

5 = Single most important factor

4 = Very important factor

3 = Moderately important factor

2 = Minor factor

1 = Do not consider

**49**

## Table 2.3
### REASONS FOR THE IMPORTANCE OF ADMISSIONS FACTORS

| | Percentage of Sample Citing Each Reason | | |
| --- | --- | --- | --- |
| | Public | Private | All |
| Admission on the basis of certain factors, such as grade point average, creates a positive incentive for high school students. | 32.5% | 31.1% | 31.8% |
| The use of certain factors best predicts the academic success of students at our institution. | 78.0 | 84.8 | 82.4 |
| The use of certain factors best predicts the later professional success of students who attend our institution. | .8 | 10.6 | 6.2 |
| The university must meet standards of fairness or equality required by the state or federal government. | 46.3 | 12.6 | 27.7 |
| I have an idea about what I think is a fair selection process. | 7.3 | 11.9 | 9.9 |
| It costs too much or takes too much time to use other factors. | 4.1 | .7 | 2.2 |
| The use of these factors protects the institution from adverse publicity. | 5.7 | 1.3 | 3.3 |
| The use of these factors will protect the university from litigation. | 5.7 | 2.0 | 3.6 |
| The use of these factors will channel quality applicants to the university in the future. | 25.2 | 37.1 | 31.8 |
| The use of these factors will improve the financial well-being of our institution now and in the future. | .8 | 5.3 | 3.3 |
| Other | 6.5 | 7.9 | 7.3 |
| No answer | 12.2 | 6.6 | 9.0 |
| $N$ = | 123 | 151 | 274 |

## Table 2.4
### PERCENT REPORTING ROUTINE EXCEPTIONS
### TO FORMAL ACADEMIC REQUIREMENTS

| Institutions | Control of Institution | | |
| --- | --- | --- | --- |
| | Public | Private | All |
| Athletes | 39.8% | 13.9% | 25.5% |
| Alumni relatives | 17.1 | 24.5 | 21.2 |
| Faculty/staff relatives | 21.1 | 31.8 | 27.0 |
| Racial/ethnic minorities | 55.3 | 30.5 | 41.6 |
| First generation to college | 12.2 | 9.9 | 10.9 |
| Women | 6.5 | 1.3 | 3.6 |
| Adult students | 48.8 | 26.5 | 36.5 |
| Handicapped students | 29.3 | 11.3 | 19.3 |
| Students with special talents (e.g., art, music) | 39.0 | 16.6 | 26.6 |
| Veterans or active military personnel | 26.0 | 8.6 | 16.4 |
| Students who can pay the full cost | 3.3 | 1.3 | 2.2 |
| Disadvantaged students (as distinct from racial/ethnic minorities) | 38.2 | 24.5 | 30.7 |
| International students | 10.6 | 12.6 | 11.7 |
| Percent reporting no exceptions | 28.5 | 46.4 | 38.3 |
| $N =$ | 123 | 151 | 274 |

officers at public institutions reported making more exceptions. Over half of the public institution sample reported making routine exceptions for minority students. Almost half reported exceptions for adult students, most likely not requiring SAT or ACT scores for older applicants. Over a third of the public school sample also reported routine exceptions for athletes, the disadvantaged, and students with special talents. Private university respondents reported exceptions mostly for minorities, faculty/staff relatives, alumni relatives, adults, and disadvantaged students. Once again, however, only about a quarter of the private school respondents cited routine exceptions in any of these categories. Twenty-eight percent of the public-university sample reported making no exceptions; 46 percent of the private university sample reported making no exceptions.

Admissions officers make exceptions to academic requirements for several reasons. Some indicators are not thought to predict well for specific groups of applicants.[73] Public institutions must meet state or federal government standards. Campus diversity could be a goal. As one officer put it, "the quality of the class is determined not only by the collection of talented individuals but also by the characteristics of the class as a whole." Admissions officers want to channel quality applicants and resources to the university in the future. Financial constraints and group pressures are at work.

### Procedures

While the goals and criteria of undergraduate admissions are similar across institutions, there is great variety at the level of implementation. In this section I draw upon my interviews with 15 admissions officers to discuss the major theoretical and practical issues of implementation. As I noted in the introduction, all of these institutions are "selective." That is to say, they receive many, many more applications than spaces available and hard choices have to be made.

***The initial sorting of the applicant pool.*** Admissions decisions at highly selective institutions may be thought of as tradeoffs between academic merit and desired nonacademic qualities. In practice, many institutions use a grid system as illustrated in Figure 2.1. Applicants are placed in the blocks of the grid depending upon their "scores" on the axis variables, which I will refer to as *academic* and *nonacademic* scores.

Some institutions use the placement of applicants only as a

### *Figure 2.1*
### ADMISSIONS GRID

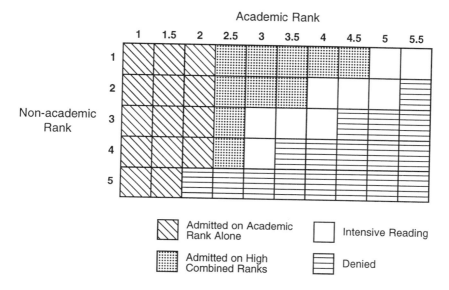

sorting system. It helps to look at the strength of the whole pool of applicants, and individual cells bring "like" applicants together to be evaluated. The job of accepting and rejecting is then working in diagonally from the best (in the upper left section) and the worst (lower right section). All applicants in the upper left-hand cells, for instance, are not necessarily automatically accepted; applicants in the lower right-hand cells are not automatically rejected. A more detailed look at the applicant's record, for example, might reveal personal problems or a competitive high school in which few students have grade point averages above 3.5, so that the student is bumped too far down on an academic scale. Overall, however, the best and the worst parts of the applicant pool are the easy choices. It is the applicant in the middle whose fate is most likely to be debated in committee or read by more than two admissions officers. These are the cases where more information may be requested about the applicants because they all look very similar.

Other institutions use placement on the grid to create tiers of admitted students. One university, for example, accepts 40–60 percent of the freshman class on the basis of academic merit alone. With respect to Figure 2.1, this implies that applicants would be admitted starting from the left side and moving to the right until this percentage of the class is reached. The remainder of the class is filled, as before, moving diagonally toward the middle.

*Academic considerations.* Academic ratings are formed either purely quantitatively or by using profiles. For example, one university forms academic ratings by entering the applicant's class rank, SAT scores, science achievement test, math and science grades, and humanities and social science grades into the computer, which then sorts the students into quintiles. Each of these elements is given equal weight in determining the final score. At other institutions, scores are assigned by matching applicants to "profiles" for each academic score. For example, the highest academic score of "one" is an applicant who has "combined SATs above 1400, is in the top 2 or 3 percent of his or her high school class, has very strong recommendations, and has taken advantage of available advanced placement courses." The task of matching applicants to score profiles does involve some discretion. Admissions officers are told, for instance, to "feel free to rate a student higher or lower than statistics might seem to dictate if personal qualities make this student more or less desirable than he/she seems statistically."

Many state universities, with large numbers of applicants, use highly mechanized procedures. At one such university, the admissions officers ask the Educational Testing Service in Princeton to regress first-year grades on high school grades, SAT scores, rank in high school class (if honors program), and ACT scores. They then use the regression coefficients as weights in selecting students for the next year, given (1) a target number of enrollment, (2) the expected distribution of applicants' scores, and (3) the expected yield rate.

Academic scores are also adjusted as high-school grades are reinterpreted. Many admissions officers recalculate grade point averages in order to eliminate "nonacademic" classes and standardize the grading scales. A few weight grade point averages by the "quality" of the high school, believing that a strong student from a private school that gives practically no A's could have a misleading grade point average. Those who avoid assigning weights to high school quality do so for two major reasons. One director argued that there was simply no way to tell if a student at the top of her class at a "poor" high school wouldn't also be at the top of her class at an "excellent" high school. Another director said that high school weights were avoided for political reasons, because if the list of weights were to get out, some high school officials would no doubt be annoyed and argumentative about their relative standing. At one public institution, grade point averages are adjusted for high school quality and, in addition, the admissions officers look at the success of freshmen from the applicant's high school.

***Nonacademic considerations.*** Nonacademic scores are also formed by using either computerized point systems or profiles. However, while the criteria used in academic ratings are fairly constant across universities, the criteria used in nonacademic ratings are not. Nonacademic ratings are formed using either positive personality attributes or indicators of disadvantage or both. I offer three examples.

The first institution is private and uses "personality ratings" that are assigned by the use of profiles similar to those used in assigning academic scores. The final personality rating used as the nonacademic rank on the grid is the average of three subscales. The first subscale measures "academic initiative." The desirable intellectual qualities include "curiosity, creativity, focus, sense of commitment, discipline, initiative, motivation, perseverance, resilience, and energy." These are to be gleaned from recommendations, essays, research experience, and academically oriented extracurricular activities. The low-score profile is the applicant who has not taken challenging courses, has lukewarm references, and shows little sense of intellectual curiosity. The high-score profile is the applicant who has taken unusually challenging courses, has superlative recommendations, and has achieved nationwide or state recognition in an independent project.

The second subscale measures "personal attributes," such as the ability to relate to others, maturity, sense of humor, and sense of social responsibility. This relies mostly on recommendations. The low-score profile is the applicant with negative qualities and a limited ability to relate to others. The high-score profile is the applicant who deeply impresses and inspires others. The final sub-scale measures "personal accomplishments," such as special talents (athletes, musicians, artists), organizational leadership, hobbies, and jobs. The low-score applicant has no apparent skills or accomplishments while the outstanding applicant has an extraordinary depth and/or breadth of talent or national recognition.

My second example, a public institution, uses a nonacademic rating that is computer-generated from three types of criteria. The first criterion is "diversity," defined as ethnic identity and state of residence. As a public institution it must give priority to in-state applicants. This institution is also required, however, to serve the state by having its student population reflect the ethnic proportions of the state population of graduating high school seniors. Points are therefore given to applicants for being members of underrepresented minorities. The second criterion is "hardship," meaning disabilities, educational disadvantage, and low-income status. Educational disadvantage takes into consideration whether or not the applicant's parents attended college and the resources available at the applicant's high school. The third criterion is "special talents, interests, and experiences," which takes into account athletic, musical, and artistic abilities.

The final example is a public institution that is less selective than the previous two. At this institution, nonacademic factors are incorporated as part of an overall grade point average. First, each applicant's grade point average is recalculated after deleting non-academic classes. Then, students with very high grade point averages and test scores are accepted with no further ado. About 33 percent of the applicants are automatically admitted in this fashion; about 10 percent are rejected. Points are added to the recalculated grade point average for applicants in the middle group according to how they rate on five additional factors. First, applicants are assigned points according to the quality of their high school. Next, they receive points if they are from an underrepresented geographic location. Third, an applicant will receive a bonus point for being the offspring or sibling of an alumnus. Fourth, the applicant is judged on how well he or she took advantage of the high school curriculum. Finally, an applicant's grade point average is upgraded if he or she possesses any "unusual or unique" characteristics. This includes athletic or musical ability, economic hardship, and membership in an underrepresented minority group. After this process is completed, about 10 percent more applicants will be accepted, and the rest deferred until enrollment goals are evaluated.

### Final Decisions

After students have been evaluated on academic and nonacademic criteria, the decision to admit, reject, or "hold" each applicant is made. Even when a grid is not actually used, the applicant pool divides itself into the easy cases and the hard choices in the middle range where all of the applicants are very much alike. Often, it is not a question of who can do the work at the university. Nearly all of the admissions officers that I interviewed claimed that the self-selection of applicants ensured that most would be able to graduate from their institution. The middle-range decisions are usually made by building a case for applicant admission on the basis of the objectives outlined earlier in this chapter. The percentage of applicants that fall into each of the "easy admit, easy reject, and difficult decision" categories depends on the nature of the applicant pool, the selectivity of the institution, and institutional estimates of the yield rates for different kinds of applicants. A waiting list is often used to fine tune the process. Most institutions take care of the final decisions in the course of two or three months while a few use rolling admissions.[74]

There is great variation among institutions with respect to the mechanics of the process, such as the number of admissions officers who read each file, whether or not the hard decisions are made in committee, and whether or not admissions officers are assigned to files on a regional basis. In the survey, I asked respondents to describe the process in terms of one or more procedures. The first of these procedures is a quota or benchmark system in which targets are set to determine the composition of various groups in each entering class. The second procedure is a point system in which points are awarded to candidates based upon valued attributes, and then those with a certain number of points are admitted. The third procedure is a tiered system in which the first tier is evaluated against academic standards and the second tier

*Table 2.5*

**THE ADMISSIONS PROCESS**

| "How would you describe the admissions process at your institution?" | Control of Institution | | |
|---|---|---|---|
| | Public | Private | All |
| We have a quota system in which we set targets to determine the composition of each entering class. | 10.6% | 6.6% | 8.4% |
| We award points to candidates based upon valued attributes and then choose those with the highest number of points. | 11.4 | 11.9 | 11.7 |
| We have a "tiered" system in which the first tier is evaluated against academic standards and the second tier is evaluated on both academic and qualitative considerations. | 25.2 | 26.5 | 26.0 |
| These responses do not accurately describe the admissions process. | 56.9 | 49.7 | 53.0 |
| N = | 123 | 151 | 274 |

is evaluated on both academic and qualitative considerations.[75] I allowed admissions officers to select a combination of procedures or offer their own description if the listed procedures were not accurate.

The results are presented in Table 2.5.[76] A majority said that none of these alternatives captured the process. Written comments revealed certain standard modifications of each category. For instance, respondents wrote that the tiers are malleable and contain both quantitative and qualitative considerations. Some of the point systems are very strict, centralized, and computerized processes used in isolation, while others are used as a first cut, followed by a qualitative review of the applicants. Some officers noted explicit comparisons between each applicant and the entire pool, while others required applicants to meet a series of thresholds without explicitly comparing them to the rest of the applicant pool. Most denied using quotas, and instead wrote of using "goals within an expected range" or "objectives" like average SAT scores, male/female distribution, geographic diversity, and percentage on financial aid. Apparently, admissions officers use more flexible versions of the procedures that were presented in the survey questions.

***Group representation.*** The representation of ethnic constituencies that are underrepresented vis-à-vis their proportions in the state or nation was a top priority at the institutions I visited. Efforts to achieve racial parity are focused on increasing applicant pools or altering admissions procedures to increase the number of minority students on campus. Affirmative action was defined by these admissions officers as heightened recruitment. Institutions will purchase only the names of minority students from testing agencies in order to send out brochures and recruitment materials. Admissions officers do recruitment visits to high schools in heavily minority-populated school districts. Some colleges offer special scholarships to promising minority students or pay for minority students to visit campus. Minority student application files are given special attention, with admissions officers making phone calls to teachers or counselors to clarify the details of the application.

In addition, most selective institutions have a policy regarding the way in which underrepresented minority status enters the admissions process. The determination of whether or not an ethnic group is underrepresented is based upon the percentage of graduating high school seniors or adults in that ethnic group in the state or the entire nation. About half of the admissions directors I spoke with claimed to have no special policy for minority students aside from intensive recruitment efforts; these were mostly private schools. The other half used one of three different methods. I offer three examples.

The first case is one of the public institutions that I described previously. Its admissions policy is based upon the grid that trades off academic merit and educational disadvantage. In that setup, race is one criterion among many others. When questioned about the details of the weighting process, however, an admissions officer revealed that his office had carried out computer simulations on previous applicant pools to know "where the chips were gonna fall" in the aggregate. Adjustments in the weighting scheme were made on the "educational disadvantage" side in order to get an acceptable distribution of minority groups at the end of the process. When confronted with the possibility that this is a de facto quota system, he replied: "They can say that but they still have to demonstrate that what we're doing is illegal. And they're going to have a hell of a time doing that."

The second case is the public institution described previously that gives points to the grade point average of minority students since membership in an underrepresented minority group, like being an athlete or musician, counts as being "unique." The director of admissions told me that, though they may be rated in the same way, underrepresented groups do not compete with other students. "If we're going to provide this country leadership," he argued, "we have to acknowledge that underrepresentation is what it is." In fact, he pointed out, without points for geographic diversity and hardship, the entering class would be lopsided geographically and economically too. His institution doesn't have a large enough pool of minority applicants to have the "luxury" of having all applicants compete with one another. When asked if this practice violates the *Bakke* decision, which states that each student must compete against every other, the director told me that "If you really want to challenge this issue, you could take every school in the country to court."[77]

The final example is a public institution that utilizes a system of targets for various kinds of students. Fifty percent of all students are selected on an academic index that combines grade point average and test scores. The rest are selected on the basis of educational and economic disadvantage, special talents, gender, ethnic identity, and residence. Within this second group, the school uses a series of targets for different categories. Of all target category slots, 50 percent go to underrepresented minority students, 18 percent to the socioeconomically disadvantaged regardless of race, 11 percent to those who just missed the first tier cut, 8 percent to athletes, and the rest are distributed among rural students, adults, the disabled, and students with special talents. Within each category, the top half is admitted on the basis of the academic index alone. The other files are read noting the essay, special strengths, and contribution to the diversity of the overall class.

The targets are rough lower and upper bounds that may be adjusted if the applicant pools change over time. The number of applicants accepted yearly in each target group will also change depending upon the strength of the applicant pool in that category. No individual will be automatically admitted. The target numbers were originally set based upon the number of admitted candidates in each category in previous years. An admissions officer told me that "in order to build consensus [over the policy], they had to demonstrate that it would not severely alter the existing distribution of benefits."

I asked an admissions officer how cross-category interpersonal comparisons were made. He described a procedure by which, starting from the top of each category, students are admitted one by one. Each is compared to those being admitted in other categories. "If the person is competitive we let them in, if not they stop admitting from that category." He goes on to say:

> The key of course is what question does a person ask to determine cross-category competitiveness. . . . We will have to rely on some notion of professional judgment or something, which is what happens all the time. At some point you can't quantify it and someone has to make a judgment based on experience, hunches, all those things.

Asked whether targets are not simply quotas in disguise, the admissions officer says there is no difference between this system and those that use weights. But he adds, "The lawyers keep saying 'maybe it doesn't make a difference in concept but it sure does make a difference in public relations.' "[78]

Apparently, the use of quotas is perceived to be as publicly unacceptable as it was in the beginning of this century, even though the purpose is to include those who have historically been excluded. The defensible means of honoring commitments to racial diversity focuses on the individual. Ironically, this was also the preferred screening method of those who meant to exclude groups in the beginning of this century. As Harold Wechsler notes, "Societal rejection of grouping and quotas in favor of individual decision-making, however, meant that for better or worse, the burden of proof fell upon the victims of discrimination rather than upon the discriminators."[79] Admissions officers see little difference between quotas and the three methods outlined above, except for the fact that quotas would be legally or publicly indefensible.

Clearly the *Bakke* ruling does not strictly determine how admissions procedures will work.[80] Admissions officers readily pointed out its ambiguity. In *Bakke,* Justice Powell contrasted the U.C.-Davis two-track system with the Harvard practice of assigning points to race as one of many factors. For Harvard, selection on merit was inadequate because so many applicants were well qualified. Therefore, other objectives such as diversity came into play, and race was treated as a bonus point toward one of these other objectives. Justice Powell wrote that the Harvard system was both acceptable and superior:

> It has been suggested that an admissions program which considers race only as one factor is simply a subtle and more sophisticated—but no less effective—means of according racial preference than the Davis program. A facial intent to discriminate, however, is evident in the petitioner's preference program and is not denied in this case. No such facial infirmity exists in [the Harvard program]. And a court would not assume that a university, professing to employ a facially nondiscriminatory admissions policy, would operate as a cover for the functional equivalent of a quota system.[81]

Justices White and Blackmun had a different view. Justice White wrote:

> There is no sensible and certainly no constitutional distinction between, for example, adding a set of points to the admissions rating of disadvantaged minority applicants as an extension of preference with the expectation that this will result in the admission of an approximately determined number of qualified minority applicants and setting a fixed number of places for applicants as was done here.[82]

The admissions officers that I interviewed agreed with Justices White and Blackmun. They must try to treat applicants as individuals at the same time that they attribute group characteristics to individuals.[83]

The problem of increasing minority and disadvantaged applicant pools at selective predominantly white institutions is a systemic one. The probability of going to college is affected in large part by family income. Over two-thirds of students in families with incomes over $38,000 per year attend college; only 38 percent of those students in families with incomes less than $7,000 per year do so.[84] Moreover, in 1988, only 28.1 percent of black high school graduates and 30.9 percent of all Hispanic high school graduates chose to go on to college.[85] Thirty-seven percent of all whites go on to college.[86] Many blacks attend either predominantly black colleges or community colleges, where they are overrepresented in relation to their proportion in the general population.[87] Overall, the college system is segregated. In 1979, 22 percent of all four-year institutions accounted for 82 percent of all the baccalaureate degrees awarded to blacks and 80 percent of all baccalaureate degrees awarded to Hispanics.[88]

Admissions officers expressed frustration about having to deal with problems that have their roots earlier in the educational system and in society as a whole. They must also confront the issue of the relationship between groups of applicants. One group's "floor" is another group's "ceiling." Increasing the number of individuals in one group means decreasing the number of individuals in another group.

There is a continuing debate over the proper objectives and implementation of admissions policy. While the debate often focuses on race, most institutions select for the right mix of regions, athletes, and alumni legacies as well. The "quota" controversy should therefore be placed in the context of a larger debate about all kinds of preferences and the predictive validity of criteria for different kinds of students across different kinds of institutions.[89] Historically, academic merit has never been the only criterion for admittance, and to implement it now would be to introduce a bias toward the most economically and culturally advantaged segments of society. Admissions officers do the best they can to operate amid these conflicting claims, in the midst of these theoretical and practical debates.

*Table 2.6*

**DISCRETION**

| "Do you use a formula to make decisions or more personalized methods?" | Control of Institution | | |
|---|---|---|---|
| | Public | Private | All |
| Admission practices are formula-driven with unambiguous requirements. | 61.0% | 14.6% | 35.4% |
| Admission practices are personalized, with ambiguous requirements. | 17.9 | 70.2 | 46.7 |
| Use a combination of methods. | 12.2 | 5.3 | 8.4 |
| $N =$ | 123 | 151 | 274 |

## Admissions Officers' Consistency and Accountability

As one director put it, "Admissions officers are supposed to be mysterious but nobody will let them be." The concern that the public and the press has with the admissions process involves not only the criteria that are used to make decisions but also the application of criteria. Implementation procedures may be placed on a continuum from purely mechanical procedures to those that involve a great deal of discretion on the part of the decision maker. As Table 2.6 shows, in general, public-institution officers tend to use formulaic procedures while private-institution officers claim to use more personalized methods.

The discretion of admissions officers may be evaluated on the basis of three consistency criteria. First, the actual decisions and rankings of each individual officer are internally consistent. Statistical analysis of rankings made by an individual officer might give evidence of inconsistent or whimsical behavior.[90] Second, the way in which the officer actually chooses among applicants is consistent with the way that officer believes he or she is choosing. Studies of decision making have shown that decision makers usually overestimate the importance of minor cues and underestimate their reliance on a few major cues.[91] Third, there is consistency in ranking across admissions officers both within and between institutions.[92]

I explored consistency across officers at one institution using their most recent applicant files.[93] I constructed a data set from a random sample of 302 applicant files, of which 57.3 percent were accepted, 8.3 percent were waitlisted, and 34.4 percent were rejected. I collected information concerning each applicant's basic demographic characteristics, test scores, class rank, type of high school attended, and socioeconomic status. I also recorded whether or not the applicant was an alumnus relation, athlete, or first generation to attend college.

The undergraduate admissions process at this particular private university works as follows. Each applicant's file is randomly assigned and evaluated by two to five admissions officers. Each applicant is evaluated on the basis of both academic and nonacademic criteria; a summary rating is formed for both sets of criteria. The academic scale, which ranges from a low score of one to a high score of six, is based upon test scores, class rank, breadth and depth of coursework, trends in academic achievement, and writing samples. The academic rating is not, therefore, a simple proxy for test scores. The nonacademic or "personality" rating scale ranges from a low score of one to a high score of four. The applicant is evaluated in terms of leadership ability, motivation, and the potential contribution of the student to the university community. Evidence of sustained achievement in one activity or involvement in a variety of activities is desirable. Officers are given examples or profiles for each score on the academic and nonacademic scales.

After completing these two evaluations, the admissions officer suggests a decision to accept, waitlist, or reject the applicant. Two or three officers read each file. They usually agree on the fate of the applicant; a small number are decided in a committee meeting. The director of admissions assigns a final academic and personality rating and makes the final decision, on the basis of the officers' ratings.

I regressed the final decision to accept or reject the applicant on various applicant characteristics.[94] A linear probability model is presented here since it is easily interpreted and probit estimation yielded the same substantive conclusions.[95] The final academic and personality ratings are included as independent variables.[96]

## *Table 2.7*
### LINEAR PROBABILITY MODEL

| Independent Variable | Full Sample | Officer 1 | Officer 2 |
|---|---|---|---|
| Academic rating | .11*** | .14*** | .23*** |
| | (.02) | (.04) | (.05) |
| Personality rating | .12*** | .19** | −.07 |
| | (.02) | (.06) | (.08) |
| Class rank | −.01*** | −.01*** | −.01* |
| | (.001) | (.003) | (.004) |
| SAT math score | .004* | −.01*** | .01* |
| | (.002) | (.003) | (.004) |
| SAT verbal score | .006** | .01*** | −.01* |
| | (.002) | (.003) | (.004) |
| Gender | .04 | .08 | .18** |
| | (.02) | (.06) | (.06) |
| Private school | .07* | .05 | .14 |
| | (.03) | (.07) | (.09) |
| Parochial school | .23*** | .34*** | .24** |
| | (.04) | (.07) | (.08) |
| Black | .20*** | .65*** | .11 |
| | (.04) | (.15) | (.10) |
| Hispanic | .31*** | .37** | .41** |
| | (.04) | (.13) | (.15) |
| Asian | .07* | .21** | −.12* |
| | (.03) | (.07) | (.06) |
| Interview | .05* | .01 | .09 |
| | (.02) | (.07) | (.07) |
| Athlete | −.01 | −.02 | .09 |
| | (.05) | (.08) | (.17) |
| Alumni relative | .09* | −.26 | .27 |
| | (.04) | (.16) | (.18) |

## Table 2.7 (Continued)

| Independent Variable | Full Sample | Officer 1 | Officer 2 |
|---|---|---|---|
| Socioeconomic status | .01 | −.01 | .05 |
| | (.01) | (.02) | (.03) |
| First generation | .07* | −.06 | .12 |
| | (.03) | (.06) | (.11) |
| West | −.03 | .04 | .11 |
| | (.03) | (.06) | (.13) |
| South | −.00 | −.16 | .19 |
| | (.03) | (.12) | (.11) |
| Northeast | .06* | .02 | .08 |
| | (.02) | (.06) | (.06) |
| Constant | −.85*** | −.31 | −.18 |
| | (.11) | (.28) | (.32) |
| N = | 298 | 63 | 64 |

Note: The dependent variable equals 1 if the applicant was accepted and equals 0 if the applicant was rejected. Entries are regression coefficients with corrected standard errors in parentheses.

* p < .05        ** p < .01        *** p < .001

Table 2.7 presents results for the full sample and for two individual admissions officers. Looking at the full sample of applicants and officers first, it seems that SAT scores have little impact on the decision, controlling for the officers' overall academic assessment. A 10-unit change in the verbal SAT score, for example going from a score of 51 to 61 (510 to 610), would yield only a 6 percent (.006 × 10) increase in the likelihood of admission. A similar increase in an applicant's math score yields only a 4 percent increase in the likelihood of admission.[97] Class rank is substantively and statistically significant. A ten percentile change in class rank, for example going from the 5th to the 15th percentile, implies a 10 percent decrease in the likelihood of admission.[98] It is the admissions officer's own academic ratings that are the most important academic predictor of acceptance or rejection. A one unit increase in the academic rating scale on average increases the probability of admittance by 11 percent. The personality rating has about the same effect.

The type of high school attended also matters, with parochial school students 23 percent more likely and private school students 7 percent more likely than public school students to be admitted. Students who were the first in their families to go to college were 7 percent more likely to be admitted than non-first-generation applicants. The largest effect is that of applicant race. Blacks are 20 percent and Hispanics 31 percent more likely to be accepted than whites, controlling for the other variables. Asians are no more likely to be admitted than whites. In the full sample, the effect of athletic ability, socioeconomic status, gender, and region are insignificant.[99]

The same regression carried out on two individual officers reveals significant individual differences.[100] Officer One is a white woman in her twenties with only a couple of years of experience, while Officer Two is a white woman in her forties with several years of experience in college admissions. The two officers differ with respect to reliance on their own academic and personality ratings. Specifically, the personality rating of applicants by Officer Two seems to have no effect on the likelihood of admission, while a unit increase in her academic rating on average increases the probability of admission by 23 percent. On the other hand, Officer One's personality rating has a strong and significant effect on the likelihood of admission, slightly stronger than the effect of her academic rating.

The admissions officers also differ with respect to the effect of applicant gender and race. Being female increases the probability of acceptance by 18 percent for Officer Two, but has no significant effect on decisions by Officer One. For Officer One, the probability of acceptance increases on average by 65 percent for blacks, 32 percent for Hispanics, and 22 percent for Asians as compared to whites. For Officer Two, the probability of acceptance for blacks is no different than that of whites, and the probability of acceptance for Asians is 12 percent less than that of whites. Hispanics are 40 percent more likely to be accepted than whites. Finally, the coefficients for alumni relatives and Southerners are substantively different for both officers, although these coefficients are not statistically significant.

The difference between officers raises the issue of the accountability of decision makers. How do we know that principles of allocation will be followed in practice? Admissions officers might claim publicly to follow certain principles and yet, individually, follow different principles in practice. It may also be the case that a particular individual does not consistently apply any principles in practice. The consistent application of principles may be protected by either making decision makers accountable or giving applicants more insight into the selection process.[101]

Offices of admissions usually share responsibility for setting broad guidelines for admissions with a board of trustees or chief executive officer, while specific policies are the result of decisions within the admissions office itself.[102] The difficulty with holding admissions officers accountable is in finding a measure of success. The later final grades of accepted students will not suffice if students are graded on a curve or if academic excellence is neither the sole basis for selection nor the only desirable characteristic of students on campus. Retention rates might be used. In some of the cases mentioned above, the office is held accountable for the ethnic composition of the incoming class. Admissions officers are also pressured if there are too many pre-meds, or if the average grade point average of incoming classes declines. Most admissions offices do internal reviews of procedures in such circumstances.

Applicants could be informed about the admissions process and allowed to contest or appeal decisions. Some applicants do. Generally, however, any individual student has little incentive to invest time and energy reforming allocative procedures. Most students apply to more than one institution and are accepted somewhere, though it might not have been a first choice. Organization of a large, transient, and geographically dispersed population would make collective action extremely difficult if not impossible.

## Conclusion

The study of college admissions in the United States offers one example of the ways in which decision makers at decentralized institutions translate abstract principles into concrete procedures that allocate a scarce good. Variation across educational institutions is a function of two major factors. First, admissions officers have multiple objectives and there is no consensus on their relative weights. Second, in practice, any particular objective may be achieved through the use of a variety of criteria and procedures. The underdetermination of procedures by abstract principles allows for modifications due to institutional and personal idiosyncrasies, public opinion and interest groups, and legislation. Admissions policies are revised over time in accordance with social and institutional changes.

As I noted early in the chapter, most four-year institutions accept a majority of those students who apply, provided that they meet a specified threshold of academic achievement. Indicators of academic merit such as grade point average, high school rank, and prior coursework are cited as the most important factors in the selection process. Admissions officers at both public and private institutions report being motivated also by notions of fairness and equity with respect to members of minority groups and the economically disadvantaged. They report exceptions for athletes, students with special talents, adults, and relatives of alumni.

Admission to the most selective institutions appears to be a two-stage process. Applicants first pass a "floor," or threshold of academic ability, independent of each other. The self-selection of applicants ensures that most will pass this test. The remaining applicants pass through a selection process where the most emphasis is placed on the individual's contribution to the composition of a freshman class. After the academic ability threshold there is no single dimension of talent or potential to contribute. Admissions officers want diversity of all kinds. They also strive to maintain the particular character of their institutional community.

Though various aspects of the college admissions process continue to be controversial, it is unlikely that it will be radically different in the future. It would be impossible to return to a system of open admission to *all* institutions of higher education. It is highly unlikely that the United States will embrace principles such as queues or lotteries that are used in other countries. Nor will college admissions become a nationally centralized process. Universities have a long tradition of institutional autonomy. As Supreme Court Justice Felix Frankfurter wrote in 1957, the "four essential freedoms of the university [are] to determine for itself who may teach, what may be taught, how it should be taught, and who may be admitted to study."[103] Evaluating whether or not the discretion of admissions officers should be limited (and by whom) can be addressed only by examining both the historical context of college admissions in the United States and the details of the process as it exists today.

## Appendix: Undergraduate Admissions Survey

The survey of undergraduate admissions was mailed in November of 1989 to a random sample of 500 directors of admissions at four-year public and private institutions. The sample was randomly selected from the *1988–89 College Handbook.* The survey questions concerned the characteristics of admissions officers, the mechanics of decision making, perceived group influences, and constraints on the individual decision maker. The survey was developed and pretested with the help of admissions officers at the University of Chicago.

Two hundred seventy-four admissions officers, or almost 55 percent of the original sample, responded. Almost 50 percent of all public institution admissions officers surveyed responded. Sixty percent of all private institution admissions officers responded. Overall, 55 percent of all respondents worked at public institutions and 45 percent worked at private institutions.

Fifty-three percent of all respondents worked at liberal arts colleges as opposed to doctoral-granting institutions. A majority of the sample (74 percent) characterized their undergraduate population as primarily within state or regional area. A little over 19 percent claimed to have primarily national undergraduate populations. Thirty-two percent of all respondents worked at institutions in the Midwest, 25 percent worked in the Northeast, 23 percent worked in the West, and 20 percent in the South.

The survey was funded by the Russell Sage Foundation, the Spencer Foundation, and the College Board.

## NOTES

1. Access to higher education in the United States is not usually considered a "scarce" good, given our extensive system of public and community colleges, but admission to selective institutions does offer access to the "rewards of prestige, status, and substantial earnings." See W. Manning, "The Pursuit of Fairness in Higher Education," in *Selective Admissions in Higher Education,* Carnegie Council on Policy Studies in Higher Education, San Francisco: Jossey-Bass 1977, p. 27. A "selective" institution is one in which only a limited number of qualified individuals are admitted.

2. College admission could also be evaluated from the perspective of the applicant or from the perspective of the system as a whole. B. Alden Thresher, *College Admissions and the Public Interest,* New York: College Entrance Board 1966.

3. AACRAO/College Board, *Undergraduate Admissions: The Realities of Institutional Policies, Practices, and Procedures,* New York: CEEB 1980; *Demographics, Standards, and Equity: Challenges in College Admissions,* New York: CEEB 1986.

4. The appendix to this chapter describes the respondents and the response rates according to region and institutional type.

5. Five of the admissions officers worked at public universities, nine worked at private universities, and one worked at a private liberal arts college. The institutions were distributed almost equally between the midwestern, northeastern, and western regions of the country. All interviews were conducted between September 1989 and June 1991. I chose the sample of institutions on the basis of scheduling and cost considerations, though I was also interested in interviewing officers from institutions involved in public controversies over admission policies. Every admissions officer that I contacted agreed to be interviewed.

6. The majority of the admissions officers that I interviewed (13 out of 15) were middle-aged men. All of the men were white, with the exception of one African American and one Asian American. I interviewed only two women. All were assured that their responses would be completely anonymous, and most were very forthcoming about the details of the admissions process.

7. In an open-door policy, all applicants are admitted. An admissions procedure is one in which applicants pass acceptable thresholds of admission independently of one another. A selection procedure is one in which individuals are ranked and evaluated relative to one another. See W. Hofstee, "Allocation by Lot," *Social Science Information* 29 (1990): 745–763.

8. For a documentary history of higher education from the establishment of Harvard in 1636 to the Civil War, see R. Hofstadter and W.

Smith, *American Higher Education: A Documentary History,* Chicago: University of Chicago Press 1961, Volume I.

9. The following draws heavily on H. Wechsler, *The Qualified Student,* New York: Wiley 1977, Chapter 1.

10. D. Oren, *Joining the Club: A History of Jews and Yale,* New Haven: Yale University Press 1985. He quotes a Yale historian who says, "Success was really their goal, not Veritas. What they were surely preparing for in their competition was the struggle of making a living."

11. The effect of this phase of admission practice, even after it was abandoned, was to bring consideration of the high school record or transcript into the process. It became appropriate to evaluate students over time and in different subjects. See Wechsler, *The Qualified Student.*

12. From text of the Morrill Act in R. Hofstadter and W. Smith, *American Higher Education: A Documentary History,* Chicago: University of Chicago Press 1961, Volume II, p. 568. Land grant institutions were supported by three additional federal Acts: the Morrill Act of 1890, the Bankhead Jones Act of 1905, and the Nelson Amendment of 1907.

13. D. O. Levine, *The American College and the Culture of Aspiration: 1915–1940,* Ithaca: Cornell University Press 1986, p. 139.

14. Levine, *The American College,* p. 145. He quotes a Depauw professor who said "The most desirable clubs, and the ones that are the hardest to get into, have the longest waiting lines. The same is true for colleges."

15. Wechsler, *The Qualified Student,* p. 149.

16. Wechsler, *The Qualified Student,* p. 78.

17. Oren, *Joining the Club,* p. 52.

18. Hopkins quoted in Levine, *The American College,* pp. 141–142.

19. Levine, *The American College,* p. 143.

20. Oren, *Joining the Club,* p. 43.

21. Oren, *Joining the Club* pp. 45–48; M. G. Synott, *The Half-Opened Door,* Westport, CT: Greenwood Press 1979.

22. Oren, *Joining the Club,* pp. 48–56.

23. Ibid., p. 55. In 1927, alumni relatives made up 13.7 percent of all students in Yale College. By 1936, alumni relatives made up 29.6 percent of all enrolled students.

24. "The number of scholarships allotted to this unassimilable element should be strictly limited upon the understanding that they are not so good an educational risk as the sons of the cultured, salaried class of native stock who hesitate to ask for aid but whose children will not reach college without such aid." Oren, *Joining the Club,* p. 53. The amount of financial aid given to Jews had been covertly monitored for years.

25. Thresher, *College Admissions,* pp. 51–52.

26. As noted previously, this amounts to an admissions procedure, not a selection procedure. Hofstee, "Allocation by Lot," pp. 745–763.

27. C. Jencks and D. Riesman, *The Academic Revolution,* Chicago: University of Chicago Press 1968, p. 280, report that faculty viewed this kind of admissions process as so inefficient that they used the freshman year of coursework to "weed out the misfits." They report that both public and private colleges had extremely high dropout rates.

28. *Higher Education for American Democracy: A Report of the President's Commission on Higher Education,* GPO 1947, Vol. I, pp. 25–27.

29. Oren, *Joining the Club,* pp. 161–166. He writes that "It would have been unAmerican, unthinkable to invoke a Limitation of Numbers policy, restricting the number of those who had risked their lives for their nation."

30. Levine, *The American College,* pp. 216–217; Synott, *The Half-Opened Door,* p. 201. The four reports were published by the Truman Commission on Higher Education, The New York State Commission on the Need for a State University, the Connecticut State Inter-Racial Commission, and the American Council on Education.

31. *Higher Education for American Democracy,* Vol. I, p. 35.

32. Ibid.

33. Thresher, *College Admissions,* pp. 9–15.

34. Ibid., p. 5.

35. Katherine M. Jones Loheyde, "Considerations for Decision-Making in Selected Admissions," *College and University* 55 (1980): 200–201.

36. Jencks and Riesman, *The Academic Revolution,* p. 282.

37. Lewis Mayhew, *The Legacy of the Seventies,* San Francisco: Jossey-Bass 1977, p. 30.

38. *Regents of California* v. *Bakke,* 438 US 265 (1978). The case and friends-of-the-court briefs are described in detail in T. O'Neill, *Bakke and the Politics of Inequality,* Middletown, CT: Wesleyan University Press 1985.

39. Also in dispute was Title VI of the 1964 Civil Rights Act, which states that no person shall be subjected to discrimination on the basis of race, gender, or handicap in any program receiving federal financial assistance.

40. The stated implication of *Bakke* according to the American Association of Collegiate Registrars and Admission Officers (AACRAO) and National Association of College and University Attorneys, in *Legal Guide for Admissions Officers and Registrars,* Washington, D.C.: AACRAO 1985.

41. M. S. McPherson and M. O. Schapiro, *Selective Admission and the Public Interest,* New York: CEEB 1990, p. vii.

42. The statistics in this paragraph are based upon the 1985 AACRAO/College Board survey of undergraduate admission practices.

43. This paragraph draws upon the 1989 survey described in the appendix. Of the respondents, 92.5 percent were white, 5.2 percent black, 1.5 percent Hispanic, and 0.7 percent Asian; 68 percent were male.

The AACRAO/College Board surveys did not ask about the personal characteristics and experience of admissions officers.

44. F. Zuker, "The Persistence of Anxiety: Life as a College Admissions Officer," *College Board Review,* no. 140 (1986): 25–28.

45. E. Shils, *The Academic Ethic,* Chicago: University of Chicago Press 1983.

46. The AACRAO/College Board surveys and my own survey find that indicators of academic excellence are consistently cited as the most important indicators in the admissions process.

47. Figures provided by an admissions director at an Ivy League university, based upon his most recent applicant pool.

48. R. Klitgaard, *Choosing Elites,* New York: Basic Books 1985, p. 60.

49. McPherson and Shapiro, *Selective Admission,* Chapter 3.

50. Klitgaard, *Choosing Elites,* Chapter 3.

51. Levine, *The American College.*

52. Diversity in the service of intellectual excellence is also the logic behind arguments to sort students throughout the college system by intellectual ability. In the current system, those students with the best resources prior to college end up being concentrated in the very best universities. Mixing high- and low-ability students might prove to be most beneficial to the learning environment of all students. An affluent or "gifted" student could advance the intellectual excellence of those students with fewer resources before college. McPherson and Shapiro, *Selective Admission,* Chapter 5.

53. Levine, *The American College;* comments by Stirling Huntley in S. McGowan and S. McGinty, eds., *50 College Admissions Directors Speak to Parents,* New York: Harcourt Brace Jovanovich 1988.

54. AACRAO/College Board, *Demographics, Standards and Equity,* pp. 34–36.

55. Klitgaard, *Choosing Elites,* p. 26.

56. C. Manski and D. Wise, *College Choice in America,* Cambridge, MA: Harvard University Press 1983.

57. McPherson and Shapiro, *Selective Admission,* p. 6.

58. In 1989 a federal district court in New York ruled that the use of the SAT test as the sole criterion for the awarding of state merit college scholarships violated Title IX regulations. *Sharif* v. *New York State Department of Education,* 709 F. Supp. 345 (S.D.N.Y. 1989). On average, women score 50 points below men on the math portion of the test and 10 points below men on the verbal portion of the test at the same time that women have slightly higher high school and college grades. Cited in S. D. Ross et al., *The Rights of Women,* 3rd ed., Carbondale: Southern Illinois University Press 1993.

59. The Office of Civil Rights investigation of Harvard University

determined that giving preference to alumni children was justified, even if this has a disparate impact on groups such as Asian Americans. J. Karabel and D. Karen, "Go to Harvard, Give Your Kid a Break," *New York Times,* 8 December 1990.

60. One director of admissions suggested the implementation of something akin to the medical residency matching program, in which both applicants and institutions are "matched" on the basis of expressed preferences for one another.

61. A poster with the phrase "First Do No Harm" hung above the desk of one director of admissions. He had spent months responding to rejected students: "How you treat the people you turn down in this job is more important than how you treat the people you admit. The people you admit, they don't think it's anything special. They assume that was the right decision in the first place."

62. S. Chira, "Smith Decision on Student Aid: 'Tip of the Iceberg,'" *New York Times* 16 May 1990, p. B7.

63. See B. Mellers and E. Hartka, "Fair Selection Decisions," *Journal of Experimental Psychology* 14, no. 4 (1988): 572–581, for a discussion of the ways race is used to evaluate other indicators.

64. Approximately 94 percent of four-year institutions require a high school diploma according to the 1985 AACRAO/College Board survey.

65. For example, Ohio State University, which has an open admissions policy for in-state applicants, recommends that applicants have taken at least four courses in English, two in a foreign language, three in mathematics, two in social science, and two in science.

66. Ninety-three percent of four-year public and 88 percent of four-year private schools require admissions test scores. AACRAO/College Board, *Demographics, Standards, and Equity,* 1986.

67. For example, "high school reputation" has been included as an indicator of academic merit, but it might also be an indicator of economic disadvantage or individual welfare. Evaluations of academic and personal qualities are hard to separate. Essays, interviews, or patterns of coursework might be used to gauge personal qualities.

68. AACRAO/College Board, *Undergraduate Admissions: Demographics, Standards, and Equity.* These surveys asked about "GPA or rank in class." The 1989 survey suggests that GPA is slightly more important than class rank.

69. The use of indicators of individual welfare may be underestimated because they are typically mediating variables. The question was worded so that respondents were encouraged to treat these factors as traits in their own right. Socioeconomic status would probably be considered important if economic diversity were a goal.

70. See Klitgaard, *Choosing Elites,* Chapter 7.

71. The "admission factors" are those listed in Table 2.2. The question asked was "Why are some factors more important than others?" Respondents were able to select more than one statement, so the percentages listed refer to the percent selecting that particular response (and the columns will not total to 100 percent). Ninety-one percent of the sample selected at least one response, 62 percent selected at least two responses, 35 percent selected at least three responses, 15 percent selected at least four responses, and roughly 6 percent selected five responses.

72. "Are exceptions to formal academic requirements for admission routinely granted to any of the following groups?" Compared to the AACRAO/College Board surveys, I find fewer exceptions for adults and the handicapped. I find a slightly higher percentage of exceptions for racial and ethnic minorities. In 1985, 26 percent of all private and 45 percent of all public institutions reported making exceptions for minority applicants.

73. See J. Crouse and D. Trusheim, *The Case Against the SAT,* Chicago: University of Chicago Press 1988; S. Huff et al., "The Definition and Measurement of Competence in Higher Education," in *The Assessment of Higher Education Competence,* G. Klemp (ed.), Boston: McBer 1980; Klitgaard, *Choosing Elites.*

74. Those who use rolling admissions readily acknowledge that some of the advantages of the process—such as committing good students early—wouldn't persist if the majority of institutions used rolling admissions.

75. Tiered systems operate in two ways. First, the same applicant pool may be progressively thinned. The first round of evaluations narrows the pool on the basis of academic standards; this narrowed pool of applicants is then evaluated on nonacademic criteria in order to make the final admissions decisions. Alternatively, the best students evaluated on the basis of academic standards may be guaranteed admission and the rest ("runners up" on the first principle) returned to the pool for evaluation of other criteria.

76. Respondents were allowed to circle more than one response.

77. A different institution's admissions brochure states that "A few categories of applicants receive special consideration provided they meet basic requirements of academic excellence and personal achievement." The brochure goes on to mention underrepresented minorities, children of faculty and staff, and athletes as those categories receiving special consideration. The implication is that these kinds of students are admitted if they meet a specific academic threshold, without necessarily comparing them to other applicants. The children of alumni, on the other hand, "receive preference in choices among applicants of approximately equal qualifications." Alumni status serves as a tiebreaker when comparisons with other applicants are being made.

78. For a discussion of the distinction between *quotas* and *goals* see the Carnegie Council on Policy Studies in Higher Education, *Selective Admissions in Higher Education*, San Francisco: Jossey-Bass 1977, p. 15.

79. H. Wechsler, "The Rationale for Restriction: Ethnicity and College Admission in America, 1910–1980," *American Quarterly* 36, no. 5 (1984): 643–667. On page 662 Wechsler notes a 1945 court case in which the American Jewish Congress challenged Columbia University for discriminating against Jews. The Court did not accept as evidence the lower aggregate admit rates for Jews. Instead, it argued with Columbia that the law provided only for a rejected *individual* who could demonstrate he was unlawfully denied admission.

80. J. H. Choper, "Continued Uncertainty as to the Constitutionality of Remedial Racial Classifications," *Iowa Law Review* 72 (1987): 255–285.

81. *Regents of California* v. *Bakke*, 438 US 265 (1978), pp. 2762–2763.

82. Ibid., p. 2793.

83. Wechsler, "The Rationale for Restriction"; Loheyde, "Considerations for Decision Making."

84. J. Lee, "The Equity of Higher Education Subsidies," unpublished, 1987, cited in McPherson and Shapiro, *Selective Admission,* p. 7.

85. Edward Fiske, "Lessons," *New York Times* 25 April 1990, p. B6.

86. "Blacks in College: Number and Rate," *New York Times,* 30 April 1990.

87. Predominantly black colleges accounted for about one-third of all the baccalaureate degrees awarded to blacks in 1981. R. Richardson and L. Bender, *Fostering Minority Access and Achievement in Higher Education,* San Francisco: Jossey-Bass 1987, Chapter 1.

88. Ibid.

89. Klitgaard, *Choosing Elites: Elitism and Meritocracy in Developing Countries,* Baltimore: Johns Hopkins University Press 1986.

90. This could happen, for example, if the officer compares applicants on three dimensions and in pairwise rankings always chooses the one that is superior on two or more dimensions. If applicant A is superior to B on dimensions I and III, B is superior to C on I and II, whereas C is superior to A on II and III, the officer will rank A before B, B before C, and C before A.

91. This self-insight result is reported in P. Slovic and S. Lichtenstein, "Comparison of Bayesian and Regression Approaches to the Study of Information Processing in Judgment," *Organizational Behavior and Human Performance,* 6 (1971): 649–744.

92. Intra- and inter-officer consistency are distinguished by J. E. Coons in "Consistency," *California Law Review* 75 (1987): 59–113.

93. Most of the directors I interviewed had extensive experience in admissions at another selective institution. They all agreed that policy is driven more by individual institutions than by the in-breeding of admis-

sions officers or any "professional norms" of admissions officers as a group.

94. The small percentage (8.3 percent) of waitlisted applicants was divided on the basis of the final outcome of their case. Sixty percent of waitlisted applicants were eventually accepted. The decision to accept is coded as one, rejection as zero.

95. Standard errors have been corrected for heteroskedasticity. The constant term is uninterpretable and the $R^2$ is of limited value.

96. Colinearity is not a problem, given the size of the correlations between these ratings and other variables. The only effect may be to inflate the standard errors of the coefficients, but the coefficients themselves will be unbiased. The correlation between the academic rating and personality rating is only .18. The correlation of the academic rating with math SAT scores is .65, with verbal SAT scores is .63, and with class rank is .50.

97. SAT scores are thought to have a greater effect on both the applicant's decision to apply to college and the quality of schools selected than on the admissions decision. The self-selection of applicants means that test scores of a particular university's applicant pool will not be a powerful means of discriminating among applicants. C. Manski and D. Wise, *College Choice in America*, Cambridge, MA: Harvard University Press 1983.

98. Class rank is measured in percentiles; an increase in class rank means the applicant's rank is getting worse.

99. The baseline category for the dummy variable region is Midwest. For gender, the baseline is male. The baseline categories for interview, alumni, athlete, and first generation to attend college are those who do *not* fall into those categories. Socioeconomic status is most likely insignificant due to measurement error. This variable was coded on an eight-point scale on the basis of parental occupation and fee waivers. If this measure is not an adequate control for socioeconomic status, the coefficients for variables such as race could be biased upward.

100. The statistical significance of these results must be viewed cautiously given the low number of cases. Files were randomly assigned to admissions officers. Characteristics of the two officers were found to be insignificant and not systematically related to the characteristics of the applicants they were assigned to evaluate.

101. Elster, *Local Justice*, pp. 162–165.

102. AACRAO/College Board, *Demographics, Standards, and Equity*, pp. 17–19.

103. *Sweezy v. New Hampshire* 354 US 234 (1957), p. 263.

# CHAPTER THREE

# Scarce Medical Resources: Hemodialysis and Kidney Transplantation

## *J. Michael Dennis*

THIS CHAPTER tells the story of the distribution of scarce medical resources for saving the lives, or improving the quality of life, of end-stage renal disease (ESRD) patients in the United States. The aim is to account for the clinical, organizational, and political factors that influence how many lives and which lives are extended or improved.

Hemodialysis and kidney transplantation are examples of organ substitution therapy. These procedures substitute an artificial or healthy human kidney for the patient's diseased kidneys. Today there are over 200,000 ESRD patients in the United States who survive by virtue of hemodialysis and transplantation, and the incidence of ESRD-causing diseases has been increasing by about 10 percent per annum in recent years. Hemodialysis is the only therapy that is available to back up transplantation; artificial hearts and livers are, respectively, impractical and nonexistent. Of the solid organs that are transplanted, kidney transplantation is by far the most widely practiced. Three in four solid-organ transplants involve kidneys.

Hemodialysis and transplantation are paradigmatic instances of tragically scarce medical resources. Historically, not all who can benefit have had access to these life-extending treatments. In 1990,

2,206 patients died while waiting for a kidney or a nonrenal (heart, heart-lung, liver, and pancreas) transplant.[1] This element of tragedy has inspired numerous examinations of the politics and ethics of the distribution of kidney substitution therapy.[2]

Kidney replacement therapy has developed in recognition of political-ethical objections to patient selection practices. The therapies are applied in a cultural context in which doctors are viewed simultaneously with respect and distrust. Following Rothman, I shall emphasize the culture of distrust in explaining the political response to the medical community's methods for distributing organs among its own members and waiting patients.[3] In *The Doctor's Dilemma*, George Bernard Shaw captures this combination of distrust of physicians and recognition of their curative powers:

> Well, Mr. Savior of Lives: which is it to be? that honest decent man Blenkinsop, or that rotten blackguard of an artist, eh?

Although there is a general willingness to recognize our nephrologists and transplant surgeons as "Saviors of Lives," we do not necessarily trust them to select patients without bias.

By saying that there is a culture of distrust I mean that there is a politically influential population composed of patients, members of the news media, academics, politicians, government regulators, and interested citizens who suspect that patient-selection decisions reflect bias, discrimination, narrow self-interest, or other irrelevant concerns. In response to expressions of distrust, clinicians protest that their decisions originate in a genuine concern for the long-term individual and aggregate welfare of patients. Because of the cultural context of distrust, nonclinicians often perceive that the clinicians' protestations are insincere or are rationalizations for deep-seated biases and self-interest.

Accordingly, the story of kidney replacement therapy can perhaps be best understood as a product of the historical tension between science and democracy. Commonly, scientists are accused of an undemocratic arrogation of allocative privilege. While doctors claim that their selective distribution of the benefits of medical progress is medically justified, democrats rejoin that the doctors are prejudiced, show favoritism to some patients, or even discriminate systematically. Scientists claim that organizational diversity or pluralism is for the long-term good of patients; democrats rejoin that diversity reflects the individual ambitions of clinicians. Scientists claim that differences of clinical opinion across subspecialties reflect medical indeterminacy; democrats rejoin that they reflect organized medical interests. The cultural context of distrust informs the local justice of kidney replacement therapy in America in these and other ways. The result is political action leading to state regulation, abridging the autonomy of medical professionals to act on their own conceptions of local justice.

Although most of the story will involve the modern era of kidney transplantation, which began with the widespread use of the immunosuppressant drug cyclosporine in 1983, I also discuss earlier important developments in hemodialysis and transplantation that make current practices intelligible. The material is organized so as to give the reader a feel for past and present struggles to find locally just and politically acceptable distribution in kidney substitution therapy. The reader is provided a lot of the organizational history of transplantation in order to equip him or her with the tools to make an informed judgment of the adequacy of the public-policy response to private distribution of organs, as well as to make understandable the pre-reform methods that determined who received—and who was denied—"the gift of life."

In telling the story it is difficult to overemphasize the role of medical innovation in propelling organizational and political change. For instance, as discussed later, advances in tissue typing and organ preservation technology are making more practical the ethical ideal of the national (as opposed to merely local) distribution of kidneys from cadavers. Whereas in the past the national distribution of organs was seen as medically risky for patients, the proposal gathers strength as objections based on the dictum "ought implies can" are met by medical innovations and medical research on their consequences.

This is not to say that all ethical disputes in medicine can be reduced to issues of medical efficacy, only that patient well-being inevitably constrains policy proposals based on ethical reasoning. Conversely, ethics-based action can push the technology further. The scientific imperative to innovate is strengthened by political influentials who press the federal government to leave no research stone unturned in the pursuit of solutions to ethical problems such as the inequitable distribution of organs. A causal simultaneity between medicine and ethics necessarily creates a politics of organ transplantation, which is responsive to the culture of distrust of medical professionals and organizations.

A brief note on method is in order. The author interviewed approximately 100 transplant practitioners, including surgeons, transplant immunologists, organ procurement specialists, and transplant nurses between 1988 and 1992. Much of the history of organized transplantation, as described below, is based on interviews and correspondence with the "grand old men" of transplantation. Because transplantation is a relatively recent area of endeavor, many of the fathers of transplantation were available for interviews, with the conspicuous exception of the late David Hume. For the period 1968–1988, primary documents regarding organ distribution were acquired from major regional organ-sharing organizations. Between 1989 and 1992, as an observer and afterward as a member, the author participated in committee meetings that advise the Board of Directors of the United Network for Organ Sharing (UNOS), the federal contractor administering the Organ Procurement and Transplantation Network. UNOS was a reliable source of policy statements and data related to organ distribution. The author, then, became to a qualified extent a "participant-observer," facilitating the collection of evidence on the local justice motivations that make intelligible organ-distribution practices.

## Hemodialysis Versus Kidney Transplantation

Although they have distinct histories as well as distinct professional career paths and organizations, hemodialysis and kidney transplantation are competing therapies for the same end: the functional replacement of diseased kidneys. Transplantation is usually considered to be the superior treatment because hemodialysis treatments are time-consuming and exhausting for the patient. This explains why transplant recipients are more likely to return to work and have higher subjective assessments of well-being.[4] A common error is to mistake kidney replacement therapy for a "cure." ESRD patients are never cured. Even the most successful of kidney transplant patients require a careful dietary, lifestyle, and medication regimen in order to prevent rejection of the kidney graft.

Long-term dialysis and transplantation are last-resort therapies. They are needed when irreversible destruction of kidney tissue compromises renal function to the point where death would occur without one of them. We need kidneys because blood cells are messy. Blood cells have "exhaust systems" that "discharge waste by-products into the rivers of body fluid that finally empty outward via the liver and the kidney."[5] The liver can break down some of the toxic by-products, but processing the urea is the kidneys' function alone. Before the 1940s, all ESRD patients—usually diabetics, hypertensives, and victims of glomerulonephritis and polycystitic disease—had shortened lives.

Figures 3.1, 3.2 show the impact of kidney replacement therapy in extending life in America. From a handful of hemodialysis patients in 1960 to the estimated quarter of a million ESRD patients expected to need care in the year 2000, the rise of kidney replacement therapy is one of the most dramatic developments in American medicine. Note that healthy kidneys for transplantation can be acquired from living and brain-dead, heart-beating cadaveric donors.

The top figure shows the number of patients dependent on dialysis in a given year. As the bottom line shows, the great majority of these patients receive hemodialysis treatment in hospitals or freestanding clinics on an outpatient basis, while a minority choose to rely on home dialysis. About 10 percent of the dialysis population receives a kidney transplant each year. Because of kidney graft rejection, about 20 percent of this transplanted population becomes dialysis-dependent within a year of the operation. The number of transplants from living donors has remained essentially flat since 1980, while transplants using cadaver kidneys took off about the same time. Figure 3.2 shows that the gap between the demand for and supply of kidneys has worsened considerably since 1986.

This section will examine the clinical developments that brought kidney replacement therapy into the medical mainstream.

*Figure 3.1*
**NUMBER OF DIALYSIS PATIENTS, 1974–1990**

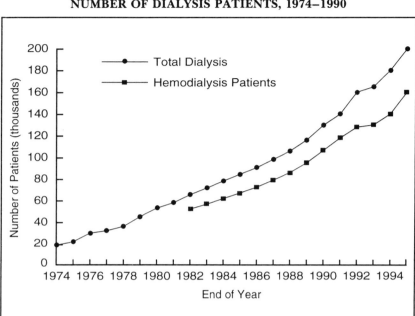

SOURCES: U.S. Department of Health and Human Services. Health Care Financing Administration. Bureau of Data Management and Strategy. *The End Stage Renal Disease Research Report, 1989.* Washington, D.C.: U.S. Government Printing Office, September 1991; U.S. Department of Health and Human Services. Health Care Financing Administration. Bureau of Data Management and Strategy. *Annual ESRD Facility Survey.*

Note: The figures for 1993–1995 are projections.

### Hemodialysis

Hemodialysis is the process of using a machine to filter waste by-products from blood. The term *dialysis* was first used in the 1860s to describe the separation of crystalloids from colloids in solution by diffusion through a semipermeable membrane.[6] In 1913 at Johns Hopkins, Abel, Rowntree, and Turner reported the use of an "artificial kidney" for the dialysis of blood of animals. Haas performed the first human dialysis in 1924. Dr. Willem J. Kolff in the Netherlands developed the first modern hemodialysis machine in the early 1940s. Working with physicians and bioengineers at Peter Bent Brigham Hospital and Harvard Medical

*Figure 3.2*

**WAITING AND RECIPIENT GROUPS
FOR KIDNEY TRANSPLANTATION**

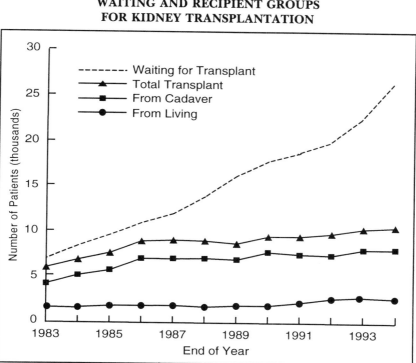

SOURCES: U.S. Renal Data System. *USRDS 1991 Annual Data Report.* Bethesda, MD: The National Institutes of Health, National Institutes of Diabetes and Digestive and Kidney Diseases, 1991; *1994 Annual Report of the U.S. Scientific Registry for Transplant Recipients and the Organ Procurement and Transplantation Network–Transplant Data: 1988– 1993.* UNOS, Richmond, VA, and the Division of Organ Transplantation, Bureau of Health Resources Development, Health Resources and Services Administration, U.S. Department of Health and Human Services, Bethesda, MD.

School, Dr. Kolff designed a new model that became the standard for American practice in the 1950s.[7]

The Kolff-Brigham artificial kidney could provide effective relief from acute kidney failure. For these patients, the Kolff-Brigham model could keep a patient healthy long enough for kidneys to heal on their own, but it was useless for the patient with chronic kidney disease. The Kolff-Brigham model required an invasive procedure for "plugging in" the machine to an artery and return vein. Each artery or vein could be used only once. In a short period, the patient would exhaust available blood vessels. Without the resumption of normal kidney function, the patient would die.

In 1960 Dr. Bernard Scribner and his colleagues at the University of Washington Medical School in Seattle invented an arteriovenous, U-shaped shunt that could be implanted permanently in the patient's arm.[8] This solved the problem of vascular access for most patients, making possible the treatment of chronic kidney disease for the first time. (We shall return later to how the Kidney Center in Seattle admitted patients for treatment.) In 1965 Dr. Brescia and his associates introduced the arteriovenous fistula for blood access, further enabling the large-scale implementation of dialysis.[9] By 1968 artificial kidneys were available to sustain an estimated 550 ESRD patients.[10]

In the 1970s and 1980s, great strides were made in reducing the amount of time the patient had to spend in the hemodialysis center. Thrice-weekly, 4-hour visits were sufficient for most patients. Home dialysis, particularly using peritoneal dialysis (dialysis through the stomach lining), became steadily less attractive to patients as the efficiency of center hemodialysis rose. The greater efficacy of hemodialysis in the 1970s permitted the liberalization of admission criteria. One leading nephrologist said that the 1972 hemodialysis population was an "ideal population": young and otherwise healthy.[11] By 1978, the hemodialysis population had become vastly sicker and older. In the early 1970s, diabetics comprised 5 percent of the ESRD group; by 1988 they comprised 20 percent. Sixty-two percent of new ESRD patients in 1989 were 55 years or older.[12]

### Kidney Transplantation

The concept of tissue replacement can be traced back to the basic text of Hindu medicine, written about 600 B.C. Experimentation with autologous skin grafts (tissue from the same person) was common during the ninteenth century. By 1900 Alexis Carrel had perfected surgical anastomosis, the joining together of blood vessels, and began transferring kidneys between cats. In 1902 Ullman attempted the first renal graft of an ESRD patient. Four years later the first qualified surgical success occurred when Jaboulay anastomosed kidneys from a pig and a goat to an artery and vein in the arms of two patients. The grafts ceased to function after an hour of diuresis (production of urine). A Russian surgeon, Voronoy, reported the first renal transplant using a human donor in 1936. The graft produced some urine for two days. For transplantation to succeed, surgical skill alone was insufficient.[13]

In the 1920s Holman discovered that when a skin-graft patient receives a second graft from the same donor, the second graft is rejected faster than the first. Why did this happen? In 1937, the plastic surgeon Brown transferred full-thickness skin between two identical twins. The grafts had complete survival for 3 years. The significance of immunological rejection began to be realized. Asked by the British government to address remedies for severely burned aircraft pilots, Peter Medawar, a zoologist, conducted his famous experiments during World War II. He confirmed and detailed the "second set response" initially described by Holman: the immune system "remembers" the first graft and is prepared to reject subsequent grafts from the same donor.[14] Medawar then embarked on a series of studies that established the basis for transplant biology. Medawar and colleagues later concluded that tolerance for homografts (grafts from other people) can be "actively acquired."[15] All grafts need not be rejected by the host recipient. Their particular method of fetal inoculation (in mice) was impractical for humans, but the conclusion that the immune response could be suppressed inspired new efforts.

Meanwhile, kidney transplant surgeons at Peter Bent Brigham Hospital in Boston and Necker Hospital in Paris performed numerous human kidney transplants in the early 1950s. (Recall that Peter Bent Brigham had use of the Brigham-Kolff artificial kidney, which provided relief for short-term kidney failure. The limitations of hemodialysis pushed the surgeons there to experiment with transplantation.) David Hume performed the first series of transplants. All of them failed with the exception of one patient who survived for 175 days. The Brigham doctors guessed that this patient had a good tissue resemblance with the donor.[16] Searching for an explanation of the failures in the first series, Brigham clinicians speculated that using kidneys from identical (monozygotic) twins would allow them to overcome the immunological barrier.

Acting on this theory, Joseph Murray at the Brigham performed the first kidney transplant with long-term success. Murray's operation in late 1954 transferred a kidney from a living, healthy donor and placed it in the donor's sick identical twin.[17]

Transplanters relied on genetically matched living donors until 1962. In the year before, Boston surgeons succeeded in controlling the rejection response of a transplant patient by using a chemical immunosuppressant, azathrioprine (or Imuran). The success of the drug gave transplantation a great boost. Hume then showed that adequate immunosuppression made practical the use of cadaveric kidneys and also retransplantation.[18] From this time on, kidney transplants from cadaver donors became more common. By 1990, only some 19 percent of kidney transplants used kidneys from live donors.

Simultaneously with advances in chemical immunosuppression, histocompatibility testing was developed by Amos, Russell, and Terasaki in the United States, Dausset in Paris, and van Rood in Leiden. The theory behind histocompatibility is that if the donor and recipient genetically match on the strong transplant antigens, the immune response of the recipient is blunted. The recipient is unlikely to reject the graft if the donor and recipient are matched on the "strong transplant antigens." Identical twins, for instance, are perfectly matched. The identification of transplant antigens started in earnest in 1958, when Dausset discovered the first transplant locus—HLA-A, that is, Human Leucocyte Antigens grouped at the A locus.[19] In subsequent years tissue typers mapped two other loci, B and Dr. In the standard case for humans, each locus has two sites that are occupied by alleles (alternative forms of genes). These alleles are expressed as, or more precisely, define the antigens found on the surface of blood cells. Barring allele "blanks" (see below), each person has six transplant antigens (two alleles multiplied by three loci). These Human Leukocyte Antigens are used in donor-recipient "antigen matching." In cadaver donation, organ recovery teams send a quantity of donor leukocytes to the tissue typers, who then identify the HLA of the donor and attempt to find a recipient whose six transplant antigens are the same as the donor's. Rejection can occur when the transplant recipient's graft-rejecting lymphocytes (white blood cells) perceive that donor HLA are foreign or different from his or her own.

Histocompatibility experts in this period made two other discoveries that had a lasting impact. First, they found that donors and recipients should share the same blood group (A, B, O, or AB).[20] The "ABO barrier," however, was and is not always respected. Most O kidneys function well in A and B recipients, but not vice versa. Even today, there are circumstances where O kidneys go into A and B recipients, creating an imbalance between the number of O and A patients waiting for transplantation. A second discovery involves the "crossmatch test."[21] This is a direct test of the immunological compatibility of the donor and recipient. Crossmatch tests mix blood sera of the donor and potential recipient and observe whether the recipient has an antigenic response specific to the donor. With infrequent exception, a positive result is an absolute contraindication to transplantation. The crossmatch test is vital for potential recipients who are sensitized. Highly sensitized patients have a build-up of antibodies that make them immunologically imcompatible with most donors.

The sharing of cadaveric kidneys between transplant programs became more feasible in the late 1960s due to advances made in organ preservation. Unless precautions are made, kidney cells expire rapidly with ischemia (absence of blood flow). Belzer's perfusion machine and Collin's preservation solution permitted *ex vivo* preservation for up to 48 hours.[22] Given sufficient organization, kidneys could be recovered from brain-dead donors, tissue-typed, crossmatched at the donor's laboratory, matched with a recipient, shipped to the recipient's laboratory, crossmatched again, and transplanted. The second crossmatch test is routinely done because even under the best of circumstances the first crossmatch test uses dated recipient serum that may not accurately describe the immunization of the patient.

In the 1970s, steady improvements in surgical technique, immunosuppression, tissue matching, and organ preservation led to correspondent increases in graft and patient survival rates. In 1980, patients had roughly a 60 percent chance that their cadaveric kidney grafts would function for a year.[23] In the mid-1960s the likelihood that the grafts would function for a year had been below 40 percent.[24] Patient survival using either cadaveric or living-related donors was at 78 percent for one year in 1980.

In 1983, the Food and Drug Administration approved the use of cyclosporine, a powerful chemical immunosuppressant developed by Borel and Kis at Sandoz Ltd. Today an estimated 150,000 patients worldwide, including non-renal transplant patients, rely on cyclosporine to regulate their immune systems.[25] One-year survival rates for cadaveric kidney grafts have now reached a more comforting 81 percent; patient survival is at 92 percent.[26] Cyclosporine in large doses, however, is toxic to the kidneys. As a result, cyclosporine has not ended the use of other chemical immunosuppressants or tissue matching.

## Expanding the Pie: The Medicare ESRD Program

### Background

On October 30, 1972, President Nixon signed a complex welfare reform bill, known as H.R. 1, Nixon's highest congressional priority. H.R. 1 was battered by a divided Congress and emerged as P.L. 92-603, the Social Security Amendments of 1972.[27] Tucked away in P.L. 92-603 is Section 2991, which extended Medicare coverage on a near-universal basis to victims of one disease, end-stage renal disease. Over 90 percent of the population could satisfy at least one of the eligibility criteria. Implemented in July, 1973, the Medicare ESRD program was a miniature model of a national health insurance system. The government paid medical providers to treat ESRD patients with hemodialysis or transplantation.

The legislative history for Section 2991 is scant. The ESRD amendment was proposed by Senator V. Hartke and adopted after 30 minutes of discussion by the Senate. Neither the House nor Senate heard testimony on end-stage renal disease. In the previous year, Representative W. Mills, chairman of the House Ways and Means Committee, heard testimony on ESRD in connection with national health insurance proposals. The famous in-Congress hemodialysis session occurred in front of Mills' committee. Mills' initiative, however, was not part of the legislative history of H.R. 1.

Antecedents to the ESRD Medicare program can be found in federal health programs in the 1960s. In 1963 the Veterans Administration announced its plan to establish 30 dialysis centers in VA hospitals. By early 1972, the VA had 44 dialysis centers caring for over 800 patients. The VA averaged 150–175 kidney transplants a year by 1971. The Public Health Service supported research efforts in dialysis. The PHS also gave regional medical grants to various transplant programs to improve organ acquisition and to set up tissue-typing laboratories.

In 1966, the U.S. Bureau of the Budget appointed a committee of experts to make recommendations for federal ESRD policy. The recommendations anticipated the implementation of the Medicare ESRD program. The "Gottschalk Report," known after its chairman, enthusiastically endorsed a federal insurance program for ESRD patients. In language common to ethical discussions of patient selection in the United States, the committee wrote:

> We recommend a national program . . . for all of the American population for whom it is medically indicated. Arbitrary selection among patients competing for limited treatment facilities is no longer tolerable.[28]

The Gottschalk Report insisted that access should be universal. Discrimination among the medically indicated—for example, between patients with and without co-morbidity—was disallowed on principle. Fearing the potential expense of an ESRD insurance program, the federal government attempted to dampen interest in the report's recommendation. The effort worked. None of the leading advocates of the kidney disease amendment knew of the Gottschalk Report.[29] Five years after the release of the report, then, its central conclusion was reached independently—that kidney substitution therapy should be distributed on a nondiscriminatory basis.

### How the Program Helps Patients

The outstanding achievement of the Medicare ESRD program is to increase access to kidney replacement therapy. By eliminating the ability-to-pay criterion in the selection of patients for dialysis and kidney transplantation, the program lowered the major barrier to treatment. The program also subsidized the opening of dialysis facilities and attracted medical talent into nephrology and kidney transplantation.

The Medicare program for the first time provided a regular source of revenue for providers of ESRD services. Founded by practitioners associated with the Brigham in Boston, the National Medical Care Inc. was poised to open hemodialysis centers across the country. There was a proliferation of hospital dialysis centers, firms to assist home dialysis patients, and for-profit outpatient centers. The number of outpatient dialysis centers increased from 606 in 1973 to 1,740 in 1988.[30] For transplantation, the program provided a routine source for reimbursement of organ procurement activities. Transplant centers accordingly set up procurement agencies that coordinated the retrieval of kidneys from brain-dead cadavers. With the spread of procurement agencies (over 110 in 1983), the supply of transplantable kidneys almost doubled in the 1970s. Major university hospitals already had kidney transplant centers when the Medicare program began (there were 167 such centers in 1973).

In 1973, dialysis and transplant programs were eager to expand and began to accept increasingly older and sicker patients for treatment. This explains the tremendous growth of ESRD activity shown in Figure 3.1 above—from an original base of about 10,000 ESRD patients in 1973 to the current total of over 150,000. The definition of treatable ESRD patients changed in response to the new reimbursement environment.

### Limits to the Medicare ESRD Program

However exceptional in the context of American health care, the Medicare ESRD program does not ensure complete access to treatment. Program critics note two main areas of concern. First, there is a small minority of ESRD patients who do not meet the eligibility requirements. The best estimate is that 6 to 7 percent of the ESRD population is ineligible for Medicare. Eligibility for ESRD coverage is tied to Social Security-insured status. Ineligible patients typically have insufficient past labor-force participation to be insured by Social Security and are neither the spouse nor dependent child of an eligible person. Eligibility is also granted to persons (and their spouses and dependents) who are over the age of 65, disabled, or blind. Data are currently not collected by Medicare to determine the scale of ineligibility to ESRD coverage. Furthermore, the extent to which non-Medicare ESRD programs (state Medicaid programs, the Indian Health Service, and Department of Veteran Affairs) have offset Medicare gaps in coverage is not known.[31] Interviews with nephrologists and transplant surgeons indicate that the problem is a very small one. One inner-city surgeon said that "no one in this country dies of renal failure because of lack of money."[32]

A second set of concerns involves Medicare-eligible patients, reflecting a recurring friction between nephrologists, who are responsible for referring patients for transplantation, and kidney transplant surgeons. At issue is the transplanters' assertion that there is an epidemic of "nonreferral" by nephrologists. Are nephrologists referring all transplantable hemodialysis patients to surgeons or are they "sequestering" good transplant candidates in their for-profit dialysis clinics? Nephrologists have the power to shape dialysis patients' opinion of transplantation because of their frequent contact with them.[33] This power can be used to divert patients from the optimal treatment protocol. ESRD patients, then, are in a sense a scarce commodity for which nephrologists and surgeons compete, with transplanters having their access to patients largely controlled by their physician competitors.

Although it is apparent that some nephrologists are reluctant to encourage their patients to graduate to transplantation, the data are insufficient to determine the extent of the problem or whether it may be attributed to the conflict of interest generated by physician ownership of dialysis clinics.[34] Arnold Relman, himself a nephrologist as well as former editor of *The New England Journal of Medicine,* has repeatedly accused his professional colleagues of allowing their financial self-interest, rather than patient welfare, to dictate treatment.

Two other problems for Medicare-eligible patients arise from gaps in Medicare coverage. Program critics argue, first, that these gaps persuade some transplantable patients to remain on hemodialysis and forgo transplantation. Three years after a successful transplant, a patient loses his disability status and thus the maintenance income provided under Social Security. Interviewed transplant surgeons are convinced that this is an active disincentive for poor patients to seek a transplant.

The second problem related to gaps in Medicare coverage is that the program induces transplanted patients to violate the post-transplant treatment regimen. Patient noncompliance is induced by Medicare's limited coverage of cyclosporine. One year after transplantation, the patient must find an alternative insurer to pay for the immunosuppressant, which costs about $5,000 a year per patient.[35] Also, prospective transplant recipients who lack private health insurance might be deterred or even screened out. A committee for the Institute of Medicine inquired into access to ESRD treatment and heard anecdotal reports from transplanters that "they could not ethically advise a patient to undergo transplantation if he or she could not pay for the medications needed to ensure its success."[36] Hence, the program gaps may cause some patients to violate the graft-sustaining drug regimen as well as motivate some transplanters to reject some transplant candidates because of their inability to pay for the drugs.

## Patient Selection Practices: 1960–1984

The impetus for the Medicare ESRD program was the existence of an effective life-extending therapy that was too expensive for most needy patients. Since its inception, the program has followed a nonselective philosophy toward patient admission and selection. Given eligibility for Social Security insurance, a patient need only convince the clinician of his medical need in order to receive treatment. The program is predicated, therefore, on the unacceptability of interpersonal comparisons of need or worthiness between patients. The dedication to nondiscrimination is a reaction to the patient selection practices between 1960 and 1972. This section will discuss patient-selection practices and related developments in the organization of kidney substitution therapy.

### 1960–1972

The tragedy of scarce medical resources in kidney replacement therapy was most acute in its early years. During the first 4 years that hemodialysis became available (1960–1964), between 50 and 100 patients survived through dialysis while some 10,000 "ideal candidates" died for want of treatment.[37]

Following their invention of the arteriovenous shunt, in 1962 Scribner and his colleagues established the Seattle Artificial Kidney Center. The Kidney Center was the first facility in the world established expressly for the long-term treatment of ESRD patients. How Scribner and his colleagues decided to select patients for treatment became a precedent for how *not* to distribute artificial kidneys.

The Kidney Center in Seattle established an anonymous, unpaid committee of lay persons to make final admission decisions. The doctors at the Kidney Center gave the committee a list of medically suitable candidates, and from this list the committee chose "who lives, who dies," in the phrase popularized by Shana Alexander's exposé.[38] To narrow down the list, the committee decided to consider only those applicants who were residents of the state of Washington and below the age of 45. The final selection was based on nonmedical criteria, particularly patients' life style, marital status, number of dependents, religiosity, and potential to contribute to society. Alexander showed that the committee relied on typically "middle-class values" in their decisions. To the public, hemodialysis in Seattle became associated with a lay committee that "played God."[39]

The critical media exposure of the Kidney Center persuaded Scribner's peers in the medical community that the use of nonmedical criteria was unacceptable to the public. The nephrological community perceived that public acceptance of hemodialysis depended on finding nonarbitrary and fair methods for deciding who gets treatment. Tellingly, a 1967 survey did not find one dialysis center that used a Seattle-style lay committee that participated in the voting in the final selection of patients.[40] As hemodialysis clinics spread across the United States in the 1960s, nephrologists began to rely on ancillary staff who interviewed the patients, their families, and even persons named as references in an effort to evaluate their psychological suitability and the quality of social support. Ancillary staff included social workers, psychiatrists, psychologists, and nurses. On the whole, nephrologists tried to ground decisions in a science (however rough) of patient selection. Social workers and psychologists could provide nonarbitrary assessments of the prospective patient's ability to withstand the substantial rigors of long-term hemodialysis.

The new reliance on ancillary personnel partially but never fully legitimated the patient-selection practices of nephrologists and, later, transplant surgeons. This is because in practice the recommendations of the scientists of selection largely overlap with those offered by lay committees imbued with "middle-class bias." The correlation between socioeconomic status and "good, clean living" on the one hand and ability to benefit with treatment on the other is a durable truism in medicine. Questioning whether indigent patients make good hemodialysis candidates, two leading nephrologists wrote in 1966:

> Patient selection for motivation, intelligence, emotional stability, and rehabilitation potential appears to be necessary to obtain the degree of co-operation required for long-term success [with hemodialysis].[41]

The fact that credentialed professionals made these recommendations was not enough to make them politically acceptable. The selections were still perceived as being discretionary and as requiring discrimination among persons.

To evade this difficulty, a number of dialysis clinics used nondiscretionary selection methods. Fox and Swazey note that before 1972

> dialysis programs . . . experimented with a number of other selection procedures [besides Seattle's method] in an attempt to avoid the ambiguities and ethical problems inherent in the use of psychological and social criteria. These include ability to pay as the sole nonmedical factor; a first-come, first-served policy; and lottery or random selection.[42]

Besides the maintenance of public relations, another reason for using nondiscretionary methods is a desire to avoid the unpleasantness of deciding who lives and who dies. Alexander quotes a perceptive patient selected by the Seattle lay committee:

> I guess that as long as facilities are not unlimited, somebody has to pick and choose. And then they have to go home and sleep at night. What a dreadful decision! It's like trying to play God. Frankly, I'm

surprised the doctors were able to round up seven people who were willing to take the job.[43]

Constantine Hampers, a leader in corporate hemodialysis, recalls the pre-Medicare experience: "We [the doctors] used to sit around and decide who would go on dialysis. I felt terrible about making those decisions and tended to blot them out of my mind."[44] Nephrologists and transplant surgeons in the period were pulled by conflicting impulses: first, to use fine-grained criteria in order to optimize the amount of well-being from each treatment and second, to find nondiscretionary selection methods that could purchase both societal acceptance and peace of mind. The same doctor groups grappled with these issues while serving on the federal government's Task Force on Organ Transplantation in 1985, as we shall see.

## *1973–1984*

With the implementation of the Medicare ESRD program in July 1973, patient-selection practices changed dramatically. The program had different consequences for hemodialysis and kidney transplantation. The program relieved nephrologists of difficult decisions at both the admission and final selection stages of patient selection, since revenue constraints no longer bounded the size and number of the dialysis centers. As the Medicare program entitled all ESRD patients to government-paid care, nephrologists could expand or create new clinics to meet demand. For-profit dialysis clinics, often as part of multi-unit chains, spread across the country to accommodate the incidence of ESRD.

Transplantation was different. While the flush of government money enabled surgeons to admit poorer, older, and sicker patients into their transplant centers, they still had to select recipients of kidneys recovered from brain-dead cadavers. The necessity of final selection resulted (and results) from a chronic shortage of healthy kidneys. This situation, while leading ethicists and the government to scrutinize the distribution of organs, has motivated transplant surgeons, nephrologists, and organ procurement personnel to focus their political lobbying on organ donation and procurement reform.

This section looks at the experience of kidney transplant surgeons before 1984 in making rules of final selection. As we shall see, the regulatory movement between 1984 and 1992 has not fully eclipsed the practices of this prior era.

Transplant surgeons take seriously their charge of distributing kidneys responsibly. They interpret this charge in three ways, which unfortunately are not entirely compatible. First, they seek to optimize graft survival. Kidneys should be distributed in ways that optimize their length of function in the patient. Second, transplanters have compassion for patients who wait a long time for transplant. Kidneys should be distributed so as to reduce their length of wait. These are primarily sensitized patients (i.e., patients with preformed antibodies that make them incompatible with most recovered kidneys), O blood group patients, and persons with relatively rare and poorly defined HLA makeups.

Third, transplanters also believe that their individual programs should get their "fair share" of recovered kidneys. Interpretation of fairness here takes several forms. One influential interpretation is that the transplant programs that "work hardest" at organ procurement should get the most kidneys. This interpretation was more prevalent before the development of modern organ procurement organizations in the mid-1980s, which took over many of the background tasks. Since all but the smallest transplant programs must rely on the cooperation of many different hospitals for donors, organ procurement entails maintaining good relations with the donor hospitals in the area and timely and effective surgical removal of donor organs by the transplant surgeons or appointed surrogates.

The norm across the country used to be that the kidney transplant surgeon who performed the nephrectomy on a donor would "keep" one or both procured kidneys for use at his own center. Such a "keep-one, share-one" system was seen as positive reinforcement for the hard work of procurement.[45] The same ethical logic applies to procurement organizations that often insist on the right to serve their member transplant programs by keeping locally procured kidneys in the area. Center-respecting allocation was perceived as "fair" because of its purportedly positive relationship to increasing the *global* supply of organs and because it was only "fair" to allow the hardest working programs to benefit their own patients with their labors. To some of their critics in the early 1980s, when the federal government began to take an active interest in organ distribution, transplant surgeons who argued the merits of local distribution were said to be cynically rationalizing their interest in keeping recovered organs for use by their own centers.

The contradictions between the three goals—we shall refer to them as medical efficiency, compassion, and inter-center fairness—continue to be the bane of transplantation. The causal connections behind the contradictions are the stuff of political-ethical debate in the transplant arena, however arcane to the nonspecialist. To illustrate: A distribution system that leads to a maximum rate of graft survival (medical efficiency) will surely require reduced access for sensitized patients (because sensitized patients have a graft-survival rate lower than average) and an abridgement of center-respecting organ distribution (because organ sharing across programs can benefit graft survival).

In order to bring rationality to the organ procurement and distribution process as well as protect their programs' interests, transplant surgeons formed organizations that attempted to reconcile these contradictions. The concurrent development of these organizations presents a stunning pluralism of ways that responsible professionals have met the challenge of distributing organs fairly while simultaneously respecting the interests of member transplant programs and the limits of medical technology. Some of these organizations and their rules of final selection are described below.

In the late 1960s, transplanters set up three regional kidney-sharing networks.[46] These networks are composed of transplant centers that agree to share recovered kidneys under agreed-upon circumstances. The main reason for kidney sharing is to increase medical efficiency. The reader will recall that HLA or antigen matching is one, albeit controversial, method for neutralizing the immune response of graft recipients. Leaders of these organizations reasoned that if they could orchestrate kidney sharing on a regional or even national basis, graft recipients could be given better-matched kidneys. Because of the extreme polymorphism of the HLA complex, large recipient pools—say, patients from a whole region—are needed to find good tissue matches with any given donor. The fact that a transplant center happens to recover two kidneys does not imply that the same program cares for the two patients who have the best tissue match with the donor.

Based in Boston, Los Angeles, and Richmond, Virginia, the kidney-sharing networks asked their members to place one of the two recovered kidneys (from each cadaveric donor) into a pool for regional distribution by HLA matching. Transplant surgeons formed the Boston Inter-Hospital Organ Bank in 1968 to coordinate the recovering, preserving, and tissue typing of cadaveric kidneys for the four local transplant programs. A year later David Hume and Bernard Amos inspired the founding of the South-Eastern Regional Organ Procurement Foundation (later renamed SEOPF). The Kidney Disease and Control Agency of the Public Health Service awarded Hume and the Medical College of Virginia a grant to begin a network "to prove the feasibility of procuring a kidney in one location, tissue typing it, preserving it and distributing it to the best matched recipient."[47] Paul Terasaki, the best-known American tissue typer, founded a smaller organ-sharing program in Los Angeles.

In these areas of the country, by 1970 it was common for half of all kidneys to be distributed according to quality of tissue matching and/or recipient sensitization. This meant that the principles of medical efficiency and compassion governed the distribution of many recovered kidneys. The trend accelerated throughout the 1970s. By 1976 the South-Eastern Organ Procurement Foundation (SEOPF) had grown from a nine-center collaboration to 44 member centers. In 1977 SEOPF confirmed its status as a leader in kidney sharing by making available its computer program, the United Network for Organ Sharing (UNOS), to nonmember institutions. If electing to subscribe, a transplant program could access UNOS to find a well-matched recipient for a kidney that it declines to transplant. Some transplant surgeons were so strongly in favor of matching that they would rather export a kidney for distribution by UNOS than transplant a local patient with a poorly matched kidney.

To see how kidney sharing works, consider the (slightly edited) priority system of the Inter-Hospital Organ Bank below. (Technical terms are explained in the text immediately following the system.) The protocol regulated kidney distribution between a dozen

New England programs between October 1979 and 1984. The system belongs to the keep-one, share-one genre.

## The 1979 Kidney Priority System
## of the Inter-Hospital Organ Bank in Boston

Kidney #1: Harvesting hospital gets first priority regardless of ABO.

    (a) Harvesting hospital can be asked to yield kidney for medically urgent, negative crossmatch patient.

Kidney #2: Descending priority by:

    (a) Medical urgency, negative crossmatch.

    (b) "Highly sensitized" patient, crossmatch negative. Definition of *highly sensitized patient:* any patient who, on 3 consecutive months, has stable panel reactive antibody in excess of 75 percent would be given top priority if and when a 3-4 antigen-matched donor is identified to whom the patient is nonreactive (crossmatch negative) when tested with the most recent and three highest sera using sensitive crossmatch techniques.[48]

    (c) Full house HLA-DR antigen matched patient IOB registry.[49]

    (d) HLA A and B locus matched recipient in IOB registry.

    (e) IOB institutions in descending order of net organ credits.[50]

    (f) Full house HLA-DR antigen matched patient in UNOS registry as part of the 8th International Workshop study.

    (g) Inter-regional exchange (UNOS).

SOURCE: Inter-Hospital Organ Bank, "IOB Kidney Priority System."

    The following describes a few, but by no means all, of the nuances of the system.

    The "harvesting hospital" was the transplant center that surgically procured a pair of kidneys. The distribution of the organ recovery task was itself a complicated matter. Each of the dozen transplant centers had its own affiliated donor hospitals. (Donor hospitals have an intensive care unit or trauma center and a neuro-surgical staff.) Hospitals affiliated to a transplant program typically included its own hospital, proximate institutions, and those employing alumni from the program's associated medical school. A transplant center was the designated "harvesting hospital"—the program that surgically recovered the kidneys—for brain-dead donors respirating in its affiliated hospitals. In the Boston area, Massachusetts General Hospital's affiliated hospitals tended to be in the northern metropolitan area, Peter Bent Brigham's in the western areas of Boston. The harvesting hospital kept the first kidney; the transplant center distributed this kidney according to the discretion of the chief surgeon. If a hemodialysis patient was running out of vascular access sites, the harvesting center could be asked to give up the first kidney.

All the member centers had a chance to transplant the second kidney. The Inter-Hospital Organ Bank kept a registry of patients waiting at the member centers. The tissue typing laboratory at the Brigham was indispensable for distributing the second kidney, screening patients on the waiting list monthly to determine their level of sensitization (preformed antibodies). Unless there was a medically urgent case, the sensitized patients were given allocative priority if they were very well matched with the donor. This was a rule based on compassion for long-waiting patients. Tissue typing assisted the identification of well-matched donors with which sensitized patients would have a negative crossmatch. At the end of 1977, 70 percent of the IOB registry had preformed antibodies greater than 10 percent.[51]

Steps (c), (d), and (e) were often referred to because of the difficulty of locating good matches for sensitized patients. A "full house" referred to a perfect antigen match on all three HLA loci. The interesting rule was (e), a bow to the principle of inter-center fairness. A system was devised by which each transplant center received credit for the number of kidneys harvested from affiliated hospitals. These credits were then compared to the number of cadaveric kidneys transplanted by the center. If the center had more credits than transplants, it received priority for the second kidney. As IOB members explain, "Distribution of cadaver kidneys was partially dependent on credit priority in order to create an incentive for a more aggressive organ donor recruitment program."[52] Finally, steps (f) and (g) show the IOB's participation in a study of perfect donor-recipient matches and the UNOS computer system.

The IOB system delicately balances concerns for medical efficiency, compassion, and inter-center fairness. A not uncommon feature in the system is that it allows for the first kidney to be distributed according to the procuring transplanter's discretion. In these instances the transplanter had the freedom to act on his own conceptions of local justice. A patient's access to a kidney depended on a happy coincidence between his medical attributes and his transplanter's selection pattern. Willingness to be part of an experimental trial could be the difference between languishing on the list and receiving a kidney. Conscious of the history of patient selection in hemodialysis, transplanters understood that there was some inherent political risk in distributing about half of the kidneys according to unchecked discretion. Because of cyclosporine, they lost the gamble.

## Because of Cyclosporine

The widespread use of cyclosporine after 1982 had an enormous impact on the thinking and practice of patient selection. This section focuses on the political consequences of the immunosuppressant drug. Because cyclosporine raised transplantation into a viable therapy, the 1980s saw a resurgence of congressional and media attention toward transplantation. The drug also had relevance to practitioners' decisions regarding donor selection. I shall note this aspect before proceeding to the role of politics and the media.

The availability and efficacy of cyclosporine persuaded many transplant surgeons to steer away from using kidneys donated by living persons. Cyclosporine made possible patient and graft survival rates of cadaveric transplantation roughly equal to those of transplantation from living-related donors. The majority of transplant surgeons were never entirely comfortable with living donation. Transplanters have difficulty squaring the medical imperative "Do no harm" (*Nihil nocere*) with living donation, which puts a healthy person at a slight risk. Thomas Starzl, the chief transplanter at the University of Pittsburgh, has crusaded against the use of living donors, pointing to 20 unpublished cases of death from living donation. Moreover, transplanters in the United States have questioned the capacity of persons to choose freely to be living donors. Family pressure could compromise a person's autonomy of choice, particularly in the case of "black sheep." Their moral qualms with living donation pushed experimentation with cadaveric donors. A leading kidney transplanter, Francis Moore, wrote in *The Nation* in 1965 that

> the most important thing . . . is to move away from the living donor entirely. This requires intensive study of cadaver organ procurement, and the definition of those factors in the recently deceased that bias the health of the remaining tissues.[53]

As seen earlier in Figure 3.2, the use of the living-related donor peaked the year before cyclosporine became available; in 1982, 31 percent of kidney transplants came from living donors. In 1990 the figure had slid to just below 19 percent. One might argue that cyclosporine has an ambivalent relationship to how many kidney transplants are done. Although a spur to cadaveric organ procurement, the drug's availability has had a harmful impact in so far as the kidney shortage can be solved by more frequent use of living donors.

## The National Organ Transplantation Act of 1984 (NOTA)

In 1979 a group of transplant surgeons approached officials in the Carter Administration with preliminary evidence for the efficacy of cyclosporine.[54] They argued that the federal government should provide Medicare coverage for cyclosporine and ultimately for the budding procedures of heart and liver transplantation. Although it was not their intention, these transplanters began a political drive that culminated in the passage of the National Organ Transplantation Act of 1984.[55]

In April 1983, Congressman Albert Gore, Democrat of Tennessee, inaugurated hearings to consider several pieces of transplant-related legislation. The "Gore Hearings," as they have come to be called, became a mechanism for a detailed federal review and investigation of the medical worth of transplantation and existing practices of organ procurement and distribution. Concurrent with the hearings, a series of high-publicity transplant patients, mostly babies and children needing liver transplants, focused the hearings on two issues: the shortage of donated organs and the methods for deciding who gets transplanted. Regarding the latter issue, the hearings devoted large chunks of time to expert testimony on questions of "equity," among them being:

- Are foreign nationals receiving preferential access to organs?
- Are children with telegenic faces and politically savvy parents receiving transplants ahead of other needy children?
- Are the larger programs transplanting more than their fair share of organs?
- Are we doing enough to transplant sensitized patients?
- Are some transplant programs favoring rich patients either directly or by condoning their purchase of kidneys from poor people?

In asking these questions, Gore and other critics expressed concern over the absence of a "rational" national system for the distribution of organs.[56]

Questions of equity displaced from the policy agenda the issues of Medicare coverage of cyclosporine and of liver and heart transplants. Of the transplanters' initial set of policy goals, only federal support for organized procurement would be included in the final legislation. The Gore Hearings cast doubt on whether transplant surgeons used their discretionary authority in a nondiscriminatory, unbiased fashion. A consensus emerged in Gore's committee that although there was inconclusive evidence of systematic wrongdoing by transplanters, it was disturbing that there was no monitoring mechanism for regulating transplanters' distribution of scarce organs.

One particular exchange between Congressman Skeen and a patients' rights activist gives a sense of the committee's concern.

The issue before the committee was whether nonimmigrant aliens received preferential access to kidney transplants.

> **Rep. Skeen:** Does anyone on this panel know of anyone who was displaced as a patient because of an alien or non-alien [getting priority]?

> **Ms. Lindsay:** As I stated in my testimony, there are instances where a patient feels like they have been passed over. But at [*sic*] the present system, there is no way to verify this.

> **Rep. Skeen:** But there is a strong feeling among patients that they have been displaced, or that there has been some displacement?

> **Ms. Lindsay:** Yes. And in some instances, they can point to a specific transplant or organ [regarding which] they feel like they have been passed over.[57]

The fact that no authority monitored organ distribution generated anxiety and suspicion over the decisions of transplant surgeons. In reference to the purportedly passed-over person, Ms. Lindsay later observed that "the problem is not whether the kidney was correctly transplanted [i.e., distributed]. The problem is there is no way of determining it [retrospectively]."[58]

According to the act's résumé, NOTA is "an act to provide for the establishment of the Task Force on Organ Transplantation and the Organ Procurement and Transplantation Network [OPTN], to authorize financial assistance for organ procurement organizations, and for other purposes."[59] In later sections we shall have ample opportunity to discuss the Task Force and the OPTN, which is now referred to as UNOS, the United Network for Organ Sharing, or just "Network." UNOS regulates organ distribution.

Left out of the act's résumé is the controversial Title III. This makes it a felony "for any person to knowingly acquire, receive, or otherwise transfer any human organ for valuable consideration for use in human transplantation."[60] By prohibiting organ purchases, NOTA foreclosed a market solution to the supply of organs: Adults would neither be allowed to sell their kidneys while alive nor promise to offer them upon death in exchange for a cash payment. The market mechanism also would not be tolerated to arbitrate who gets transplanted. Only "medical criteria" should be used to "match organs and individuals."[61] NOTA acceded to an administrative or rationing model of organ distribution. Consequently, the central question became, if not by markets, how should the Network distribute organs? Congress delegated the question to the Task Force on Organ Transplantation.

In short, NOTA declared that professional self-policing is unacceptable—from here on, discretion in organ distribution would be disallowed, input into the rules of final selection would include representatives of the lay public. In contrast to the discretionary authority of the "God" committee in Seattle, the role of lay representatives would now be to offer counsel on the nondiscretionary rules used by the transplant system.

### The Pittsburgh Scandal

The Task Force on Organ Transplantation had just begun its deliberations when a scandal broke out in Pittsburgh that appeared to demonstrate conclusively that transplant surgeons should not be trusted with decisions granting and denying life. The scandal also seems to have convinced transplant surgeons that they needed federal oversight in order to purchase the trust of the public. This is a key goal of transplant surgeons, who understand that the public's support for organ donation depends on its evaluation of their actions as a whole.

On 12 May 1985 the Sunday issue of *The Pittsburgh Press* rocked the transplant world. In the first of a series of articles, the front page read "Favoritism Shrouds Presby Transplant." Thomas Starzl's transplant program at Presbyterian-University Hospital was the busiest in the world and symbolized the best of American transplantation. The article begins as follows:

> Since January 1984, transplant surgeons at Presbyterian-University Hospital have given some foreign citizens—especially Saudi Arabians—preference over Americans for kidney transplants, according to records obtained by *The Pittsburgh Press*. To ensure that the foreign citizens received the organs quicker than others on the transplant list, doctors bypassed hospital policy that sets transplant priorities, records and interviews show.[62]

Were transplant surgeons discriminating against Americans?

The authors report that in the previous 17 months, Presbyterian transplanted 35 kidneys "into patients from foreign countries." In an least 27 of these cases, there were suitable "Americans" who were passed over. An internal hospital review found that, since 1981, 61 of the 611 performed kidney transplants went into "foreigners." This is their first example:

> December 22, 1984—Two O [blood type] kidneys were donated by the family of a Pittsburgh woman. Of the 17 patients cross-matched, 11 were foreign nationals. Three foreigners and four Americans came up negative, the desirable result. The kidneys were transplanted into two Arabs, however. Of the 117 other Americans waiting for an O kidney in Pittsburgh, the 61 who were on active status were not considered.[63]

Schneider and Flaherty located a patient who could possibly die as a result of being passed over:

> Doctors say a 60-year-old Pennsylvania woman who has been waiting for a kidney transplant in Pittsburgh for three years may be running out of time because she has few remaining sites in her veins where life-saving dialysis machines can be attached. The woman was one of three Americans who matched a pair of donor kidneys that became available May 4, but she was bypassed in favor of a foreigner. An investigation . . . shows that her case is the latest example of a practice that has been a pattern for 17 months for the kidney transplant team headed by Dr. Thomas Starzl. . . .[64]

Asked for comment, Albert Gore, at that time a U.S. Senator, said "I do not think we can accept a system that can be jiggered so that foreign nationals get transplants ahead of Americans."[65]

Schneider and Flaherty's series, for which they shared a Pulitzer Prize, was followed by a federal grand jury investigation of the hospital. Spurred by the *The Press* exposé, the Office of Inspector General (OIG), the investigations branch of the Department of Health and Human Services (DHHS), conducted its own study, "The Access of Foreign Nationals to U.S. Cadaver Organs" (released in August 1986). It estimates that 300 or 5.2 percent of the cadaveric kidney transplants in 1985 were for nonimmigrant aliens. Receiving widespread media coverage, the OIG report appeared to confirm the allegations made by Schneider and Flaherty. As for Starzl, he denied involvement in any wrongdoing and was reportedly perplexed by the newspaper's motivation for its prolonged investigation of his program.[66] In his memoir, *The Puzzle People*, Starzl points to his disgruntled procurement assistant, Donald Denny, as the information conduit for a "gullible" news media.[67] After a year's deliberation, the federal grand jury, as well as a hospital-appointed oversight committee, cleared Starzl of charges of wrongdoing.

### The Task Force on Organ Transplantation

Schneider and Flaherty's initial report appeared in May 1985. The timing was excellent for influencing the agenda of the Task Force on Organ Transplantation. Six of the eight Task Force meetings and both public hearings occurred after its publication. Congress charged the Task Force with making recommendations to the forthcoming Network "for assuring equitable access by patients to organ transplantation."[68] Although charged with other responsibilities, such as identifying barriers to organ donation, the Task Force focused on organ distribution. In doing so, the Task Force responded to a feeling in Congress—a feeling encouraged by the *Press* exposé—that there was a crisis in public confidence regarding the distribution of organs. Congress attempted to build in sensitivity to public opinion by mandating that a majority of the Task Force members be drawn from lay fields such as law, ethics, social science, theology, health insurance, organ procurement, and federal health policy.[69]

In making its recommendations, the Task Force relied on the premise that "donated organs [should] be considered a national resource to be used for the public good."[70] The Task Force's reasoning is as follows:

Central to the question of fairness is the issue of controlling the disposition of donated organs. Organs are donated on behalf of all potential recipients; this implies that the organ is to be used for the good of the community, and ultimately the community must decide what best serves the public interest. Although the gift is presently

made to a person, agency, or institution, surgeons and organ procurement agencies should view themselves as stewards or trustees of
this resource. The physicians who select the recipient of a donated
organ are making decisions about how a scarce resource should be
used. Such a decision should be determined by criteria based on
need, effectiveness, and fairness that are publicly stated and publicly
defended.[71]

The Task Force identified certain problems in the existent
system. Again, to quote in full:

> There are several questions that have been raised about the current
> system of allocating organs. It has a strong bias in favor of patients
> in the community where the organs are procured, even if there is a
> better [tissue] matched patient for the organ elsewhere. In addition,
> the perceived commitment of the transplant team to their patients
> sometimes leads to locally procured organs being used in local cases
> for medical urgency, retransplants, or in presensitized patients, when
> the organ could have been used in a better-matched patient else-
> where with more likelihood of success. There are also cases in which
> patients may have provided financial incentives to obtain organs
> ahead of others on the waiting list, though these are exceptional.
> Finally, where medical efficacy is roughly equal, a variety of consider-
> ations, from source of organ and time on the waiting list to social
> and economic factors, have influenced selection of the transplant
> recipient.[72]

The Task Force, then, leaned toward two conceptions of local
justice, "procedural justice" and medical efficiency. Procedural justice means that patients that are equal along relevant dimensions
should have an equal chance to be transplanted. As noted already,
medical efficiency requires that selection be based on relative ability to benefit from treatment. The Task Force resolved that geographical inequity and favoritism interfered with these conceptions. Procuring organs in their locales, transplant surgeons
favored their own patients over others, often allowing their compassion to persuade them to give priority to high-risk cases such
as retransplant and sensitized patients. To the Task Force, such
practices violate procedural justice and medical efficiency. Justice
requires that all persons have access through the same allocative
procedure; one's chance for transplant should not depend on a

single transplant team's efficiency in organ procurement and singular philosophy of organ distribution. Medical efficiency suggests that the decision procedure have a substantial fit to the goal of preventing the rejection of kidney grafts—that is, through genetically matching donors and recipients.

The Task Force recommended that the forthcoming Network develop selection policy "based on medical criteria that are publicly stated and fairly applied." In cases where patients are equally qualified medically, the tie-breaking criterion should be length of time on the waiting list. "In the interests of the effective and efficient use of organs and justice," the Task Force held out the "ideal" of complete national kidney sharing on the basis of tissue matching.[73] But after looking at the clinical evidence regarding tissue matching and at the "technical, practical, and ethical limitations on sharing organs," the Task Force agreed that only perfectly matched kidneys (i.e., less than 10 percent of recovered kidneys) should be "mandatorily shared" on a national basis.[74] The identified ethical limitation foreshadowed a later controversy in transplantation. The Task Force worried that if too many kidneys are shared according to quality of tissue match, minority populations would be deprived access to kidney transplants.[75] We shall return to this topic.

The Task Force grudgingly conceded that for the time being "the majority of kidneys will remain under the jurisdiction of regional organizations." The Task Force's conception of equity ran up against an established tradition of local and regional hegemony in organ distribution. The politics of the United Network for Organ Sharing have been shaped by interests positively and negatively disposed toward the ideals of the Task Force.

## How Cadaveric Kidneys are Distributed: 1987–1992

After much procrastination, the Reagan Administration in 1986 awarded the contract for running the Network to the United Network for Organ Sharing. UNOS began formal operations in September 1987. The first three-year contract required UNOS to develop and administer a set of policies designed to ensure equitable and efficient access to kidney, liver, heart, and other solid-organ transplants. Although a private, not-for-profit organization, UNOS was given public regulatory power. By federal law, transplant programs and histocompatibility laboratories must be members of UNOS and hence comply with its bylaws.[76] To enforce its bylaws, federal law granted the Network the right to deny Medicare eligibility to any hospital whose transplant center is found to violate Network bylaws. Most hospitals would either close or face major cutbacks in the absence of Medicare reimbursement. The Network had this authority until December 1989, when the Assistant Secretary for Health and Human Services announced that the policies of the Network are in fact voluntary. Since that time, the transplant professionals have waited for Health and Human Services to issue formal regulations that the Network would carry out.

Hence 1987 was an historical turning point in American transplantation—the determination of organ distribution rules and their enforcement had been assigned to a single visible and federal accountable Network. Although compliance with Network policies became voluntary in 1989, transplant programs have retained their membership in the OPTN and, with some conspicuous exceptions, followed its policies.

In this section we review UNOS bylaws and local transplant policies that have influenced the distribution of cadaveric kidneys between 1987 and 1992. (The use of kidneys from living donors is privately arranged.) The controversies and interesting policy disputes will be discussed in later sections. I shall not consider the factors that influence which patients go from dialysis to a transplant waiting list, such as the effects of Medicare policy, patient self-selection, referral practices of nephrologists, and admission criteria used by transplant surgeons. We are interested primarily in institutional rules that are both manifestations of local justice and influence who receives kidneys and who languishes on dialysis. The analysis incurs an inevitable risk of inadequately describing present practices and policies, not only because of their complexity but by their rapid supersession. Nevertheless, the reasoning and politics behind the rules are likely to remain representative.

In kidney transplantation, the rules of final selection have two components. The first involves the construction of waiting lists; the second the definition of the rules themselves. For purposes of local justice, how waiting lists are organized is just as important as how patients are sorted by rules.

### Who Distributes Kidneys: The Construction of Waiting Lists

Since its formation in 1987, the national registry of waiting kidney transplant patients has almost doubled in size. Over 24,000 now wait for cadaver kidneys, while the available supply of cadaveric kidneys has varied between 6,900 and about 7,800 in recent years. There are several ways to subdivide the national registry into local waiting lists. The inclusiveness of a waiting list determines which patient population is eligible to receive a given pair of kidneys.

To illustrate how the system works, suppose you are a kidney-seeking patient and that your transplant surgeon works for Northwestern Memorial Hospital in Chicago. Waiting lists, in theory, could then be organized so that you are one of (1) about one hundred patients on a Northwestern transplant center (TC) list; (2) 700 patients on the list maintained by the Regional Organ Bank of Illinois (ROBI), the local OPO; (3) about 2,400 patients on the list kept by Region VII of UNOS (which represents the upper Midwest); and (4) 24,000 on the national list. The current local arrangement would place you on three waiting lists: the OPO list, which includes patients under the care of six major transplant centers in Illinois; a little-used list for regional kidney sharing; and the UNOS national registry.

As a well-informed patient you know that ROBI is distinguished from many other procurement organizations in that it collapses local transplant center lists into a single waiting list. ROBI is referred to as a "single-list OPO." This puts patients listed at local transplant centers on an equal footing to be transplanted with kidneys procured by ROBI.[77] Procedural justice is achieved at the local level; a point system is evenly applied in ranking potential recipients from across Illinois.

A single-list OPO is one of three ways that transplanters organize local waiting lists. In transplant parlance, a single-list OPO is referred to as "patient-driven" rather than "center-driven." More clumsily put, a single-list OPO is devoted to "inter-patient fairness" rather than "inter-center fairness." It matters more that patients have equal chances to receive kidneys than that centers have equal chances to transplant them.

Multiple-list OPOs and keep-one, share-one OPOs are less directed toward equalizing patient chances for transplantation. In a multiple-list OPO, the operational waiting list is the transplant center list. The OPO is in charge of organ donation programs and allocates the privilege of procuring kidneys. The transplant team that procures the kidneys keeps both, using its own center waiting list to determine the identity of the recipients. In a keep-one, share-one OPO, as seen in the example of the Inter-Hospital Organ Bank of Boston in the 1970s, each transplant program maintains one list for distributing the first procured kidney and uses the OPO-wide list for the second kidney. In either a multiple-list or keep-one, share-one OPO, there is a risk that the best-matched local patient (or, for that matter, a crossmatch negative sensitized patient) might not receive priority, because he or she could be under the care of a transplant team different from the procuring team.

Although the trend is toward the use of single lists, keep-one, share-one and multiple-list OPOs still exist in significant numbers and, more tellingly, in larger OPOs serving a disproportionate number of waiting recipients. The growing number of single-list OPOs reflects the federal mandated consolidation of over forty procurement agencies in the mid-1980s and congressional amendment of the Transplant Act in 1990 to mandate single-list OPOs. Mirroring congressional worry that allocation remains center-regarding, the Government Accounting Office surveyed 68 OPOs (the number designated by HCFA) in 1992, finding that 17 of them used a transplant center waiting list for distributing cadaveric kidneys. Of the 17, 12 were based on the keep-one, share-one model, while 5 were multiple-list OPOs (i.e., there was no OPO-wide list).[78] The largest of these include the California Transplant Donor Network (San Francisco/Northern California), Delaware Valley Transplant Program (Philadelphia), and the New England Organ Bank (six-state New England area).

Federal pressure to winnow out the use of center-respecting distribution appears to have been marginally effective, as evidenced by an earlier survey (conducted 2 years before the GAO effort) showing 24 OPOs using keep-one, share-one or multiple-list schemes.[79]

Well timed to influence the hearings for the Reauthorization of the National Organ Transplantation Act, the GAO recommended to Health and Human Services that the government require single, OPO-wide waiting lists for allocating organs.[80] The GAO's concern reflects the "localness" of kidney distribution in the United States. Since only about one in five procured kidneys is distributed outside the OPO, center-driven distribution comes into play for a significant plurality of recovered kidneys.

In this connection we should note that in 1990 the Office of Inspector General (for DHHS), which we shall discuss later in the context of racial inequality, found considerable variance in the length of time patients wait for a transplant. Of 202 transplant programs reviewed, 79 had a median waiting time of less than 6 months for nonsensitized patients, while at 15 transplant centers the median was over 18 months. The OIG speculates that the variance is related to bias in local kidney-sharing arrangements.[81]

In addition to the system used for organizing waiting lists, patients' chances for transplantation depend in part on the relative efficiency of the local procuring organization and the relative demand for organs. In 1989, OPOs procured on average about 19 donors per million population with a standard deviation of almost 5.[82] As tabulated by Medicare for 1982–1987, the incidence of end-stage renal disease varies widely across states, from a high of 275 new Medicare ESRD enrollees a year per million population in the District of Columbia to a low of 56 in Wyoming.[83]

### Mandatory Kidney Sharing

Cadaveric kidneys are a heterogeneous good in the sense that they differ in value for different persons. For the patient whose transplant antigens match those of a donor, the recovered kidney is especially valuable because it is expected to provide longer relief than other kidneys. Following the recommendation of the Task Force on Organ Transplantation, UNOS implemented a bylaw for the "mandatory sharing of six-antigen matched kidneys."[84] The bylaw means that if a patient on the national registry has a perfect tissue match with a donor, that patient's transplant surgeon has first-refusal rights to one of the two kidneys. After kidney procurement, donor tissue is typed and entered into the UNOS Organ Center computer. If there is not a six-antigen matched recipient on the national registry, the two kidneys are then freed for local distribution. The emerging consensus in the transplant community is that first-year graft survival for mandatorily shared kidneys is in the neighborhood of 10 percent higher than for poorly matched kidneys.

The mandatory sharing rule probably represents the most complex inter-hospital collaboration in all of American medicine to date to maximize the expected benefit of a medical procedure.

### UNOS Point Systems

For the distribution of cadaveric kidneys at the local level, that is, at either the transplant center or procurement organization, UNOS bylaws have sanctioned two point systems. A point system is a decision procedure composed of criteria having various degrees of emphasis. A point system ranks applicants according to their relative fit with the criteria. "Patients are to be offered kidneys in descending sequence with the patient with highest number of points receiving the highest priority."[85] Patient's age, race, and gender are not entered on the registry and because of federal antidiscrimination law are not permitted as allocative criteria in transplantation. The two UNOS point systems illustrate how subtle changes in criteria definition and weights can alter patterns of distribution. We go through each point system thoroughly and then discuss their impact on waiting patients.

Both point systems strive for medical relevance and ease of monitoring. The latter condition rules out the use of various discretionary medical criteria that correlate well with desirable patient outcomes. Such criteria include the presence of comorbid conditions, psychological stability, and social support. In the cultural climate of distrust they are unacceptable. Critics of the UNOS point systems sometimes contend that monitorability takes precedence over medical relevance.[86]

The first UNOS point system was initially developed by Thomas Starzl and his colleagues at the University of Pittsburgh.

Starzl developed his "multifactorial system for the equitable allocation of organs" in order to insulate his program from further
negative publicity.[87] The reader will recall that Starzl's program
was cast as the villain in Schneider and Flaherty's reports in *The
Pittsburgh Press* in 1985. Starzl's point system was the only tabled
proposal in UNOS meetings in 1986–1987. The second UNOS
point system is called the Terasaki point system after its author,
the UCLA tissue typer, Paul Terasaki. It replaced Starzl's model
in February 1989. Briefly stated, the Terasaki point system upgraded the criterion of tissue matching and downgraded patient
length of wait.

Table 3.1 summarizes the two point systems. The systems are
similar in that recovered kidneys are offered to patients in order
of their point total. A common exception to this rule occurs when
the patient with the highest point total has a positive crossmatch
with the donor.

Now to explain the criteria in Starzl's model. Tissue matching:
Two points are awarded for each antigen on the A, B, and Dr loci
that matches with the donor's. Each locus will have 0, 1, or 2
identified antigens. PRA: This stands for *panel reactive antibody*,
which is a measure of the reactivity of a patient's serum against a
panel of antigens randomly drawn from the population. A sensitized patient has preformed antibodies against 80 percent or more
of the paneled antigens. These patients are given an additional
point for each decile of panel reactive body (e.g., 8 points for
sensitization to 80 percent of assembled donor antigens). Points
for sensitization are awarded automatically, even though a crossmatch test is likely to indicate the patient's incompatibility with the
donor. Points for length of wait are also given on a percentile basis,
though with the difference that a patient's comparative ranking is
determinate. For instance, in a 100-patient queue, the patient who
is the 75th person to be listed would receive 7.5 points, while the
patients waiting longest would receive 10. Point calculations are
made for each kidney placement.

Awarding points for tissue matching is a straightforward concession to medical efficiency. Less obvious is how the criteria of
PRA and length of wait originate in compassion for unlucky patients. In order for sensitized patients to have a negative crossmatch, it is usually necessary (but not always) for the patient to

*Table 3.1*

**UNOS POINT SYSTEMS**

| Distribution Criteria | Points Awarded | |
|---|---|---|
| | "Starzl" 10/1987 | "Terasaki" 2/1989 |
| Tissue Match (M) | | |
| 6 HLA M | 12 | |
| 5 HLA M | 10 | |
| 4 HLA M | 8 | |
| 3 HLA M | 6 | |
| 2 HLA M | 4 | |
| 1 HLA M | 2 | |
| Tissue Mismatches (MM) | | |
| 0 ABDr MM | | 10 |
| 0 BDr MM | | 7 |
| 0 AB MM | | 6 |
| 1 BDr MM | | 3 |
| 2 BDr MM | | 2 |
| 3 BDr MM | | 1 |
| PRA (Sensitization) | 0–10[a] | |
| Length of Wait | 0–10 | 0–1[b] |

SOURCE: UNOS, "Memorandum: Kidney Allocation Policy."

NOTE: Two rarely used criteria are omitted: medical urgency and logistics.

[a] For patients PRA ≥ 80, points are awarded on condition of a negative preliminary crossmatch.

[b] One point is awarded to the patient with the longest waiting time; fractions of a point for those with shorter tenure. For each additional year after one year of waiting time, 0.5 points are awarded.

have a closer-than-average genetic match with the donor. As a result, sensitized patients wait longer. Thus, for sensitized patients, points for tissue matching, PRA, and length of wait tend to be mutually reinforcing.[88] By giving sensitized patients so many additional points, the intention is to ensure that they receive priority ahead of similarly matched nonsensitized patients. Both the Starzl and Terasaki point systems accomplish this much. The length-of-wait criterion is not only a tiebreaker for equally well-matched patients but actually ranks hard-to-match patients over all but the best-matched patients. The criterion benefits persons who have obscure HLA and are difficult to match with the average donor. Finally, both point systems include an "O-kidneys-for-O-recipients" rule. For an O donor kidney, if the highest ranked patient is an A blood type, and the second is an O, then the O patient gets priority. The goal is to redress an imbalance in the waiting list population between A and O blood type patients.

The Terasaki formula emerges from a more positive assessment of HLA matching. It involves a different method of measuring genetic similarity between donor and recipients. Terasaki and the UNOS board of directors argued that only actual antigen "mismatches" should be counted. The reader should be alerted to the potential for misunderstanding: having fewer antigen mismatches is the desired objective. Terasaki argued that if a recipient or a donor has an unidentified antigen or a "blank," the resulting lack of antigen match should not be held against the recipient. A zero ABDr mismatched (MM) recipient may have fewer than six antigens matched with the donor on the three HLA loci but—and this is the point—possess no antigens that are different from the donor's. This seemingly slight alteration in accounting has the effect of doubling the frequency of best-matched donor-recipient pairs.[89] While facilitating the awarding of points for HLA, the Terasaki system diluted the value of patient length of wait. Relative to Starzl's system, the Terasaki point system gives approximately one-quarter as much weight to patient length of wait (see Table 3.1).

The Terasaki formula is not warmly regarded by a substantial proportion of kidney transplant surgeons. To them the formula simply gives too much weight to tissue matching in the current clinical environment, which, in addition to tissue matching, also emphasizes the fine-tuning of chemical immunosuppression.

### Tissue Matching
### in an Age of Chemical Immunosuppression

As I said earlier, graft rejection can be countered in two ways: either by suppressing the immune response through the ingestion of drugs or by preempting the rejection response through donor-

## Figure 3.3
### SEOPF KIDNEY SHARING: 1977–1991

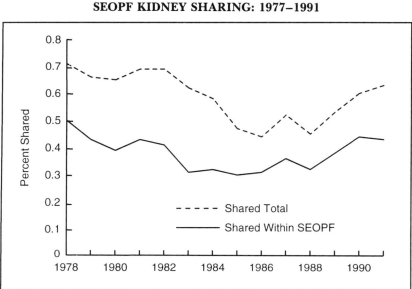

Source: South-Eastern Organ Procurement Foundation. "Statistical Summary, 1991" D [photocopy]. SEOPF, Richmond, VA.

recipient HLA matching (by using living-related donors or selectively distributed cadaveric kidneys). For purposes of organization, the two methods have radically different implications because controlling graft rejection by immunosuppression does not require large recipient pools, kidney sharing, or large numbers of living donors. HLA matching, on the other hand, does require pooling or living donors to be effective. If chemical immunosuppression is adequate, then kidney sharing is unjustified except insofar as it benefits hard-luck patients and is ethically grounded.

In the early 1980s, kidney sharing declined in proportion to the availability of cyclosporine. Beginning at the University of Pittsburgh, the trend later included other members of the South-Eastern Organ Procurement Foundation.

SEOPF members increasingly relied on locally recovered kidneys because they believed they could achieve medical results with these kidneys as good as those attained with well-matched, shared ones. Much of the kidney sharing that remained was for the explicit benefit of sensitized patients.[90] The medical premise of kidney sharing was challenged at a time when the Task Force on Organ Transplantation argued that more kidney sharing was required by equity.

The success of cyclosporine and other drugs has led some transplanters to oppose kidney sharing and the use of living donors on any grounds besides that of helping immunized patients. A few, for instance, still resist the conclusion that six-antigen matched recipients do better than other patients. But, on the whole, transplant leaders agree that sharing these kidneys is justified medically. The points of contention are (1) whether medium-grade matched recipients do better than low-matched recipients and (2) whether well-matched, "shared" kidney grafts do better than poorly matched, "local" kidney grafts. Tissue typers affirm, while immunosuppression advocates deny, the value of matching in both cases. For over 20 years defenders of immunosuppression have argued that kidney sharing involves prolonged cold ischemia (iced-down kidneys without blood flow), which ends up offsetting any post-operative benefits from tissue matching.[91] The massive collaborative studies conducted by Terasaki (1991), Opelz (1991), and UNOS and SEOPF personnel contradict this line of defense. They affirm the superiority of medium-grade matches, typically concluding that "grafts that function very well at 1 year follow-up, in spite of poor HLA match, have not overcome the risk of failure associated with tissue compatibility."[92] Long-term graft function, it is argued, is highly correlated with the quality of HLA match. In comparing the graft survival of zero with four-to-six mismatched recipients, the difference at 5 years posttransplant is sizable—on the order of 13 to 20 percent. A major SEOPF study also finds that prolonged ischemia from kidney sharing does not offset the benefit of tissue matching.[93]

Immunosuppression advocates argue that the huge collaborative studies obscure an essential truth—the "center effect." The "center effect" is "a reflection of a single transplant center's standards and policies for the care of the donor and recipient."[94] Some transplant centers deliver better care, particularly because of their advanced understanding of chemical immunosuppression and organ preservation. The argument is that these programs achieve better-than-average medical outcomes even when placing locally procured kidneys into poorly matched recipients. When shared, well-matched kidneys have good function at these centers of quality, the favorable outcome is also attributed to the center's experience and individualized approach to patient care. The collaborative studies, the argument suggests, make the mistake of lumping together the patient statistics of the elite and second-tier programs. The second-tier programs have no choice but to rely on HLA matching in order to achieve good results. Some of the transplant centers that classify themselves as exemplars of the center effect include university programs at Stony Brook, Pittsburgh, Madison, San Francisco, and Pacific Presbyterian Medical Center.

Advocates of tissue matching have rejoined that the center effect is in reality a statistical artifact. Transplanters who argue for the center effect use single-center studies; they examine the relationship between tissue match and graft rejection for only their own patients. Terasaki, Opelz, and other tissue typers argue that single-center studies are incapable of testing the matching hypothesis because the number of well-matched recipients in these studies is not large enough to satisfy statistical standards of significance. Only in multicenter studies are there sufficient zero ABDr mismatched recipients for hypothesis testing. In addition, single-center studies are unable to control for confounding factors. Opelz writes:

> That all large multicenter studies show a positive matching effect, and that smaller studies don't, indicates that HLA matching is just one of several factors that influence graft outcome. With very large patient numbers, the background noise of other influential factors is distributed evenly.[95]

The tissue typers are saying, in effect, "Just because you cannot prove that matching works in your program does not count as evidence against matching."

Tissue typers and transplanters favoring chemical immunosuppression accuse each other of allowing their institutional interests to influence their technology assessments. Transplanters, particularly Starzl, often argue that tissue typing is a "cottage industry" that is largely "self-perpetuating." Tissue typers, for their part, allege that the large and established transplant programs are against kidney sharing not because of their avowed disbelief in tissue matching but because of institutional pressure to transplant as many local recipients as possible. This suspicion is shared by advocates of egalitarian measures, who argue that the "territoriality" and "sense of local ownership" of transplanters interferes with the pursuit of justice.[96] Rather than a clinical dispute, the crux is thought to be a big-center-versus-little-center conflict, where the little centers favor kidney sharing as a way to pry kidneys away from the big centers.

On this second count of accusation I find little evidence to support the view that many transplant surgeons are insincere in their anti-sharing philosophy. More plausible is the hypothesis that the big centers tend to be research institutions and that their stands on tissue matching reflect their particular research histories.

The major transplant centers in the 1960s specialized in specific areas of transplant science. For example, in the late 1960s and early 1970s transplanters in Boston and San Francisco were pioneers in organ preservation. Their orientation was and continues to be that hemodynamic management of the donor, precise nephrectomy (removal of kidney), and preservation by mechanical perfusion and varying solutions are the keys to graft survival. San Francisco-based surgeons pioneered both the perfusion machine and preservation solutions. Boston surgeons engineered organizational solutions to the difficult logistics of organ retrieval, preservation, tissue typing, and distribution. Another example is Starzl's research in Denver and later Pittsburgh. Starzl experimented in mixed-drug chemical immunosuppression in the 1960s (before there was an HLA controversy) and has more recently conducted trials with a new immunosuppressant, FK-506. Accordingly, his objection to match-driven allocation is based on his belief in the value of drug therapy. In contrast, under the leadership of David Hume and sponsorship of the federal government, transplanters at the Medical College of Virginia, Johns Hopkins, Duke, Georgia, and elsewhere pioneered the feasibility of kidney sharing for HLA matching. Their organizations, SEOPF and later UNOS, continue to press for greater kidney sharing. Similarly, Terasaki's familiarity with French and German developments in histocompatibility oriented him toward kidney sharing in Los Angeles. By 1964 he had identified many of the alleles on the HLA-A locus.

The peers and students of these respected leaders have fanned out across the country, carrying the philosophies of their respective research institutions. These leaders pinned their hopes of revolutionizing transplantation through their own research efforts, and it is hard to ask them to distance themselves from these hopes at a time when clinical advances in both tissue typing and immunosuppression continue at a rapid pace.

### Point Variances

To the lay person, it is somewhat frustrating when scientists disagree. Why can't they devise a test that conclusively demonstrates the value of tissue matching? How can we begin to discuss local justice when the science of medicine is in flux? This section introduces another confusing aspect of transplantation. That is, it is not enough to know the mandatory sharing rule and the official UNOS point system for distributing kidneys. Many transplant centers and procurement organizations have succeeded in persuading UNOS to allow them to use "point variances"—i.e., decision procedures that differ from the UNOS point system.[97]

The (mistaken) impression that there is a uniform national standard for the distribution of organs is encouraged by the official role of UNOS as the contractor for a National Organ Procurement and Transplantation Network. I possess copies of a dozen variances. From these and discussions with about a hundred transplant professionals over 4 years (1989–1992), certain patterns emerge about the character of the variances. The first impression is that the biggest transplant programs use variances. Moreover, all the variances I have seen or been made aware of de-emphasize tissue matching relative to the criteria of length of wait and frequently medical urgency (i.e., failure on dialysis) and patient sensitization. These variances are intended to increase the access of "bad-luck" patients.

Variances used by the Regional Organ Bank of Illinois and the University of California at San Francisco are typical. Both variances weaken the criterion of matching by not awarding points to medium- and low-grade tissue matches. ROBI's variance is used to rank patients for priority who are under the care of six major transplant programs in the area. In contrast, UCSF's variance is for only its own patients; other programs that are served by the California Transplant Donor Network employ other variances (as does Pacific Presbyterian) or the UNOS standard. Ranked by the number of kidney transplants performed, UCSF and Pacific Presbyterian are perennial top-ten programs, while ROBI is one of the largest OPOs. Probably the largest OPO, the New England Organ Bank, used a variance between 1987 and 1990 that gave highest priority to medically urgent and sensitized patients. For a number of years another top-ten program, the University of Wisconsin, has had a policy of allocating only one of a pair of kidneys to a high-risk patient. One kidney must go to a low-risk patient. *High-risk* is defined as a first-graft patient with a PRA greater than 80 percent or a second-graft patient with a PRA greater than 50 percent. In Houston, transplant programs have deleted entirely the criterion of HLA matching. It's clear that big programs often use variances.

A recently adopted variance illustrates how transplanters look for ways to increase access to bad-luck patients with compromising graft survival rates too much. A Kansas OPO has found in a trial that donor kidneys of a common A blood type (A2) may be successfully transplanted in blood group B and O patients. The ABO barrier, then, can be broken to benefit B and O patients in certain instances. This was an important finding to the Midwest Organ Bank since, relative to their donor population, the recipient population is overrepresented in the O and B blood groups. The Organ Bank now has a special algorithm that is used for recovered A2 kidneys, giving special priority to the most needy population, B recipients, and then O patients.[98]

There are numerous other examples that could show that the rules of kidney distribution are not necessarily centrally determined. The fact is that UNOS has granted OPO boards, dominated by their medical advisory committees, the freedom to draft point variances. There is not one but tens of philosophies of local justice influencing kidney distribution. Varying mixes of medical efficiency, compassion, and inter-center fairness are embodied. The present era differs from the pre-UNOS period not as much in the principles used as in their nondiscretionary implementation.

Besides scientific indeterminacy (does matching work?), the number of point variances reflects bargaining between transplant centers with OPOs. This bargaining has intensified as more OPOs use a single waiting list for kidney distribution. In these OPOs, slight changes in the criteria weights have the potential to channel kidneys toward a subset of local transplant centers. Relevant patient values and allocative criteria can be highly correlated. A new transplant center, for instance, will lobby against the use of length of wait as the decisive criterion. A more common example is for inner-city programs serving minority populations to push for wait-driven point systems. Under the standard UNOS system, their patients would have to wait longer because they have on average a lower-grade tissue match with the donor.

### Regional Kidney Sharing

Point variances are used not only at the local level but also in inter-OPO organ sharing. On review, UNOS permits inter- and intra-Regional sharing. For example, Region 2 members, whose hospitals are in the mid-Atlantic states, decided to share kidneys across procurement organizations when a highly sensitized recipient has a preliminary negative crossmatch with the donor. Because Region 2 members share samples of the blood sera of their highly sensitized patient, each member has the ability to determine whether a donor is likely to be compatible with a particular highly sensitized patient.

In an example of inter-regional sharing, the 50-member South-Eastern Organ Procurement Foundation still runs a large kidney-sharing network. SEOPF has members in four of the eleven UNOS Regions participating in its kidney-sharing program (Armata letter to author, 1991). Through the program, SEOPF members from July 1990 to June 1991 shared more kidneys between themselves (859) than were transplanted locally (745).[99] All sharing is voluntary. Shared kidneys are distributed according to a modified version of the Terasaki-UNOS point system, giving greater emphasis to sensitized patients and explicit preference to blood group B and O patients. O groups wait longer, as mentioned, because O donor kidneys still go to non-O patients in certain circumstances (six-antigen match). B blood group patients wait longer, reflecting the representation of black patients in this

*Table 3.2*

**EFFECT OF PANEL REACTIVE ANTIBODIES
ON CHANCE OF RECEIVING A TRANSPLANT IN MAY 1989**

| | Transplanted In | |
|---|---|---|
| PRA Group | UNOS | SEOPF |
| >90% | 1.2% | 1.8% |
| 60–90% | 2.5% | 2.1% |
| <60% | 5.3% | 6.4% |

SOURCE: South-Eastern Organ Procurement Foundation, reported in J.F. Burdick, A. Diethelm, J.S. Thompson, et al., 1991. "Organ-Sharing—Present Realities and Future Possibilities." *Transplantation* 51: 287–292.

category. The role of race is discussed in the section "The Role of Patient Status."

### The Facade of Uniformity

The National Organ Transplantation Act of 1984 appeared to promise a Network that would centrally and rationally order the distribution of kidneys. But, as we have seen, where one might expect uniformity there is impressive diversity. The construction of waiting lists varies from locale to locale. Some OPOs make every local patient eligible to receive each kidney, while others limit eligibility to patients under the care of the procuring transplant program. The rules of final selection also vary substantially. The aggregate impact of local variations can be striking. For instance, diluting the criterion of tissue match and limiting kidney sharing may arguably lower the average length of function of kidney grafts and thus undo a main goal in transplantation, which is to prevent returns to dialysis. Also, inter-regional sharing, like SEOPF's program, can reduce the length of wait for sensitized patients. Table 3.2 compares the chances of a sensitized patient getting transplanted in SEOPF and UNOS as whole. Although UNOS is judged by its success in achieving equitable allocation, recipient patterns are in reality the result of policies favored by local transplant organizations.

### Summary of Distribution Process

The distribution process works in the sequence described below. (The nuances of the process are necessarily not described.) At one of these steps, one or both of the recovered kidneys is distributed to a patient for transplantation. Kidneys are released from level to level depending upon the content of the rules, the complementarity of donor and recipient values, the availability of the recipient's transplant team, and the choice of the patient when informed of an available kidney.

### Levels in the Kidney Distribution Process

1. National Distribution: Mandatory sharing of a six-antigen matched kidney, then

2. Local Distribution, provided there is a highly sensitized patient with a preliminary negative crossmatch, then

3. "Payback" Kidney: Kidney is shipped to an OPO that had earlier shared a mandatorily shared kidney. If there is no outstanding payback debt, then

4. Local Distribution: Procuring transplant team shares zero, one, or both kidneys with another local program, depending upon OPO rules for keeping the recovered kidney for transplantation at the procuring team's hospital.

5. Regional Distribution, provided there is an inter-OPO sharing agreement. If not, then

6. National Allocation by UNOS.

As noted already, local distribution (items 2 and 4) accounts for the bulk of the kidneys, while about 20 percent of the kidneys are distributed through the other levels.

## Local Justice in the UNOS Era

This section examines existing practices or recipient patterns that bear on principles of local justice such as medical efficiency, compassion for the worst-off, and racial equality.

### *Retransplantation*

The issue of retransplantation brings up a host of questions. About 20 percent of kidney transplant recipients will lose their kidney grafts during the first year. If transplanted again, chances of rejection are even higher for these patients because they lose their grafts to hyperacute or acute rejection responses. Thus, it is not the rigors of prior transplant surgery that make them suboptimal candidates for transplantation but the activation of antibody that complicates the tolerance of another graft. Patients who lose their grafts to chronic rejection, typically after 3 or more years of graft function, are not regarded as bad risks. (Note, however, that the more involved procedures of heart and liver transplantation do have an independent effect on the efficacy of retransplantation.) In 1988, about 17 percent of cadaveric kidney transplants were retransplants.[100]

As the need for retransplantation is often correlated with presensitization, policy on retransplant patients reduces to a concern as to whether sensitized patients merit preferential or even equal access. The University of Wisconsin policy is an exception to the general pattern. As noted earlier, repeat transplant candidates there are placed in the high-risk category and are therefore eligible for only one of every recovered pair of kidneys. Another OPO, which I am not free to name, has constructed two lists: one with nonsensitized patients, the other with nonsensitized and sensitized patients. The first kidney is distributed by the nonsensitized list, the second kidney by the combined list. The rationale for this move parallels Wisconsin's. Good stewardship of organs requires that preference be given to patients who can best benefit with treatment.

These two examples are aberrations. UNOS permits and encourages OPOs to give allocative priority to sensitized patients (who are often second-graft candidates). The SEOPF inter-regional sharing program is an example. The UNOS Region in the Pacific Northwest recently began a trial of regional sharing for sensitized patients. UNOS policy reflects the content of its federal contract with the Department of Health and Human Services, which specifies that sensitized patients are to receive preferential access. The UNOS Ethics Committee has also examined the issue of retransplantation, concluding that compassion compels preference be given to this class of patients.

### Multiple Listing

A persistently contentious issue is the practice of multiple listing, that is, the placement of a patient on more than one local waiting list. (A local list is either transplant center or OPO list.) Under pressure by the Reagan Administration, UNOS inserted bylaw 3.2 permitting multiple listing. A patient can multiple list in order to increase his or her chances of receiving a cadaver organ. An estimated 2 percent of cadaver kidney transplants occur through this means.[101] Usually the practice involves listing at more than one transplant center in the same OPO. This makes sense for multiple-list OPOs like San Francisco's. Patients there sometimes choose to be listed at a small program and a large program. The reason why patients might find this in their interest is that, on average, patients at the small programs do not have to wait as long for a transplant. The OIG discovered that "a patient awaiting a first transplant in a center with 25 registrants had a 7 percent better chance of receiving one at any point in time than a patient in a center with 100 registrants."[102] A rotation system distributes kidneys between programs in such OPOs, and the rotation is usually ordered to give the smaller transplant programs more kidneys than their historical patient census would justify. There are notable counterexamples where the large programs biased the rotation in their own favor. But on the whole, interviews reveal, this is how the large programs purchased the cooperation of the small new programs in the formation of OPOs in the mid-1980s.

Multiple listing, it should be made clear, does not better a patient's chance to receive a mandatorily shared kidney or other kidneys placed by the Organ Center of the United Network for

Organ Sharing. The national waiting list maintained by UNOS will not accept a patient identification number more than once.

Patients' rights activists disagree on the ethics of multiple listing. Dissension arises over whether multiple listing works to the advantage of higher socioeconomic groups. Sometimes the knowledgeable patient will list in his home town and in a second OPO having a history of efficient organ procurement. Does this work to the advantage of the well-endowed who can afford the expense of visiting an out-of-town program? Some patient advocates energetically defend multiple listing as a way for patients to remind their surgeons to be active procuring agents, and in their experience have found that poorer patients do exercise their option to multiple list. Others—including many, perhaps all, medical ethicists—argue that it is "inherently unfair" since "only those with the resources" can gain the advantages.[103] UNOS withdrew the proposal to eliminate the option of multiple listing after a stormy public hearing in May 1988 in which the majority of patients testified against the proposal.

### Geographical Inequality

Geographical inequality is a persistent thorn in the sides of justice advocates. The Task Force on Organ Transplantation and more recently Dr. Louis Sullivan, Secretary of the Department of Health and Human Services, have questioned the rationale for local kidney distribution.

Because most kidneys are transplanted in the communities where they are recovered, the luckiest patients live in areas where there is a low incidence of end-stage renal disease and a high rate of donor recovery. By this measure patients in Wisconsin and perhaps Minnesota should be the envy of the ESRD population. Unlucky patients wait longer where low donor recovery coincides with high patient demand. Metropolitan areas with large minority populations fit this profile, particularly Chicago and New York. In large multiracial cities, the families of potential cadaver donors more often refuse to cooperate with procurement organizations. There is also much anecdotal evidence to the effect that organ donation is a low priority in financially strapped, overcrowded hospital complexes in inner cities. These are sources of frustration for the transplant community, since these complexes are the care-takers of a disproportionate share of potential organ donors (i.e., victims of massive cerebral injury arising from car and motorcycle accidents, gun shots, and drug overdoses).

The federal government has isolated the problem of geographical inequality for reform. Congress amended the National Organ Transplantation Act in 1988 in an attempt to end the use of more than one waiting list in an OPO.[104] In its 1990 renewal of UNOS's contract, the Department of Health and Human Services asked UNOS to investigate the feasibility of distributing all recovered kidneys by a single national waiting list.[105] The reader may recall that the Task Force in 1986 proposed complete kidney sharing to be the "ideal" policy. Use of a single national list would iron out geographical inequalities as long as the criteria composing the point system do not have systematic overlap with patients in any particular region or variety of metropolitan area. If the current Terasaki-UNOS point system (which is driven by HLA matching) were to distribute kidneys by a national list, the effect would certainly be to replicate or aggravate the current pattern: for ESRD patients in urban areas with large nonwhite populations to wait longer for a transplant. I shall return to the connection between minority access and distribution by HLA matching later in the subsection on race.

### The Role of Patient Status

In addition to the decline of discretionary methods of allocating scarce goods, another contemporary trend is the declining use of status criteria. Age, gender, citizenship, and race are examples of status criteria, the use of which is usually considered to contradict the idea of a liberal society. I shall look at the relevance of each to transplantation, with special reference to race. I shall rely on the report of the Office of Inspector General, since it brought status issues to the forefront in recent transplant politics.[106]

*Age and Gender.* The OIG found that men and younger persons receive higher-than-average percentages of kidney transplants. For the surveyed period (October 1987–March 1989), men made up 54 percent of the national waiting list and received 61 percent of the kidneys. The respective percentages for women are 46 percent and 39 percent. Persons aged 46–65 comprised 36 percent of the waiting list and received 35 percent of the procured kidneys. Only 2 percent of the kidneys went to patients over 65 years old, while 57 percent were transplanted in persons between 19 and 45 years old. UNOS does not have control over the demographic composition of the national registry, but through its policies it can affect the final distribution.

Age discrimination is not implied at the stage of final distribution. Across age groups, representation on the waiting list is a good predictor of chances for transplantation. The aged are transplanted less frequently than their share of the general population would indicate, but this is easily explained by a combination of patient preference for hemodialysis, comorbidity, and generally bad health of the aged ESRD patients.

Gender discrimination is suggested but not established by the OIG statistics. Women receive a share of kidneys significantly less than their representation on the waiting list. The American Medical Association's Council on Judicial and Ethical Affairs has recently commented that this is an example of unacceptable "gender disparities" in medicine.[107] In contrast, the OIG report did not find cause for alarm. (The OIG has a well-deserved reputation for sensitivity to inequality in transplantation.) The OIG report argues that gender disparity can be explained by comparing male-female sensitization rates. The OIG confirmed the received wisdom that women are more often sensitized, principally because of past pregnancy. This factor reduces their chances of finding compatible kidneys. Of patients waiting for a first transplant, almost 37 percent of women are sensitized, while only 23 percent of men are. For the gender discrimination hypothesis to succeed, it would have to be true that sensitized women wait longer than equally sensitized men. The OIG found that both groups wait on average about 92 months for first kidney transplant.

***Citizenship.*** The transplant community depends on voluntary donations of organs, and for this reason has taken steps to create the impression that American transplantation is for Americans first, foreigners second. These steps were taken on the theory that public approval of the conduct of organ distribution is a sine qua non for public willingness to donate organs. Although a survey subsequent to reforms has showed that the public does not prefer a nationalistic policy of organ distribution, the ferocity of *The Pittsburgh Press* exposé and intense scrutiny by the Gore Hearings put the role of citizenship on the policy agenda.[108]

In 1986 the Task Force on Organ Transplantation recommended that "non-immigrant aliens not comprise more than 10 percent of the total number of kidney transplant recipients at each transplant center."[109] Eight members of the Task Force dissented and inserted a statement of exception in the final report. They argued that a kidney "should not be offered for transplantation to a non-immigrant alien unless it has been determined that no other suitable recipient can be found."[110] UNOS policy has followed the majority view of the Task Force. There is now in effect a 10 percent quota on the number of kidney transplants a program may perform for nonimmigrant foreigners.

**Race.** This is the major issue for transplantation politics in the 1990s. Everyone agrees that blacks receive fewer kidneys (24 percent of the total) than their share of the national waiting list (31 percent), though more than their share of the general population (12.1 percent) and contribution to the supply of cadaveric kidneys (8 percent). No one knows precisely why they receive less than their share of the waiting list. The causes of the racial inequality are inordinately complex, precluding their full discussion here. For simplicity's sake, I shall discuss just two explanations that are at the center of the on-going policy debate.

The first explanation is that transplant surgeons are prejudiced. This explanation is favored by media and governmental accounts. Inside the transplant community the usual explanation is that distributing kidneys by HLA matching has a disparate impact on blacks. These explanations are sometimes referred to as involving "racism" and "institutional racism," respectively.

The racism hypothesis rests on a faulty appreciation for the difference between the pre-Network and current era. Before 1987, there was no central computer network that tracked cadaveric kidneys to make sure that recipients were chosen by publicly stated and defended procedures. Since 1987, transplant surgeons have been deprived of the discretionary freedom to act on their personal beliefs. At the stage of admission to a program, transplanters continue to exercise discretion. Discrimination at the admission level, though, is not a contested policy issue. In addition to the check of the UNOS Organ Center computer, professional self-policing acts to constrain transplanters whose ethically inappropriate actions threaten to jeopardize the reputation of transplantation as a whole. Interviews of transplant surgeons suggest that in the pre-UNOS era it was not uncommon for transplanters to ostracize surgeons engaged in morally disreputable practices.

The institutional racism hypothesis has unclear empirical support. The case in its favor begins with the observation that distribution by tissue match clearly operates in a racially differentiated genetic population. Milford et al., among others, show that there are several transplant antigens common in the black population that are rare in whites, and vice versa.[111] Though the pattern is for racial differentiation, there are HLA elements common in both racial populations (e.g., A2, A3, and B7) that account for many of the better-matched white kidneys distributed to blacks. As antigens define a person's blood type, the distribution of ABO red blood groups also varies by race.[112] Blacks are overrepresented in the blood group B category, while whites are overrepresented for blood group A. The reader should recall that, as a rule, there is an antibody barrier preventing the distribution of A kidneys into B patients, and vice versa.

These genetic differences matter because blacks are overrepresented in the waiting population (31 percent of the total) and underrepresented in the donor pool (8 percent of the total). Blacks, then, depend on access to the predominantly white donor pool. The question is whether distribution by HLA matching reduces blacks' access to this pool.

During the last 2 years, a growing body of circumstantial and experimental evidence has sustained the hypothesis that allocation by HLA matching has a disparate impact on black recipients. For instance, the Regional Organ Bank of Illinois made a computer search for potential recipients having four or more antigens matched with a donor. Actual case records were used (352 donors, 604 recipients). Fifty-two percent of the waiting list was white, 40 percent was black. The proportions of well-matched potential recipients were 71.8 percent white and 6.2 percent black. The matching criterion led to intraracial organ flows.[113] Regarding actual distribution, the U.S. Renal Data System records the following for 376 zero-mismatched (i.e., very well matched) kidney recipients in 1988–1989: 8 percent into blacks and 92 percent into whites (including Hispanics).[114] Since blacks make up over 30 percent of the national registry, this is a striking disparity. Sanfilippo et al., however, in January 1992, published a multivariate study based on the records of over 22,000 cadaveric kidney recipients. They find patient race to be the seventh most powerful predictor of length on the waiting list. Recipient sensitization, O and B blood group, local organ procurement rate, and prior transplantation were all more powerful variables.[115] Giving other factors their due appears to lead to the conclusion that HLA matching is only one significant factor in explaining racial inequality.

If we accept the hypothesis that allocation by matching, however marginally, has a disparate impact on blacks, what should be done? Some OPOs have implemented local solutions, such as the variances put forward by the Midwest Organ Bank, the Regional Organ Bank of Illinois, and LifeGift in Texas. The latter eliminated the criterion of HLA matching entirely in its Houston section. To help blacks get transplants, equity-sensitive lay observers of transplantation tend to recommend the use of OPO, regional, and national waiting lists and distribution by first-come, first-served. They are opposed by tissue typers and many transplant surgeons.

Aware that distribution by HLA matching might have a disparate impact, in 1990 Terasaki nonetheless proposed a national keep-one, share-one policy. The first kidney would be distributed nationally according to the match-driven Terasaki point system and the second one would be distributed locally by an undictated method. Gjertson et al. deny that the proposal would have a disparate impact on black patients in terms of access, but their argument rests on a non sequitur.[116] The hypothesis that HLA-driven distribution has a disparate impact on blacks does not, however, depend on the use of local waiting lists, as Gjertson and colleagues imply. Rather, it depends on whether transplant antigens are racially correlated and whether there is equal racial representation in the donor and recipient pools. Moreover, their own data show that expanding the recipient pool increases the percentage of well-matched recipients (which are disproportionately white).

Advocates of racial equity, on the other hand, are forced by the data to concede that at least 10 percent of the recipient population receives additional benefit from HLA matching. Zero and one ABDr mismatched recipients do better than lesser-matched recipients.[117] I have not seen any evidence suggesting that, in terms of gains in graft survival, blacks benefit from matching less than whites. Tissue typers believe that a factor in lower long-term graft survival in blacks is their greater histocompatibility donor-recipient differences.[118] Impressed by the typers' data, the UNOS leadership questions the ethics of transplanting patients with poorly matched kidneys. Sometimes, they argue, it is better to leave a transplantable patient on hemodialysis.[119]

## Hemodialysis Update: Medicare Cost

Two developments that relate to the quality of life of dialysis patients lead us to discuss hemodialysis once more. First, there is the issue of whether Medicare cost cutting has compromised dialysis services to the point of harming the welfare of ESRD patients. Second, there is the introduction of recombinant erythropoietin, or EPO, in 1989. EPO corrects anemia associated with ESRD, reducing the fatigue induced by dialysis treatments.

In the 18-year history of the ESRD program, reimbursement rates for outpatient dialysis have decreased steadily.[120] Despite falling reimbursement, the number of outpatient dialysis facilities increased from 600 to 661 between 1980 and 1988. Somehow expansion was possible in a climate of cost containment. The question is: Has quality of care suffered because of cost cutting? Are profit-seeking nephrologists cutting corners in a drive to expand centers and begin new ones?

Congress asked the Institute of Medicine to address these and other questions concerning ESRD patients. Analyses for the resulting study "suggest but do not prove that quality of care may have been reduced."[121] The Institute of Medicine found that length of dialysis treatments had shortened in the 1980s, probably in response to changes in reimbursement rates. And shortened treatments did correlate with increased mortality and hospitalization, as outpatient clinics decreased staffing. Although it was unable to find a direct link between reimbursement policy and patient welfare, the Institute put stock in the general impression that "these changes are adverse to the quality of care."[122]

As a change for the better we should note that EPO is improving the quality of life of dialysis patients, although in a 10-month study period these patients were no more likely to return to work than the control group.[123] Medicare reimbursement policy for EPO is, like that of dialysis, a subject of criticism. It, too, apparently provides an incentive to undertreat patients.[124] A final point about EPO and its relation to kidney distribution politics: EPO works to the political advantage of tissue typers, since it makes dialysis more competitive vis-à-vis transplantation. Pro-matching advocates argue, as noted, that hemodialysis is a better therapy if the alternative is to give a patient a poorly matched kidney.

## The European Contrast

Before concluding I offer a brief discussion of the European experience, to demonstrate the presence of an "American exceptionalism" in kidney replacement therapy. Two contrasts are the most glaring. First, there is a greater willingness on the part of transplanters in Western Europe to embrace selectivity in the admission and transplantation of ESRD patients. And second, European transplanters have more political freedom to use discretion in their allocation of kidneys. They are both more selective and more relaxed in their distribution.

Because of limited resources made available to them at the macro-allocative level, British, French, German, and Dutch transplant surgeons use stricter medical criteria in their admission of transplant candidates. European transplanters, for instance, are still reluctant to transplant patients older than 50 or 55 years of age or who are diabetic or hypertensive. European transplanters have a history of giving preferential access to patients who do not have underlying diseases that may later pressure the kidney graft.

At the stage of final selection, European transplanters were the first to use national and international kidney exchanges in conjunction with HLA matching.[125] In comparison with the transplantation in the United States, organized transplantation in Europe has been led more by tissue typers such as van Rood, Opelz, and Dausset. They have impressed on the transplanters the value of tissue matching. The organ-sharing exchange, Eurotransplant, has shipped as many as 75 percent of all recovered kidneys in order to optimize donor-recipient matching.[126] Sells observes that, while sharing decreased across Europe after the introduction of cyclosporine, it is still much higher than in the United States.

The irony is that while most kidneys are shared by centrally administered rules, the unshared kidneys tend to be distributed according to the absolute discretion of the transplant surgeon. In the United States, by contrast, there is no discretion outside the surgeon's right to pass on a kidney offer. Ignoring the nuances of their protocols, in France and the U.K. procuring transplanters offer one kidney to the national transplant society for distribution to the best-matched patient and retain the second for their own discretionary distribution. Extremes are married in the European systems. More kidneys are selectively distributed, more are nonselectively distributed.

The obvious, but facile, explanation of this mixture of greater selectivity and discretion in Europe would be that European transplanters are not subject to legislation similar to the American National Organ Transplantation Act, nor have they been the focus of task forces and numerous legislative hearings. But what explains this absence of politics?

## Conclusion: Local Justice in American Medicine

Because there is little legitimacy in the center of the American health care system, its borders are all the more politically vulnerable.[127] Legitimacy is a resource that can shield its bearers from political challengers. This is an academic way of saying that if Americans were to approve of their health care system, organ transplantation would be freer from political pressures. Numerous public opinion surveys show widespread dissatisfaction with the American health care system. Transplant surgeons in Western Europe, in contrast, can borrow from the legitimacy of programs of national health insurance and services. This frees European transplanters to engage in micro-allocative practices that by any moral standard are greater cause for alarm than those in America. I argue, then, that the impressive local justice of American kidney replacement therapy is very much connected to the perception of the injustice of the overall health care system.

Lacking confidence in the authorities overseeing health care, the public in effect appoints lay political influentials, medical ethicists, investigative journalists, and other lay experts to monitor various areas of health care delivery. The cultural climate of distrust—the prevalent suspicion that allocators of scarce goods are biased and self-interested—may be considered a rational response to the absence of effective and vigilant statist regulation. The European public and political influentials take greater store in their state authorities' willingness and power to set things right when the border functions inefficiently and inequitably. In the United States, the rational response is distrust—without an encompassing national health service or insurance system, who else but patients and their agents can be counted on to check the power of the doctors?

In transplantation, the checking of the power of doctors has taken an exceptional form. Policies proposed by UNOS are reviewed by internal committees having public representatives, by officials in the Public Health Service and other bureaucracies of the Department of Health and Human Services, and by congressional staffers, and are printed in the *Federal Register* for public comment. A veritable mountain of paperwork rises up as part of enacting the smallest amendments to the UNOS bylaws.

In the transplant arena, an intentionalist, statist mode of development has replaced an organicist, evolutionary method for resolving local justice dilemmas. By "organicist" mode of development I refer to Hayek's conception of "spontaneous ordering" whereby individuals are free to form and dissolve combinations for meeting commonly felt problems. Relative to the European experience, this conclusion would not be mistaken. However, in an objective sense there are still politically entrenched local transplant organizations—representing the organicist, evolutionary mode of development—that effectively resist the standardization of organ distribution initiated by the state. Point variances, localism, and complicated organ-sharing schemes symbolize the continuation of the organicist past of American transplantation into the justice-centered present. If the recent politics of kidney substitution therapy is an accurate mirror for the future, the local justice of organ transplantation is likely to proceed along egalitarian lines because so much of the public and their politically influential agents believe that local diversity reflects the biases, self-interest, and discriminatory intent of transplant professionals. Regarding the public interest in controlling the costs of hemodialysis care, no one is suggesting that doctors be given authority to ration access, as had occurred before implementation of the kidney disease entitlement.

I want to acknowledge the theoretical and editorial assistance of Jon Elster and the help of my colleagues Patti Conley, Steve Laymon, and Stuart Romm. Also I want to thank and acknowledge the contributions of Drs. Tom Starzl, Oscar Salvatierra, Paul Russell, and Charles Shield III, and the following organizations: the Regional Organ Bank of Illinois, the Midwest Organ Bank, the New England Organ Bank, the South-Eastern Organ Procurement Foundation, the United Network for Organ Sharing, and the Division of Organ Transplantation, Department of Health and Human Services.

## NOTES

1. F. H. Cate and S. S. Laudicina, "Transplantation: White Paper," Washington, D.C.: The Annenberg Washington Program in Communications Policy Studies of Northwestern University and the United Network for Organ Sharing 1991, p. 3.

2. For example, G. Calabresi and P. Bobbitt include a case study in their *Tragic Choices*, New York, NY: Norton 1978. See also J. Kilner, *Who Lives? Who Dies? Ethical Criteria in Patient Selection*, New Haven: Yale University Press 1990; J. Childress, "Ethical Criteria for Procuring and Distributing Organs for Transplantation," *Journal of Health Politics, Policy and Law* 14 (1989): 87–113.

3. For a well-told account of the role of distrust in bringing laypersons into medical decision making, see D. J. Rothman, *Strangers at the Bedside: A History of How Law and Bioethics Transformed Medical Decision Making*, New York, NY: Basic Books 1991. By contrast, Paul Starr emphasizes the cultural authority in his staple of medical sociology, *The Social Transformation of American Medicine*, New York, NY: Basic Books 1982.

4. R. W. Evans, D. L. Manninen, L. P. Garrison, L. G. Hart, C. R. Blagg, R. A. Gutman, A. R. Hull, and E. G. Lowrie, "The Quality of Life of Patients with End-Stage Renal Disease," *The New England Journal of Medicine* 312 (1985): 553–559.; R. A. Rettig and N. G. Levinsky (eds.), *Kidney Failure and the Federal Government,* Washington, D.C.: National Academy Press 1991, p. 283.

5. F. D. Moore, *Give and Take,* Philadelphia, PA: W. B. Saunders 1964, p. 1.

6. C. R. Blagg, "The Role of Dialysis in the Management of End-Stage Renal Disease," in G. J. Cerilli (ed.), *Organ Transplantation and Replacement,* New York, NY: Lippincott 1988, pp. 237–252.

7. F. D. Moore, "A History of Transplantation—A Lesson for Our Time," in Cerilli, *Organ Transplantation and Replacement,* pp. 3–15. H. Sendi, M. Schurter, and G. Letterman, "The First 68 Years of Renal Transplantation," *Journal of the American Medical Women's Association* 23 (1968): 998–1013.

8. R. M. Hegstrom, J. S. Murray, J. P. Pendras, J. M. Burnell, and B. H. Scribner, "Two Years' Experience with Periodic Hemodialysis in the Treatment of Chronic Uremia," *Transactions of the American Society for Artificial Internal Organs* 8 (1962): 266–275.

9. Blagg, "The Role of Dialysis in the Management of End-Stage Renal Disease," p. 239.

10. U.S. Bureau of the Budget, *Report of the Committee on Chronic Kidney Disease.*

11. G. B. Kolata, "Dialysis After Nearly a Decade," *Science* 208 (2 May 1980): 473–480, at p. 473.

12. Calculation based on Rettig and Levinsky, *Kidney Failure and the Federal Government,* p. 67.

13. Besides Sendi et al., "The First 68 Years of Renal Transplantation," see also C. G. Groth, "Landmarks in Clinical Kidney Transplantation," *Surgery, Gynecology & Obstetrics* 134 (1972): 323–328.

14. P. B. Medawar, "A Second Study of the Behavior and Fate of Skin Homografts in Rabbits (A Report to the War Wound Committee of the Medical Research Council)," *Journal of Anatomy* 79 (1945): 157–176.

15. R. E. Billingham, L. Brent, and P. B. Medawar, "Actively Acquired Tolerance of Foreign Cells," *Nature* 172 (1953): 603–606.

16. Moore, *Give and Take,* p. 64.

17. J. E. Murray, "Organ Transplants: A Type of Reconstructive Surgery," *Canadian Journal of Surgery* 8 (1965): 340–349 at p. 345.

18. D. M. Hume, "The Immunological Consequences of Organ Homotransplantation in Man," *The Harvey Lectures (1968–1969), Series 64,* New York, NY: Academic Press 1970.

19. F. T. Rapaport and J. Dausset, "Tissue Typing in Human Trans-

plantation," *Journal of the American Medical Women's Association* 23 (1968): 1029–1040.

20. T. E. Starzl, known principally as a surgeon, described the phenomenon in his *Experience in Transplantation*, Philadelphia, PA: Saunders, 1964.

21. R. Patel and P. I. Terasaki, "Significance of the the Positive Crossmatch Test in Kidney Transplantation," *The New England Journal of Medicine* 180 (1969): 735–739.

22. J. H. Southard and F. O. Belzer, "Organ Preservation," in M. W. Flye (ed.), *Principles of Organ Transplantation*, pp. 194–215, Philadelphia, PA: Saunders, 1989.

23. Rettig and Levinsky, *Kidney Failure and the Federal Government*, p. 170.

24. J. E. Murray and B. A. Barnes, "Human Kidney Transplantation," *Journal of the American Medical Women's Association* 23 (1968): 985–990 at p. 988.

25. J. F. Borel and Z. L. Kis, "The Development and Discovery of Cyclosporine," *Transplantation Proceedings* 23 (1991): 1867–1874 at p. 1867.

26. Cate and Laudicina, "Transplantation: White Paper."

27. See R. A. Rettig, "The Policy Debate on Patient Care Financing for Victims of End-Stage Renal Disease," *Law and Contemporary Problems* 40 (1976): 196–230. Also see R. A. Rettig and E. L. Marks, *Implementing the End-Stage Renal Disease Program of Medicare*, Washington, DC: Department of Health and Human Services, Health Care Financing Administration 1981.

28. U.S. Bureau of the Budget, *Report of the Committee on Chronic Kidney Disease*, Washington, DC: GPO September 1967, p. 7.

29. See R. A. Rettig, "Origins of the Medicare Kidney Disease Entitlement," in Kathi E. Hanna (ed.) *Biomedical Politics*, pp. 176–208, Washington, DC: National Academy Press 1991.

30. Rettig and Levinsky, *Kidney Failure and the Federal Government*, p. 112.

31. Ibid., Chapter 8.

32. R. Pollak, M.D., interview by author on 20 February 1991. Pollak is a transplant surgeon at the University of Illinois at Chicago.

33. Funded by the Agency for Health Care Policy and Research, this study will include a survey of dialysis patients to determine if the opinions of nephrologists are influencing the likelihood of patients' opting for transplantation. See R. Ozminkowski, A. Hassol, J. M. Dennis, and W. D. Marder, "Access to Organ Transplantation: A Review and Proposal," Bethesda, MD: Abt Associates Inc. 1993.

34. Rettig and Levinsky, *Kidney Failure and the Federal Government,* p. 129.

35. The Omnibus Budget Reconciliation Act of 1993 amended the Medicare law so that, beginning in 1995, kidney transplant patients will have coverage of immunosuppressive therapy for 18 months, as opposed to the present 12-month benefit. For patients transplanted in 1996 and 1997, coverage will last 24 and 30 months, respectively. After 1997, coverage will last 3 years.

36. Ibid., p. 172. Criticism of the program is also based on a 1990 survey conducted by the American Society of Transplant Surgeons to determine the effect of Medicare coverage policies on patient compliance with drug regimens and medical outcomes. Eighty-five percent of the responding transplant surgeons cited the cost of drugs as a major cause of noncompliance. American Society of Transplant Surgeons, *Survey on Present Status of Reimbursement for Immunosuppressive Drugs,* 1990.

37. B. H. Scribner, "Ethical Problems of Using Artificial Organs to Sustain Human Life," *Transactions of the American Society for Artificial Internal Organs* 10 (1964): 209–212, at p. 209.

38. S. Alexander, "They Decide Who Lives, Who Dies," *Life* (9 November 1962): 102–125.

39. Ibid., p. 125.

40. A. H. Katz and D. M. Proctor, *Social-Psychological Characteristics of Patients Receiving Hemodialysis Treatment for Chronic Kidney Failure,* Washington, DC: Department of Health and Human Services, Public Health Service, Kidney Disease Control Program 1969, p. 26.

41. J. W. Retan and H. Y. Lewis, "Repeated Dialysis of Indigent Patients for Chronic Renal Failure," *Annals of Internal Medicine* 64 (1966): 284–292, at p. 292.

42. R. C. Fox and J. P. Swazey, *The Courage to Fail: A Social View of Organ Transplantation* (2nd ed.), Chicago, IL: University of Chicago Press 1978, p. 255.

43. Alexander, "They Decide Who Lives, Who Dies," p. 125.

44. Quoted in Kolata, "Dialysis After Nearly a Decade," p. 473.

45. G. Collins, interview with the author on 10 March 1991. Collins is a senior San Francisco-area transplant surgeon with a special interest in organ preservation. See also P. S. Russell, "How Can We Assure Equitable Distribution," *Transplantation Proceedings* 20, supplement 1 (1989): 1022–1024.

46. These are the subject of Chapter 3 in J. M. Dennis, *The Politics of Kidney Transplantation* [doctoral dissertation], Department of Political Science, University of Chicago, 1992.

47. The South-Eastern Organ Procurement Foundation, "Brief History of the South-Eastern Organ Procurement Foundation," Richmond, VA: SEOPF 1990.

48. Panel reactive antibody (PRA) is a measure of the likelihood of the recipient's initial compatibility with a random organ donor. PRA greater than 75 percent means the patient is likely to be contraindicated for 3 out of 4 donors.

49. I.e., a patient that is genetically matched with a donor on the A, B, and Dr loci. Dr is given special reference because of its late entry in laboratory protocols.

50. Transplant center that has shared the most kidneys and received the fewest receives distributive priority. See text below.

51. B. A. Barnes, "Development of Organ Bank Practices in New England for Renal Allografts," *Dialysis & Transplantation,* 8 (1979): 486–492.

52. S. I. Cho, R. P. DerHagopian, R. S. Krane, and D. C. Nabseth, "Regional Organ Preservation Program in the New England Area," *Surgery* 75 (1974): 528–534.

53. F. D. Moore, "Ethics in New Medicine: Tissue Transplants," *The Nation* 200 (1965), 358–362, at p. 361.

54. For Starzl's role, see T. Starzl, "Discussion," *Transplantation Proceedings* 21 (1989), 3441.

55. Public Law 98-507.

56. Congress, House Committee on Science and Technology. Subcommittee on Investigations and Oversight, *Organ Transplants: Hearings Before the Subcommittee on Investigations and Oversight,* 98th Cong., 1st sess., 13, 14, and 27 April 1983.

57. Ibid., pp. 60–61.

58. Ibid., p. 62.

59. Public Law 98-507.

60. Ibid.

61. Ibid.

62. A. Schneider and M. P. Flaherty, "Favoritism Shrouds Presby Transplant," *The Pittsburgh Press* (12 May 1985), p. A1.

63. Ibid., p. A10.

64. Ibid.

65. Ibid.

66. L. Gutkind, *Many Sleepless Nights,* New York, NY: Norton 1988, p. 94.

67. T. Starzl, personal communication.

68. Task Force on Organ Transplantation, *Organ Transplantation: Issues and Recommendations,* Washington, DC: Department of Health and Human Services, Public Health Service, Health Resources Services Administration, Office of Organ Transplantation, 1986, p. xix.

69. Public Law 98-507.

70. Task Force on Organ Transplantation, *Organ Transplantation,* p. 86.

71. Ibid.

72. Ibid.

73. Ibid., p. 91.

74. Ibid., p. 70.

75. Ibid., p. 92.

76. The Social Security Act, Title XI, Section 1138.

77. Regional Organ Bank of Illinois, "Regulations for Cadaver Kidney Distribution," Chicago, IL: ROBI, December 1988.

78. U.S. Government Accounting Office, *Organ Transplants: Increased Effort Needed to Boost Supply and Ensure Equitable Distribution of Organs,* Washington, DC: GAO April 1993, pp. 51–52.

79. J. Wolf, personal communication, on UNOS September, 1990 survey of OPOs.

80. U.S. Government Accounting Office, *Organ Transplants,* p. 45.

81. U.S. Department of Health and Human Services, Office of Inspector General, *The Distribution of Organs for Transplantation: Expectations and Practices,* Washington, DC: DHHS 1991, pp. 11–12. Hereafter OIG, *Distribution of Organs.*

82. Association of Organ Procurement Organizations, *Positions and Recommendations for Improving the National Organ Procurement System,* Washington, DC: AOPO 1990, Appendix D.

83. U.S. Department of Health and Human Services, Health Care Financing Administration, Bureau of Data Management and Strategy, *End Stage Renal Disease Research Report, 1989,* Washington, DC: GPO September 1991, p. 8.

84. United Network for Organ Sharing, *By-Laws,* Richmond, VA: UNOS 28 February 1991, Section 3.4.

85. Ibid., Section 3.5.

86. See for instance, A. L. Caplan, "Problems in the Policies and Criteria Used to Allocate Organs for Transplantation," *Transplantation Proceedings* 21 (1989): 3381–3387.

87. T. Starzl, T. R. Hakala, A. Tzakis, R. Gordon, A. Stieber, L. Makowka, J. Klimoski, and H. T. Bahnson, "A Multifactorial System for Equitable Selection of Cadaver Kidney Recipients," *Journal of the American Medical Association* 257 (12 June 1987): 3073–3075.

88. A tendency observed early by Starzl et al., "A Multifactorial System."

89. For elaboration, see United Network for Organ Sharing, "Memorandum: Kidney Allocation Policy, Final Policy Statement," Richmond, VA: UNOS April 1989.

90. T. Armata, letter to the author, 18 September 1991.

91. J. F. Burdick, A. Diethelm, J. S. Thompson, C. T. Van Buren, and G. M. Williams. "Organ Sharing—Present Realities and Future Possibilities," *Transplantation* 51 (February 1991): 287–291.

92. G. Opelz, "HLA Matching Should Be Utilized for Improving Kidney Transplant Success Rates," *Transplantation Proceedings* 23 (1991): 46–50, at p. 47.

93. F. P. Sanfilippo, W. K. Vaughn, T. G. Peters, C. F. Shield III, P. L. Adams, M. I. Lorber, and G. M. Williams, "Factors Affecting the Waiting Time of Cadaveric Kidney Transplant Recipients in the United States," *Journal of the American Medical Association* 267 (1992): 247–252.

94. M. Shabtai, W. C. Waltzer, D. Anaise, E. L. Shabtai, and F. T. Rapaport, "Relevance of the 'Center Effect' to the Utilization of Scarce Medical Resources for Renal Transplantation," *Transplantation Proceedings* 23 (1991): 1882–1885, at p. 1882. Also see Burdick et al., "Organ Sharing."

95. Opelz, "HLA Matching Should Be Utilized," p. 49.

96. See for instance Caplan, "Problems in the Policies and Criteria," and OIG, *Distribution of Organs.*

97. UNOS bylaw 3.5 reads: "The allocation of cadaveric kidneys at the local level according to the following point system is mandatory." Bylaw 3.5.8 weakens 3.5 by providing for "alternate point assignments." UNOS, "By-Laws."

98. Midwest Organ Bank, "Organ Allocation Policies, February 1991," Westwood, KS: MOB 1991.

99. South-Eastern Organ Procurement Foundation, "Statistical Summary," Richmond, VA: SEOPF 1991. This document summarizes kidney sharing by SEOPF members between 1977 and 1991.

100. U.S. Renal Data System, *USRDS 1990 Annual Data Report,* Bethesda, MD: The National Institutes of Health, National Institutes of Diabetes and Digestive and Kidney Diseases 1990, tables F.3-4.

101. OIG, *Distribution of Organs,* p. A-3.

102. Ibid., p. 12.

103. Caplan, "Problems in the Policies and Criteria," p. 3384.

104. Congress, Senate Committee on Labor and Human Resources, *Transplant Amendments of 1990,* 101st Cong., 2d sess., 1990. S. Rpt. 101–530.

105. U.S. Department of Health and Human Services, *OPTN Contract,* Washington, DC: DHHS, Health Resources and Services Administration, Division of Organ Transplantation 1990.

106. OIG, *Distribution of Organs.*

107. American Medical Association. Council on Ethical and Judicial Affairs, "Black-White Disparities in Health Care," *Journal of the American Medical Association* 263 (1990): 2344–2345.

108. Evans and Manninen concluded that the Task Force overreacted to the media scandal, having found that the vast majority of Americans are of the opinion that distribution should be by "medical need" only.

See R. W. Evans and D. L. Manninen, "U.S. Public Opinion Concerning the Procurement and Distribution of Donor Organs," *Transplantation Proceedings* 20 (1988): 781–785.

109. Task Force on Organ Transplantation, *Organ Transplantation*, p. 95.

110. Ibid., p. 137.

111. E. L. Milford, L. Ratner, and E. Yunis. "Will Transplant Immunogenetics Lead to Better Graft Survival in Blacks?," *Transplantation Proceedings* 19, Supplement 2 (1987): 30–32.

112. Blood group frequencies for blacks and whites, respectively, are: blood group O 49 percent, 45 percent, A 27 percent, 40 percent, B 20 percent, 11 percent; AB 4 percent, 4 percent.

113. See V. A. Lazda, for the Medical Advisory Committee, Regional Organ Bank of Illinois, "An Evaluation of a Local Variance of the United Network for Organ Sharing (UNOS) Point System on the Distribution of Cadaver Kidneys to Waiting Minority Recipients," *Transplantation Proceedings* 23 (1991): 901–902.

114. U.S. Renal Data System, *USRDS 1991 Annual Data Report*, Bethesda, MD: The National Institutes of Health, National Institutes of Diabetes and Digestive and Kidney Diseases, August 1991.

115. Sanfilippo et al., "Factors Affecting the Waiting Time of Cadaveric Kidney Transplant Recipients."

116. D. W. Gjertson, P. I. Terasaki, S. Takemoto, and M. R. Mickey, "National Allocation of Cadaveric Kidneys by HLA Matching," *New England Journal of Medicine* 324 (1991): 1032–1036.

117. Some respected leaders in transplant immunology will dispute this claim on clinical grounds.

118. P. I. Terasaki, M. R. Mickey, Y. Iwaki, J. Cicciarelli, M. Cecka, and J. Yuge. "Long-Term Survival of Kidney Grafts," *Transplantation Proceedings* 21 (1989): 615–617.

119. J. McDonald, former SEOPF and UNOS president and kidney transplanter, makes this argument. See J. McDonald, "Comment: Issues Related to Race in Transplantation," *Transplantation Proceedings* 21 (1989): 3411–3412.

120. In constant dollars. N. G. Levinsky and R. A. Rettig, "The Medicare End-Stage Renal Disease Program: A Report from the Institute of Medicine," *New England Journal of Medicine* 324 (1991): 1143–1148, at p. 1146.

121. Ibid., p. 1147.

122. Ibid.

123. Evans et al., "The Quality of Hemodialysis Patients Treated with Recombinant Human Erythropoietin."

124. J. E. Sisk, F. D. Gianfrancesco, J. M. Coster, "Recombinant Eryth-

ropoietin and Medicare Payment," *Journal of the American Medical Association* 266 (1991): 247–252.

125. I. Löwy, "Tissue Groups and Cadaver Kidney Sharing: Socio-Cultural Aspects of a Medical Controversy," *International Journal of Technology Assessment in Health Care* 2 (1986): 195–218.

126. R. A. Sells, "Ethics and Priorities of Organ Procurement and Allocation," *Transplantation Proceedings* 21 (1989): 1391–1394, at p. 1393.

127. I am indebted to Vincent Wright for a suggestive comment on another paper.

# CHAPTER FOUR

# Layoffs: Principles and Practices

## *Stuart Romm*

V ERY FEW PEOPLE who work for organizations are exempt from the possibility of being laid off. In this chapter I consider how criteria of age, race, sex, seniority, and ability are used or prohibited in layoff decisions, focusing on surveys of employer practices, relevant statutory and case law,[1] and case studies of corporate practices derived from confidential interviews. The focus will be on firms in the private sector.

Although many workers in recent years have lost their jobs due to a total shutdown of the operations of their employer, I do not consider this topic. The local justice project is concerned with how decisions are made when many people want or need something that only a few can have. A total shutdown does not involve such decisions, since everyone is put out of work. The focus of this chapter is on the criteria that the parties in the employment relationship, namely the firm and the workers (perhaps organized in a union), use in making workforce reduction decisions. In unionized firms, the provisions governing layoffs are formally incorporated in collective bargaining agreements, as the result of a negotiating process in which firm and worker preferences are expressed and taken into account. However, even in nonunion firms managers are constrained, albeit to a lesser extent, by worker preferences, since they must consider the incentive effects generated by one or another set of criteria. They may also mimic some of the aspects of unionized firms in order to keep unions out. In addition, the federal government, as well as most state governments, has intervened in the employment relationship with legislation and regulations concerning civil rights in order to further broader social goals embodying the principle of "equality." However, there is a continuing dispute over whether this legislation was intended to further equality of opportunity or equality of result.

The extent of the problem of workers displaced by permanent layoffs has been estimated. Hammermesh reports that during the period of 1981–1985, 5.1 million workers with 3 years or more of tenure on the job were displaced—2.8 million workers due to plant closings and 2.3 million due to layoff from continuing operations.[2] A 1993 American Management Association study found that 47 percent of the companies surveyed had reduced their staffs in the prior year by an average of 10 percent. Managers, supervisors, professionals, and technicians accounted for more than half of the positions eliminated.[3] Although new jobs appear in the economy as old ones are eliminated, many workers experience extended spells of unemployment. Furthermore, Podgursky and Swaim report that those losing their jobs due to a layoff on average experience a longer duration of joblessness than those losing their jobs to a plant shutdown. They attribute this phenomenon to laid-off workers' unrealistically high expectations of being recalled as long as their former plant remains in operation.[4]

In terms of the impact of layoffs on equal employment opportunity, a 1993 *Wall Street Journal* study found that blacks suffered a significant net loss of jobs during the 1990–1991 recession, with seniority systems, corporate relocation from inner cities, and outright racism seen as the main causes.[5] Another recent development is the tendency of relatively healthy companies to conduct layoffs aimed at "re-engineering" the corporation.[6] However, corporations often do not obtain the hoped-for improvements in productivity and profitability, the survivors of the layoffs being demoralized and shell-shocked.[7]

If the lowered demand for goods and services produced in the United States has been the bane of workers, the rising frequency of corporate mergers and acquisitions has been the bane of executives and managers. Duplicate staff and functions must be eliminated in this situation. This is functionally equivalent to a layoff—there are more people than there is work. Interviews with officials at state and federal equal employment opportunity agencies reveal that there are a large and increasing number of age discrimination complaints brought by managers eliminated subsequent to a merger or acquisition.

## Seniority and Distributive Criteria

Seniority is central in the analysis of layoffs because it is involved in two primary conflicts on layoff decision making. On the one hand, there is the tradeoff between seniority and ability/performance criteria that businesses make in selecting people for layoff. On the other hand, there is a conflict between seniority and affirmative action goals embodied in the "last-hired, first-fired" problem. Before examining the tradeoffs, however, it is necessary to ask why the actors involved in the process would favor the use of seniority in the first place. First, consider the use of seniority from the unions' perspective. Golden details three reasons why unions will press for seniority.[8] First, as democratic institutions, unions respond to the preferences of their members. If layoffs involving more than 50 percent of the firm's workers are not expected, then the most senior 51 percent of the workers at any given time will favor the use of seniority.[9] Second, unions must protect their activists from being discharged under cover of an economically motivated layoff. Many union contracts give union officials "super-seniority," which in effect exempts them from layoff during their terms. Third, a mechanical principle such as seniority allows unions to extract higher total rents from the firm insofar as better-paid senior workers are ahead of lower-paid junior workers in the job queue. Kuhn and Robert argue that a union seeking to maximize rents will favor seniority rules with this effect even if the union, taken as a unitary decision maker, has no distributional preference in favor of the senior workers.[10]

Union responsiveness to some workers' preference for seniority is consistent with senior workers' tendency to participate in union meetings and elections more than junior workers, thus amplifying the influence of those most in favor of seniority provisions.[11] Senior workers tend to place a high value on employment security,[12] so they may favor seniority-based layoffs to an even greater extent than seniority-based wage increases.

Slichter writes that workers are fearful of arbitrary managerial discretion because they believe that this discretion is "almost certain to be abused, because foremen find it difficult to resist pressure to favor friends or members of certain social groups."[13] Although seniority systems may disadvantage women and minorities because of the last-hired, first-fired phenomenon, they may also help these groups insofar as a mechanical selection criterion precludes arbitrary discrimination on the part of the supervisor. In addition, unionists argue that it is unfair "to concentrate the burden of unemployment upon a few men simply because they happen to be less efficient than others. . . . To drop them first and hire them last amounts to treating their lower efficiency as a grave social offense."[14]

Seniority is a way to limit managerial discretion in a way compatible with workers' sense of fairness. Abrams and Nolan write that workers believe that "seniority inheres in the employment relationship because justice so dictates. . . . While seniority may hinder the advancement of the junior employees, even they know that in time—when they need it most—they too will enjoy the privileges of seniority."[15] Formally, layoffs in reverse order of seniority is a queuing mechanism, but the substantive justification in the minds of the recipients seems to be the principle of prior contribution. When a worker confronting a permanent layoff states "I've given this firm the best years of my life," he is referring both to his place in the queue for job protection and to his cumulative contribution to the firm over the years. Subjectively, workers also believe that senior workers are more experienced and productive and that seniority can be used as a proxy for value to the firm.[16]

However, to a certain extent union leaders seek to maintain permanent employment levels per se as well as to extract rents from the firm.[17] Even with the unions' preference for "rigid wages, flexible employment" relative to the nonunion sector, there may be instances where the threat of permanent layoffs induces more wage flexibility to save jobs than one would observe if unions sought only to maximize rents. So, the rent maximization explanation for unions favoring seniority-based workforce reductions may be primarily applicable to temporary layoffs.

Now, consider seniority from the firms' perspective. Golden

gives three reasons why managers might want seniority to be used in layoffs. First, the system encourages workers to stay in the firm and thus reduces turnover costs. The benefits of job security and higher pay that typically come with seniority make workers reluctant to leave, since they will be lacking these benefits on any new job. Also, the expectation of long-term employee tenure allows firms to invest in training and employee development.[18] Second, seniority gives firms greater disciplinary power over their workers and discourages employee shirking and misbehavior, since exit costs are high for workers who will lose significant seniority benefits. Third, firms that are unsure of the fairness or objectivity of their first-level supervisors and foremen may use seniority as a convenient, albeit imperfect, proxy for ability and experience in selecting people for layoff.[19]

In fact, a firm might be better off using seniority than allowing first-level supervisors to make discretionary decisions even if seniority and ability are not that strongly related. Several of the decision makers I interviewed noted that giving supervisors unlimited discretion could result in expensive discrimination charges, making some check on this discretion necessary. In addition, several stated that for many unskilled jobs there is really no relevant ability information or qualification at all. The problem is not that supervisors cannot or will not give accurate information but that there is no relevant information to give. Here the use of seniority is basically by default.

However, there are three reasons why managers might not want seniority to be used in layoffs. First, it might prevent them from retaining the most able workers, if reliable information on this is available. Second, it may reduce the incentive of senior workers to perform, since the threat of job loss in the event of a downturn is weak or absent. This is the flipside of Golden's view of seniority as promoting worker discipline by making the job more valuable to the worker. Third, if promotions and raises are also in some way linked to seniority, the senior workers retained in a crisis will be the highest paid workers. The reasons why managers might not want seniority are straightforward extensions of their desire for freedom to cut the budget and maximize productivity in a crisis.

Whether a firm adopts or consents to a seniority system is a function of (1) how the firm perceives the relative importance of the advantages and disadvantages of seniority, (2) the strength of the workers' preference for seniority, (3) the positions of the two parties on other issues, and (4) their relative bargaining power. Even if on balance the firm sees the disadvantages of seniority for the company as outweighing the advantages, it may be willing to compromise with the union on this point in return for concessions from the union on other points.

So far I have assumed that there are two options: a strict last-in, first-out system or no seniority element at all. However, actual seniority systems often specify some tradeoff between seniority and ability in making layoff selections. Thus, instead of bargaining over which one of the two discrete options should be adopted, the employer and the union can bargain over modifications to the strict last-in, first-out setup, with the company typically seeking to place some weight on ability. One common modification specifies that senior employees are retained as long as they possess some minimum qualification to perform the available work. Another, which places even more weight on ability, specifies that the senior employee is retained over the junior employee if they possess relatively equal ability to perform the available work. These modifications are discussed in greater detail below.

Now, consider the case of a nonunion company deciding whether to adopt some type of seniority system. Even if there is no system under which the potential advantages for the company outweigh the disadvantages, the employer may still adopt one as part of a program to avoid unionization. If the lack of a seniority system is one of several issues that might lead employees to vote for a union, and if the employer considers a seniority system less burdensome than other union-style policies, the company may adopt a seniority system to reduce the level of support for unionization. In order for this strategy to be effective, seniority does not have to be the most important issue for most employees; it need only be important enough to enough employees to reduce support for unionization to less than 50 percent. Again, a seniority system need not be strict seniority: some tradeoff between seniority and ability can be specified.

There is evidence that the employer strategy of forestalling unionization by implementing systems that the employees see as fair or beneficial[20] in part accounts for the declining rate of success in union organizing campaigns. Fiorito, Lowman, and Nelson found that union success in organization campaigns was negatively affected by the employer's adoption of union-style policies, even when controlling for other relevant factors, such as wages and the strength of employer opposition. The authors conclude that the use of seniority-based layoffs is effective in inhibiting unionization.[21]

However, the employees might not regard the nonunion employer's promises to stick with a seniority policy as credible. Although the employees might conjecture that the employer would keep his promise because of fear of unionization, they would also know that his choice will be influenced by the rate at which he discounts the future. For all employers there exists a crisis severe enough to cause the long term to be less important than the short term, simply because the long term is irrelevant if one does not survive the short term.[22] Knowing this, workers might expect an employer faced with an acute crisis to retain the most productive rather than the most senior workers. Unionization, in fact, might be the only way for the employer to ensure that his promise to use seniority is credible. To the extent that this is the case, the use of seniority to preempt unionization is not a feasible strategy.

The use of seniority may conflict with the goals of increasing female and minority representation within the company. If a previously all-white-male company or department begins to hire women and minorities and soon thereafter conducts layoffs in accordance with seniority, most or all of the new female/minority employees will be laid off. Specifying some tradeoff between seniority and ability in selecting people for layoff could help solve this problem. A highly able female or minority employee could then be retained over a subpar white male. However, a system that takes ability as well as seniority into account may not help female or minority employees if ability is not evaluated fairly and accurately. Conscious discrimination by supervisors in conducting performance evaluations, or unconscious devaluation of work performed by female or minority employees, might result in such unfairness. Furthermore, if one assumes that seniority is to some extent correlated with ability due to the effects of experience and training, even perfectly fair performance evaluations in a system based purely on ability would result in junior female and minority employees being laid off.

In theory, evenhandedness in hiring over an extended period of time should cause the last-hired, first-fired problem to go away. Over time, the representation of females and minorities within each service cohort would mirror the percentages in the relevant labor market. In practice, however, evenhanded hiring is a distant goal. Furthermore, even if universal hiring of female and minority employees in proportion to their representation in the relevant labor market could be implemented overnight, last-in, first-out systems will continue to have a disparate impact on female employees as long as social norms dictate that women take time out of the labor market to raise children. (Empirical studies confirm that women quit their jobs at higher rates than men.)[23] If a company's female employees consist in part of young women who have not yet married or had children and older women who have reentered the labor force after raising children, then the average tenure among the female employees will be less than the average among the men, everything else being equal. Since seniority systems reward continuous employment, these systems will necessarily have a disparate impact on groups that on average experience a greater frequency of exogenous employment interruptions. In addition, the continuing extension of equal employment opportunity laws to cover previous unprotected victims of discrimination (e.g., the recent Americans With Disabilities Act) ensures a steady supply of potential last-hired, first-fired victims.

Need is not currently a significant criterion in layoff decisions in the United States, at least not in terms of the formal criteria that companies use. As of 1992, however, need is used in the determination of the amount of the individual's unemployment insurance benefits in fourteen states, workers with more dependents receiving a greater allowance.[24] Suppose one considers job loss not as a discrete variable—either one has a job or one has not—but as a continuous variable—the cost of losing one's job in dollar terms. In these states, need will generally not be a criterion used in the selection of the set of people who will bear these costs. But need will be used in the determination of how large these costs will be for different individuals within this set. If two people in the same pay category are laid off, the one with more dependents will experience a lower net cost (previous salary minus unemployment insurance benefits). In this sense, these states use need as a criterion in the distribution of the costs of job loss, although it is not used in determining who will lose their jobs.

It is unlikely that seniority itself is directly related to need in some way. There is no reason why having worked at a particular job for a length of time should be directly correlated with an individual's need, if we define need as an individual's level of financial obligation or family responsibilities. However, a relationship between seniority and need may exist to the extent that (1) age is correlated with seniority, and (2) needs so defined increase or decrease with age. Despite the Age Discrimination in Employment Act (ADEA), older workers permanently laid off may face greater difficulty in obtaining new employment. Losing the health benefits associated with employment is more burdensome for older workers, who need medical care with greater frequency. In this sense, they need their present jobs more than the younger employees. In terms of family responsibilities, however, it is workers of child-bearing and -rearing age who have the greatest need. So, the correlation between age and need changes as one changes one's definition of need.

## Seniority in Practice

In this section I describe the scope and use of seniority in the union and nonunion context. Data on the frequency of various clauses in union contracts are available from the Bureau of National Affairs. There have also been statistical and descriptive studies of practices in the nonunion sector. Before presenting the data, however, it is necessary to review the typical ways in which seniority and ability are traded off and the various ways in which seniority units can be defined.

In terms of the seniority/ability tradeoff, there are four basic types of clauses in collective bargaining agreements governing workforce reductions. Some specify "strict seniority," under which ability is not a criterion. The "minimum qualifications" clause specifies that the senior person should be retained over the junior as long as he or she has the ability to perform the available work at some minimum level. The "relatively equal" clause states that seniority governs only when the senior employee is relatively equal to the junior employee in ability to perform the available work, while the "tradeoff" clause states somewhat vaguely that both seniority and ability are to be taken into account in layoff decisions.

Under all contracts, seniority is "compared" in the sense that one employee is ranked higher on the seniority list than the other employee. This, however, establishes only an ordering. In theory, under the strict seniority, minimum qualifications, and relatively equal clause types, this aspect of seniority is the only one that should matter. Only under the tradeoff clause type should seniority be taken into account cardinally as well as ordinally by examining the magnitude of the seniority difference between the two employees. This is the dictum given to labor arbitrators in *How Arbitration Works* by Elkouri and Elkouri, often cited as the "Bible" of labor arbitrators. The authors do not discuss taking the magnitude of seniority difference into account in cases arising under strict seniority, minimum qualifications, or relatively equal clauses. However, with respect to the tradeoff clause type, which they refer to as a *hybrid* clause, they write that

> in comparing two or more qualified employees, both seniority and ability must be considered, and where the difference in length of service is relatively insignificant and there is a relatively significant difference in ability, then the ability factor should be given greater weight; but where there is a relatively substantial difference in seniority and relatively little difference in abilities, then length of service should be given greater weight.[25]

It is difficult to specify a simple ideal-typical process for the tradeoff clause type, since these clauses tend to specify vaguely that "seniority and ability shall be taken into account." It is possible for the employer to implement a point system under which individuals' seniority and ability are combined into a composite score, with those scoring the highest assigned layoff protection. Under such a system, the most senior employees are assured of receiving at least some return for their years of service in terms of protection from layoffs. A high cardinal level of seniority could compensate for a low cardinal level of ability in terms of one's relative score.

In comparing these four clause types, it is apparent that, in theory, the relatively equal clause is the only one under which the most senior employees are not assured of receiving first consideration for protection from layoff and that the tradeoff clause type is the only one under which seniority counts in a cardinal as well as an ordinal sense. Under a relatively equal clause, one's seniority can come into play only if one is at least as good as every junior employee. This might not always be the case. Under a minimum qualifications clause, however, one conceptually starts at the top of the seniority list and assigns "protection" to those able to perform the available work, working one's way down the list until the number of protections assigned equals the number of employees to be retained. Here, the most senior employees, rather than the most able, are first in line to be protected, as long as they can meet some minimum criterion.

The definition of the unit within which layoffs are conducted varies from contract to contract. Under companywide seniority, there is only one seniority list for the entire enterprise, and selections for layoff are made from this list, subject to the specified ability qualification. Plantwide seniority implements a similar procedure for an entire plant. However, seniority units can be defined in a narrower way. Under departmental seniority, when there are reductions in a particular department, selections are made in accordance with the seniority list of that department only. For example, selections could be made in accordance with people's length of time in the department, or the plantwide seniority of the people who happen to work in that department could be compared. Under occupational or classification seniority, the relevant seniority list would detail dates for all people working in a particular classification, e.g., electrician, mechanic, and so on. When a reduction occurs somewhere in the plant that affects members of this classification, the most junior members of the classification will be laid off, even if this means that senior workers from the department that has been reduced replace junior employees in unaffected departments. Again, occupational or plantwide seniority can be used. It is also possible for layoff selections to be made by seniority within both classification and department.

In general, the more specific the seniority units, the less one has to worry about imposing some ability criterion in making lay-

*Table 4.1*[26]

**CONSIDERATION OF SENIORITY IN LAYOFF**
**(frequency expressed as a percentage of contracts)**

|  | Applied in Some Degree | Sole Factor | Determining Factor | Secondary Factor |
|---|---|---|---|---|
| All Industries | 88 | 47 | 27 | 14 |
| Manufacturing | 96 | 48 | 33 | 16 |
| Nonmanufacturing | 74 | 44 | 19 | 11 |

off selections. All employees working in a particular classification within a particular department will generally have at least minimum qualifications to perform the work remaining in that classification/department cell, or else they could not be working there. However, if one has a large plant and one implements layoffs in accordance with strict plantwide seniority by figuring out how many people will have to be laid off and then lopping off enough junior men from the bottom of the seniority list, plant operations may be negatively affected.

People laid off in accordance with some type of seniority narrower in scope than plantwide seniority sometimes have the ability to "bump" junior employees in parts of the plant unaffected by the layoffs. In general, the laid off senior employee may only bump into a lower classification or skill level. Bumping is regulated by clauses specifying some manner in which both seniority and ability are to be taken into account in deciding whether or not to allow a bump. These clauses are analogous to those governing layoffs, with minimum qualifications and relatively equal clauses being the most common types. For example, a minimum qualifications bumping clause might state that an employee laid off from one job classification has the right to displace a less senior employee in a lower rated classification, provided that the senior employee has the ability to perform the job adequately with a minimal break-in period.

Data from 1992 on contract type from the union sector are presented in Table 4.1. In 47 percent of the contracts in the BNA sample, seniority is the sole factor in determining who will be laid off. It is the determining factor in 27 percent of the contracts and a secondary factor in 14 percent of the contracts. These figures are different for manufacturing and nonmanufacturing jobs. In 96 percent of manufacturing contracts, seniority is applied in one way or another, while this is true for only 74 percent of nonmanufacturing contracts.

Contracts in which seniority is the determining factor are minimum qualifications contracts, in which the senior employee retains his job provided he is able to perform at some minimal level. Contracts in which it is a secondary consideration are relatively equal contracts.

The greater frequency of seniority clauses in manufacturing industries can perhaps be explained by the greater vulnerability of the manufacturing sector to cyclical swings in demand.[27] When employment is more unstable, there is more of an incentive to fight for contract provisions controlling how the employer responds to this instability.

In terms of recall from layoff, 86 percent of contracts specify procedures in this regard. Forty-one percent recall employees in reverse order of layoff, and 50 percent recall employees in reverse order of layoff only if they are qualified to perform available jobs. In 35 percent of the contracts containing recall provisions, laid-off employees have priority over new hires.

Sixty-one percent of the agreements in the BNA sample permit bumping—75 percent in manufacturing and 40 percent in nonmanufacturing. Of the contracts giving bumping rights, 71 percent state that an employee must be qualified to do the job he seeks. Bumping on a plantwide or companywide basis is permitted in 29 percent of the contracts specifying a permissible bumping area; the rest restrict bumping to the employee's department or classification. Ninety-two percent of the agreements permitting bumping specify who may be displaced within the permitted area. Fifty-three percent of these specify the least senior employee, and 45 percent specify any less senior employee.

So, in a typical layoff situation, the evaluation of which jobs will be eliminated and which incumbents of those jobs will get to stay is only the start of the process. Those who do not get to keep their present jobs may bump a less senior employee in another area or department, then this employee may bump another less senior, and so on. The disruptive phenomenon of "chain bumping" may then result. This can take two forms. Either A bumps B, B bumps C, and so on, or A bumps B but fails to do the job adequately, then bumps C and tries to perform adequately in this position, and so on. Employers will generally try to limit this disruption.

As will be seen in the section on affirmative action below, the scope of the unit in which seniority is calculated is often important in both layoff and bumping cases. Prior to Title VII, many employers segregated their workforces by race and/or sex. Seniority was calculated within each segregated department. A contract which specifies that upon transferring to a new department the employee starts at the bottom of the seniority list in his new department, losing the seniority accumulated in his previous department, results in a variant of the last-hired, first-fired problem. A woman or minority person taking advantage of new opportunities opened up by Title VII by transferring into a formerly all-white and/or all-male department is vulnerable if layoffs are conducted in accordance with departmental seniority.

The degree to which prior contribution is rewarded with job protection is in part dependent on the scope for the exercise of bumping rights. Given a heavily departmental seniority system, only companywide or plantwide scope for the exercise of bumping rights places primary emphasis on rewarding this contribution. Limiting the scope of bumping rights to avoid disruptive cross-department or classification bumping is, in effect, trading off the prior contribution ethic against efficiency criteria. In terms of queuing, however, narrowing the scope of seniority rights simply redefines the queue. There may be several queues within a company under a heavily departmental system. It should be kept in mind that in most cases the right to bump is contingent on the employee's ability to do the job he or she seeks to bump into, or to qualify for the job within some specified time period.

However, the employee may have discretion in using his or her bumping rights. If a layoff is short-term in nature, an employee might want to accept being laid off instead of bumping into another department, as long as he or she is assured of recall and can collect unemployment benefits. More generally, even if a senior worker was not originally slated for layoff, he or she may want to waive his or her seniority rights if the above conditions are satisfied. In some collective bargaining agreements, senior employees are allowed to elect to be laid off while maintaining their eligibility for recall. Almost one-fourth of the collective bargaining agreements in a Bureau of Labor Statistics sample allowed an employee to waive his or her seniority rights and take layoff.[28]

In terms of the use of seniority in the nonunion context, Abraham and Medoff found in a survey of both union and nonunion employers that seniority was a factor in permanent layoff decisions in nonunion as well as unionized firms, albeit to a lesser extent.[29] They present data from a survey of a sample of firms from Standard and Poor's Register concerning written provisions governing permanent layoffs of nonunion employees. As is seen in Table 4.2 below, 16 percent of all respondents stated that they had a contract or written provision specifying that seniority is the most important

*Table 4.2*[30]

**POLICIES GOVERNING USE OF SENIORITY
FOR UNION AND NONUNION EMPLOYEES**

|  | Union Hourly | Nonunion Hourly | Nonunion Salaried |
|---|---|---|---|
| Proportion of respondents reporting that contract or written policy specifies role of seniority in permanent layoff decisions. | .92 | .24 | .07 |
| Given contract or written policy specifying seniority's role, proportion of respondents reporting that seniority stated to be the most important factor. | .84 | .68 | .43 |
| Proportion of all respondents reporting that a contract or written policy specifies seniority as the most important factor in permanent layoff decisions. | .78 | .16 | .03 |

*Table 4.3*[31]

**USE OF SENIORITY IN PRACTICE
FOR UNION AND NONUNION EMPLOYEES**

|  | Union Hourly | Nonunion Hourly | Nonunion Salaried |
|---|---|---|---|
| Proportion reporting senior employee never laid off before junior. | .84 | .42 | .24 |
| Proportion reporting senior employee laid off first if junior believed to be worth *significantly* more on net. | .14 | .44 | .57 |
| Proportion reporting senior employee laid off first if junior believed to be worth more on net. | .03 | .14 | .19 |

factor in permanent layoff decisions for nonunion hourly employees, while 78 percent responded that they had a contract or written provision specifying that seniority is the most important factor for union hourly employees in permanent layoff decisions. Only 3 percent stated that they had a contract or written provision specifying that seniority is the most important consideration for nonunion salaried employees.

The authors also report results concerning actual practice (as opposed to written provisions). These data are presented in Table 4.3. The data show that 84 percent of the respondents stated that a senior union hourly employee would never be laid off before a junior union hourly employee, while 42 percent of the respondents said that a senior nonunion hourly employee would never be laid off before a junior nonunion hourly employee. Fourteen percent of the respondents indicated that, for union hourly workers, a senior employee would be laid off first if the junior employee is believed to be worth significantly more on net, while this was the response with respect to nonunion hourly employees for 44 percent of the respondents. It is interesting to note that, while only 7 percent of the respondents said their companies had a contract or written policy specifying the role of seniority in permanent layoffs of salaried employees, 24 percent claimed that a senior salaried employee would never be let go before a junior.

Freed from the constraints of a union contract, employers do not discount seniority completely; they will, however, accord it less weight as opposed to ability. However, only written contracts between employer and employee are clearly enforceable under U.S. law. There are some states that will recognize a written statement of policy on the part of the employer as an implicit contract between employer and employee;[32] nevertheless nonunion employees are to a great extent dependent on the willingness of employers to live up to their promises.

In addition to senior workers being more favored in layoff situations under unionism, the use of layoffs, according to Medoff, is greater in union firms. He finds that nonunion firms adjust to a decline in product demand with a greater emphasis on wage cuts and reliance on normal quit rates. Under unionism, quit rates are too low and wages too sticky for these responses to be possible.[33] Blau and Kahn also find that unionism increases the probability of an employee being subject to either temporary or permanent layoff, with younger, less senior employees significantly more at risk. They also report results consistent with the hypothesis that sometimes senior workers waive their seniority rights and take temporary layoff.[34]

So, layoffs are both more based on seniority and more widely used in union firms, reflecting the disproportionate influence wielded by senior members in unions. They tend to participate at a great rate and with a greater degree of intensity than less senior workers, behavior which is explicable in rational choice terms as "protecting their investments," that is, as protecting their stake in jobs in which they have already "invested" many years of their labor. However, in addition to the tendency for unions to favor rigid wages and flexible employment, there may also be some tendency for unions to arise in industries subject to employment fluctuations in order to extract a wage premium as compensation for the risk of unemployment.[35]

One aspect of the use of seniority that is found only in the union context is the practice of granting "superseniority" to union representatives and officials. In BNA's sample, about 38 percent of the contracts contain exceptions of this sort. Under superseniority, union officials and local stewards are the last to be laid off. The primary justification for retaining union officials is that their presence is necessary in a layoff situation in order to aid in the process of the inevitable grievances and conflicts. Although the National Labor Relations Act prohibits employer retaliation against participants in union activities, the inability of the employer to punish union representatives and officials by slating them for layoff is a not unwelcome further protection.

If, in a unionized firm, the union believes that the conduct of layoffs by the company violated the terms of the contract, it can file a grievance. Contracts ordinarily specify a multistep grievance procedure terminating in binding arbitration. Typically, after a layoff the union will bring a grievance on behalf of senior employees who claim that they were laid off when, under the terms of the contract, they should have been retained. If the parties cannot resolve the issue themselves, a labor arbitrator will be called in to evaluate the evidence and decide whether or not the company's actions violated the contract. Conversations with managers and union officials confirm that the majority of conflicts resulting from layoffs are resolved during the grievance phase.

The expense of hiring an arbitrator provides an impetus to settle prior to arbitration. In addition, several managers expressed dissatisfaction with the quasi-judicial nature of the arbitration process, in particular the fact that the arbitrator, like a judge, must find either that the company is "guilty," that is, that their selection of employees to be laid off was contrary to the terms of the contract, or that the company is "innocent." Although the arbitrator has some flexibility in specifying the terms of the award, in general he cannot supervise "horse trading" between the company and the union. Yet several managers of unionized manufacturing firms stated that they desired to engage in such horse trading with the union and that they frequently did so in the pre-arbitration grievance process.

Nevertheless, some layoff disputes do make it all the way to arbitration. According to one experienced arbitrator, cases involving permanent layoffs are more likely to go to arbitration than those involving temporary layoffs. The employer is more concerned with retaining the best worker in a permanent layoff situation, and the aggrieved employees face a permanent loss of their employment.

The arbitrator also noted that the weight of tradition is very great in the incorporation of layoff provisions in union contracts, with many firms and unions content to let the same ambiguous and confusing provisions be retained in the agreement year after year. In particular, the union does not want to open the Pandora's box of layoff provisions at a time when they want support for their wage-and-benefit demands. The routine prolongation of these clauses creates considerable work for arbitrators. An ambiguous clause may hinder pre-arbitration horse trading or, to put it the other way around, trading is facilitated if each party has some general idea as to how likely it is that they would prevail in arbitration. Unclear contracts are both more likely to spark disputes and less likely to facilitate pre-arbitration resolution of these disputes.

## Historical Overview

Prior to the rise of unions and the bureaucratization of the employment relationship, selections for layoff were ordinarily made in an arbitrary fashion by foremen and supervisors subject to very weak central control. The legal framework governing the employment relationship, which the United States inherited from English common law, is known as the doctrine of *employment-at-will*. This doctrine holds that an employment contract of indefinite duration is terminable at will by either party, allowing employers very wide discretion in dismissing or laying off workers. The historical development of policies governing workforce reductions is characterized by the progressive restraint of employer behavior (and employer abuses) in this regard.

In Jacoby's reconstruction of the history of labor relations in U.S. manufacturing, by about 1880 the factory had become the dominant model of production.[36] However, the organization of work in these factories was highly decentralized. Many firms were organized on the basis of internal contracting, in which production tasks, although performed within the physical confines of the factory, were performed by contractors who hired their own employees and received a piece rate from the company.[37] In factories where foremen directly supervised workers, they enjoyed authority similar to that of the independent contractor.[38]

The foreman had complete and arbitrary control over employment decisions such as hiring, pay levels, layoff selections, and dismissals. This strong foreman control over employment decisions remained the dominant mode of organization during the period of 1880–1915.[39] Employment was highly unstable, resulting in many layoffs and periodically high unemployment. An employee's relationship with the firm was ordinarily severed as a result of a layoff, so there was little hope of being recalled when business picked up.[40] Workers were sometimes forced to bribe the foreman in order to keep their jobs.[41] Foremen would use their authority over layoff and discharge decisions to sexually harass female employees.[42] When news of a forthcoming reduction would spread among the workers, each would increase his or her efforts to the maximum in an effort to be retained. The resulting increase in per-worker productivity would enable the employer to eliminate even more employees than had originally been planned.[43]

Workers who were organized in unions (a distinct minority of workers during the 1880–1915 period) were not subject to such arbitrary foreman power.[44] Unions attempted to lessen the impact of employment fluctuations through seniority-based layoffs and, the more preferred system, work-sharing.[45] According to Jacoby,

> employment was so volatile in many industries that seniority rules would have divided the union into two groups, those who had steady jobs and those who did not. Further, seniority layoffs were unsuited to those trades with a tradition of mobility, where few workers remained with an employer for any length of time.[46]

Either worksharing or seniority-based layoffs limited the foreman's power to extract favors from workers, to pit them against one another, or to discriminate against union members or activists. The existing unions were primarily craft unions. Unskilled workers had little capacity to sustain any sort of organization and thus had little bargaining power. The only option of an unhappy worker was to quit; turnover rates were very high among unskilled workers.[47]

However, during the period of 1880–1915 there was a trend toward greater scale and complexity in manufacturing operations. More centralized and systematic control over operations was needed, typically provided by production engineers who significantly reduced the foreman's autonomy in administering production. Although control over employment matters remained, by and large, vested in the foreman,[48] the costs of the high turnover rates resulting from that system were increasing.[49] After 1900, some large firms tried to rationalize employment policy via the establishment of personnel departments to oversee employment decisions.[50] Advocates of personnel management wanted to constrain the foreman's power over discharge and layoff decisions, attributing much labor unrest and turnover to abuses of this authority. Foremen and production managers wanted to retain the old system, believing that the flexibility arising from unquestioned discretion and the discipline instilled by fear of the foreman's authority outweighed the considerations stressed by advocates of reform.[51]

The arbitrary power of the foreman was used to make employment decisions in a discriminatory fashion on the basis of ethnic stereotypes, successive waves of immigration having created a labor force composed of many different groups.[52] However, opportunities to discriminate on the basis of race and sex in layoff selections were limited by the segregation of the labor market resulting from discrimination in hiring and promotions. Participation by women in the labor force expanded during this period, especially in the textile and needle trades. The development of corporate bureaucracies also created a demand for clerical workers, many of whom were female. Starting around 1900, however, legislation restricting the hours and conditions of women's labor was implemented in many states, ostensibly to protect them but having the effect of segregating them from male-dominated occupations.[53] Black employment in nonagricultural, nondomestic service occupations also increased during this period. However, most black workers remained segregated in unskilled occupations.[54]

During World War I, demand for labor accelerated at a time when conscription reduced the labor supply. This made some employers more receptive to systematizing personnel practices in order to promote labor stability and peace. The government, in order to ensure continuity of production, encouraged employers to deal with the unions rather than fight them and to improve working conditions. The trend toward centralized personnel administration accelerated.[55]

In the postwar period of the 1920s, management endeavored to roll back unionism's gains.[56] Some tried to keep unions out with increasingly centralized and regularized personnel policies (the "union substitution" strategy); many also used a variety of legal and illegal means to forestall unionization.[57] In general, the movement toward systematized personnel administration was uneven, and there was some resurgence in the arbitrary power of the foreman in this period. This resurgence was clear in the area of layoffs. In 1927, only one-third of the companies in a sample of large firms stated that their personnel managers were involved in layoff decisions, most responding that decisions were made by foremen and line managers.[58] Although 40 percent of these firms responded that seniority was the primary criterion used in selecting at least some employees for layoff, most placed restrictions on when and where it could be applied.[59]

At the beginning of the Depression in 1929, employers to a certain extent tried to avoid layoffs via a commitment to work-sharing and employment stabilization policies.[60] However, by 1931–1932, employers began to abandon these commitments, implementing layoffs and wage cuts. Seniority played a limited role in layoff selections. Table 4.4 presents data on the criteria used in

*Table 4.4*[61]

**LAYOFF POLICIES
OF MANUFACTURING ESTABLISHMENTS IN 1932
(N = 224)**

| Primary Basis of Retention | Percent |
| --- | --- |
| Efficiency | 51.8 |
| Seniority | 18.3 |
| Family responsibility | 20.5 |
| Other factors | 9.4 |
| Total | 100.0 |

layoff selections from a 1932 Bureau of Labor Statistics survey of manufacturing firms.

There were more firms claiming to take "family responsibility" (a measure of need) into account than firms claiming to use seniority.[62] However, the degree to which these criteria were incorporated in formal procedures rather than informal practice is unclear. As late as 1935, most companies did not have any formal procedures for layoffs.[63] Foremen still had considerable control over layoff selections, resulting in the expected abuses.[64] Age discrimination in layoffs was common in the Depression. There was a widespread belief that older employees would be unable to keep up with employers' demands for speed.[65]

With the passage of the National Labor Relations Act (NLRA) in 1935,[66] which made it easier for workers to organize, the arbitrary power of the foreman was diminished. Nonunion companies sought to forestall unionization by centralizing and systematizing personnel management and by increasing their use of seniority, although its use remained weaker and less frequent than in the union sector.[67] Increasing the use of seniority in layoff, recall, and promotion decisions ranked high on the agenda of the newly invigorated unions. Limitation of the foreman's authority, prevention of discrimination against older workers, and constraining employers from using layoffs to eliminate union activists (still important despite the theoretical protections granted by the NLRA) motivated the unions' emphasis on seniority. Table 4.5 presents the results of a 1937 National Industrial Conference Board survey (two years after the NLRA) concerning seniority practices in union and nonunion manufacturing firms. Although a little over half of the nonunion firms used seniority in some way, most of those who did so used it in an informal or qualified way. Approximately 70 percent of the unionized firms used formal seniority procedures, and only about 5 percent had no established use of seniority.

Within the framework of the NLRA, the power of unions increased in the bargaining over the relative weights to be placed on seniority and merit in the design of layoff practices, with the unions, as before, seeking layoffs in reverse seniority order and management seeking greater emphasis on ability. Nonunion employers operating in this new environment faced a similar problem. Now that the capacity of unions to organize had increased,

*Table 4.5*[68]

**USE OF SENIORITY IN LAYOFFS
IN UNION VS. NONUNION FIRMS IN 1937
(N = 475)**

|  | Union Firms | Nonunion Firms |
|---|---|---|
| Formal seniority procedure used in layoffs | 69.8 | 12.5 |
| Informal or qualified use of seniority in layoffs | 24.8 | 39.5 |
| No established use of seniority | 5.4 | 48.0 |
| Total | 100.0 | 100.0 |

they gave more careful consideration to the benefits of policies incorporating seniority, such as generating employee loyalty and making the workers less inclined to bring in a union, as opposed to the costs of limiting their discretion to retain their most productive employees.

However, a significant minority of firms continued to counter unionization with confrontational, sometimes violent, tactics and legal challenges to the new framework, which were generally unsuccessful.[69] In addition, the mobilization of the war economy during World War II shifted the balance in favor of the unions. As in World War I, the government intervened in labor relations in order to ensure continuity of production, compelling employers to deal with unions and more actively enforcing the NLRA's protection of the right to organize while simultaneously pressuring unions to moderate wage demands and forgo strikes.[70] By 1945, approximately 70 percent of all workers in manufacturing were organized in unions.[71] By the end of the war, only 11 percent of the firms in one study still gave their foreman unchecked authority to dismiss workers.[72]

The period from the end of World War II to the early 1960s marked the height of the power of unions. In 1960, about 31 percent of the nonagricultural labor force was unionized.[73] This has declined to about 17 percent today. But during the unions' heyday, firms seeking to avoid or contain unionization made their personnel administration more systematic and centralized, with an emphasis on employment security in the personnel policies adopted.[74] For example, about 96 percent of the nonunion firms surveyed in a 1950 National Industrial Conference Board study stated that they somehow incorporated seniority into their layoff selection criteria. However, about 89 percent of the firms using seniority stated that they used it in a qualified way, most commonly when merit and ability were relatively equal between two employees.[75]

Although the percentage of the workforce organized by unions began to decline around 1960, employers could not, in theory at least, return to decentralized and arbitrary employment decision making. The Civil Rights Act of 1964, which mandates equal employment opportunity for women and minorities, created strong disincentives (e.g., lawsuits) to doing so.[76] The interviews with personnel executives summarized below indicate that one of the main functions of contemporary centralized personnel administration is to review the decisions of managers and supervisors in order to minimize corporate exposure to discrimination suits. Furthermore, after the passage of the Civil Rights Act of 1964, a conflict arose between status criteria such as race and sex and the seniority criterion, namely the last-hired, first-fired phenomenon.

After the passage of the act, employers began to adopt formal equal employment opportunity (EEO) policies and to form specialized EEO departments. Edelman contends that in doing so employers attempted to impose an interpretation of the law which focused on fair and objective procedures, and on rules and bureaucracies to implement them, as opposed to an alternative interpretation based on equality of result.[77] The increasingly conservative courts have over time made the procedural view the dominant one. While the position of women and minorities in the workforce is clearly better today than it was in 1964,[78] it is not what it would be had the equality-of-result view been adopted.

The problem of selecting workers for layoff can be avoided if an alternative to layoffs can be used. There is always the option of adjusting wages rather than employment levels. With respect to temporary layoffs, there are more equitable burden-sharing devices such as worksharing. Historically, the practices of union and nonunion firms with respect to worksharing prior to layoffs diverged from around 1930. In 1938, about 60 percent of union firms and 53 percent of nonunion firms reduced hours prior to implementing layoffs; by the early 1950s, 30 percent of union firms and 63 percent of nonunion firms reduced hours prior to implementing layoffs.[79] Over time, unions developed a preference for "rigid wages, flexible employment." With respect to a permanent contraction of the workforce, the alternative of early retirement (ER) is increasingly popular. Still, an employee's years of service, an absolute length-of-service measure rather than a relative one like seniority, is typically an important component in determining eligibility for these ER programs. Furthermore, there is some dispute over whether these programs constitute age discrimination under the Age Discrimination in Employment Act (ADEA).[80]

## Overview of the Legal Framework Governing Workforce Reductions

Modifications to the "employment-at-will" doctrine relevant to workforce reductions arise primarily from the National Labor Relations Act (NLRA) and various antidiscrimination statutes and regulations. The NLRA, apart from compelling employers to recognize and deal with unions, also places certain direct restraints on their decision making in workforce reductions. Employers are prohibited from discriminating against pro-union employees by formulating some sham justification for selecting them for layoff during a business downturn, or by disguising their discharge as an economically motivated layoff. The National Labor Relations Board (NLRB), which decides cases arising under the NLRA, has recently held that employers have a duty to bargain in good faith with the union over impending layoffs to determine if these layoffs can be avoided via concessions from the union on issues such as wages and benefits.[81] An employer attempting to counter a union-organizing campaign cannot state that layoffs will result if the union is brought in unless such layoffs are in fact a demonstrably probable consequence of circumstances outside of the employer's control.[82]

In deciding cases arising under the NLRA, quasi-judicial procedures play an important role in the initial phases. Cases are first decided by an administrative law judge and reviewed by members of the NLRB, although decisions can be appealed in the courts.[83] However, the enforcement of the federal antidiscrimination laws is more heavily weighted toward the federal courts.

Federal legislation, particularly Title VII of the Civil Rights Act of 1964 and the Age Discrimination in Employment Act, has greatly affected the way in which employers must take into account status criteria such as race, sex, and age in all employment decisions, including layoffs.[84] With respect to layoffs, the primary conflict concerning the use of these criteria is the last-hired, first-fired problem. The primary question is the extent to which the costs of remediating a past wrong, viz., past discrimination resulting in underrepresentation of women and minorities in certain occupations, may be placed upon a group that had little role in perpetrating that wrong, viz., white males in these occupations who will be vulnerable to layoff if seniority protections are reduced or eliminated as part of an affirmative action program. This is a complex issue from a legal perspective, given that seniority systems enjoy a measure of protection under Title VII which other employment practices do not. Section 703(h) of Title VII reads:

> it shall not be an unlawful employment practice for an employer to apply different standards of compensation, or different terms, conditions, and privileges of employment, pursuant to a bona fide seniority or merit system . . . provided that such differences are not the result of an intention to discriminate because of race, color, sex, religion, or national origin.[85]

The original motivation for the Civil Rights Act of 1964 was to help rectify historic injustices to blacks. Although forbidding religious and ethnic discrimination seems a logical complement to prohibiting racial discrimination, the inclusion of sex might seem somewhat progressive for 1964. It resulted, in fact, from a failed strategic move by a Southern legislator who believed that adding sex would diminish support for the act. Much to his surprise, once he proposed it the small number of female members of Congress started a bandwagon in favor of its inclusion, although none of them had even considered such a provision.[86] Recently, the Americans with Disabilities Act has extended legal protection to people with disabilities. It requires covered employers to make "reasonable accommodations" for such individuals and forbids standards and tests that tend to screen them out, unless the disability so screened can be shown to preclude effective job performance.[87] It is not at all clear how this legislation will work out in practice, since there is no clear definition of what a "disability" is.

Although the Equal Employment Opportunity Commission (EEOC) is empowered to investigate complaints and to press for a settlement of the issue between the parties, they do not have the same power to decide cases and to mandate awards that the NLRB has. Either the EEOC or the aggrieved party must instead bring the case to federal court.[88]

There is another set of federal regulations guiding employers, namely a series of executive orders prohibiting discrimination based on sex, race, age, religion, or national origin on the part of contractors doing business with the federal government.[89] If the amount of business a company does with the government exceeds $10,000 a year, the company must comply with the nondiscrimination requirements. Furthermore, if the company does more than $50,000 a year of business with the federal government and has 50 or more employees, the company must develop a specific affirmative action plan. There is a monitoring and audit procedure aimed at ensuring that progress is made toward achieving numerical representation goals. In addition, two other laws affect federal contractors. The Vietnam Era Veterans' Readjustment Act of 1974 forbids discrimination against disabled veterans and Vietnam era veterans on the part of federal contractors and mandates plans for increasing employment of these groups.[90] The Rehabilitation Act of 1973 requires contractors to develop affirmative action plans for people affected by physical or mental disabilities.[91]

The compliance-monitoring process is overseen by the Office of Federal Contract Compliance Programs (OFCCP), which is part of the Department of Labor. However, layoffs that, if conducted in accordance with a seniority system, work against the achievement of representation goals do not receive specific attention in the OFCCP guidelines, perhaps because winning a federal contract marks an expansion rather than a contraction of one's business. A vague reference is made to nondiscrimination with respect to "layoffs and terminations," but conversations with managers confirm that specific guidance from OFCCP in the event of layoffs is lacking. However, an employer who is concerned with maintaining compliance with minority representation goals must keep an eye on these figures when conducting layoffs.

Federal contract compliance is the most direct form of government intervention in the private employment relationship aimed at achieving affirmative action goals. This seems consistent with American values: The person who signs the checks gives the orders. As will be detailed below, Title VII usually requires positive action on behalf of the complainant; someone must bring a charge before the government can step in. But federal contract compliance is proactive; employers in theory must meet representation goals in order to keep their contracts. They must submit compliance reports, and they may be selected for a compliance review or audit. If an audit reveals that goals have not been met, the employer may be barred from federal contracts.

Interviews with employers reveal that there is some dissatisfaction with the perceived arbitrary nature of the audit process. How strictly one will be held to the achievement of these goals depends on the particular auditor who is drawn. Some auditors are strict, others simply tell the company to try to do better next year. Several managers stated that there are varying types of strictness within the set of strict auditors. One auditor may be most concerned with race, another with sex, and so on. One manager, in describing this phenomenon, stated that in his perception female auditors were most concerned with sex discrimination, black auditors with racial discrimination, and so on. However, equal employment opportunity advocates contend that OFCCP enforcement of compliance with affirmative action guidelines has generally been weak, especially after 1980.[92]

Focusing specifically on workforce reductions, one OFCCP official I spoke with stated that OFCCP is more concerned with ensuring that employers take advantage of opportunities to improve representation of the groups covered than with maintaining these gains during a workforce reduction. In particular, OFCCP does not expect employers to modify seniority practices in order to maintain these gains.

With respect to layoff alternatives, there is a potential conflict between early retirement incentives and the ADEA, which protects workers aged 40 and over. Early retirement incentive programs promise eligible employees a level of benefits superior to retirement under the regular terms of the pension plan. They can also make employees not eligible under the regular terms of the pension plan eligible to receive retirement benefits if they elect to retire within some specified period. Typically, eligibility for early retirement will be determined by some combination of age and length of service, often correlated with but distinct from age as a criterion. Section 623(f)(2) of the ADEA states that it is not unlawful to observe the terms of a bona fide seniority system or retirement plan.[93] Mandatory retirement of most employees is prohibited under the ADEA, so employees must choose the early retirement option voluntarily.[94] But the issue of what is and is not a voluntary choice remains unresolved. If the employer uses coercion or pressure, there can be an ADEA violation. But whether or not a statement embodies coercion or pressure is dependent on context, in this instance the context of an older worker facing an uncertain employment situation.

### Seniority and Equal Employment Opportunity

The last-hired, first-fired problem is the primary focus of the conflict between seniority and civil rights law in terms of layoffs. I will review the development of federal law on this question, which has resulted in strong current protection of seniority systems under section 703(h). Although states also have their own fair employment practice laws, the federal law is the baseline that state laws must meet in order to be "deferral agencies" (described below). But first, I will outline the process by which antidiscrimination laws are enforced.[95]

The Equal Employment Opportunity Commission (EEOC) is the federal organization charged with overseeing this issue area. Virtually all states also have their own fair employment practice laws and associated agencies. Alabama, Arkansas, and Mississippi are the only states without a law covering private employers. The federal and state agencies work together, if the state's equal opportunity laws provide coverage not less than that provided by Title VII. In almost all cases, however, the state laws extend the scope of the antidiscrimination effort. For example, some state equal opportunity laws include homosexuals, people with foreign accents, and even people with unpleasant personal appearances. State agencies providing sufficient coverage are designated as "deferral agencies." These state agencies process the aggrieved party's initial complaint, but if they do not achieve a resolution within 60 days, either finding no cause to believe the charge is true or, if cause is found, conciliating the dispute and achieving a settlement, the charging party may take the case to the EEOC. However, virtually nothing is ever resolved in 60 days. The complainant therefore has some ability to engage in "forum shopping." One official of the Illinois Human Rights Commission commented that, with the conservative turn in the federal judiciary, complainants were more likely to continue to seek relief on the state level, given the greater expected value of continuing the case on this level. It is also possible for the state or local agency to waive its 60-day exclusive jurisdiction period pursuant to a work-sharing arrangement with the EEOC. The EEOC itself may make a charge if an official has reason to believe that a violation has occurred.

Title VII sets out strict procedural guidelines and time limits for processing a charge. The first step in processing a charge is an investigation conducted by an EEOC investigator, to determine if there is "reasonable cause" to believe the charge is true.[96] If the EEOC finds reasonable cause, they attempt to achieve conciliation between the employer and/or union and the aggrieved party or parties. If there is no finding of reasonable cause, the complainant is issued a right-to-sue letter informing the charging party that he or she may continue to seek relief in a federal court. If the EEOC is able to achieve a conciliation, they may obtain a court-approved consent decree, which commits the parties to provide relief for the victims and possibly to fulfill the terms of an affirmative action plan. If conciliation is not achieved within 30 days, the EEOC may bring civil action in the appropriate federal court. If the EEOC does not bring this action within 180 days, it issues a right-to-sue letter, notifying the aggrieved party that he or she has 90 days to file suit in the appropriate district court.

Many managers I spoke with stated that in any reduction in the workforce they could expect some charges claiming that selections for layoff were made in a discriminatory manner. There are two basic orientations of managers to this process: deterrence and settlement. Managers who believe in deterrence say that it is important to fight charges when they arise, even though the costs may be high, to deter future aggrieved employees from filing more charges. These tend to be the managers who claim that their company has never had a weaker case than the charging party and that their company is almost always in the right. Managers who settle, while not admitting directly that the decision in question may have been wrong, do state that often the paper trail needed for a strong defense is not in place and that they will simply try to pay the charging party a sum of money to satisfy him or her. One legal official of a large manufacturing firm stated that it was their policy to fight charges very strongly up until just before litigation, at which point they try to settle.

The relief that can be obtained by an aggrieved employee under Title VII is as follows: In addition to prohibiting the unlawful practice and ordering an affirmative action plan, the court may award reinstatement with back pay, attorney's fees, and retroactive seniority.[97] These are "make-whole" provisions. An award of retroactive seniority grants victims of discrimination in hiring seniority equal to that which they would currently hold had they not been discriminatorily denied the employment in question. Until the Civil Rights Act of 1991, this make-whole relief was all that was available to victims of sex or religious discrimination. Victims of race discrimination could obtain compensatory and punitive damages under a long-dormant Civil War statute, but other victims were left out.[98] The 1991 Act, however, allows limited compensatory and punitive damages to be awarded to all victims in cases of intentional discrimination.[99] A facially neutral practice that has a disparate negative impact on a protected group, but which was not implemented with an intent to discriminate, may have to be modified but cannot result in compensatory or punitive damages.

A seniority system that is not bona fide (that is, which is formulated with intent to discriminate) or which is differentially applied falls outside of the protection of 703(h), and therefore falls into the category of cases that could involve compensatory and punitive damages. Although it is difficult to prove actual intent, courts have found that a seniority system is not bona fide when the arrangement of seniority units is irrational and out of line with industry practice, its only possible purpose being its negative impact on a protected group.[100] When there are two seniority progressions and, for example, blacks are segregated into one and whites into the other, courts are likely to find that these systems are not bona fide.[101] When female or minority employees are not granted the same seniority benefits as white males of equal seniority, it will be found that the system is differentially applied and not bona fide.[102]

The most difficult problem is that of a bona fide system that, although facially neutral, has an adverse impact on protected groups. As mentioned above, some such systems are currently prohibited or proscribed. For example, the use of an IQ test to select employees for hiring or promotion would be regarded as a violation in the majority of circumstances. But the fact that intent is specifically referred to in Section 703(h) of the act gives seniority systems much stronger protection than other practices, at least in the eyes of conservative jurists. This seniority systems exception was a response to the fear that the act, as originally drafted, would compromise the seniority rights of employees covered by collective bargaining agreements.[103]

In the subsequent sections I will trace the development of judicial thought on this issue, focusing (although not limiting) my attention on important Supreme Court decisions. These cases fall into two categories: first, cases that directly address the question of whether routine application of a bona fide seniority system is protected by 703(h); second, cases that arise from disputes over modifications to seniority systems and lists made pursuant to an affirmative action plan in order to avoid the last-hired, first-fired problem. In both categories, the prevailing doctrine has over time become quite conservative.

### Extending the Protection of Seniority Systems

Cases involving a conflict between seniority and Title VII arose soon after the act went into effect. In *Quarles* v. *Philip Morris,* an oft-cited early case, a Virginia District Court in 1968 ruled that the seniority rights of whites were not vested and indefeasible but subject to modification, and that a departmental system originally set up for the purpose of segregating blacks could never be bona fide even if currently administered neutrally.[104] In another influential early case, *Local 189 United Papermakers and Paperworkers* v. *United States,* the Fifth Circuit in 1969 articulated a "rightful place" theory of remediation which rejected the radical view that white incumbents should be displaced but also rejected the conservative view that fair application of a facially neutral system was necessarily sufficient to satisfy the purposes of the act.[105] The opinion states that a seniority system that is facially neutral nevertheless still violates the Civil Rights Act if the inevitable effect of the system is to perpetuate the effects of prior discrimination. Both of these cases involved departmental rather than plantwide seniority systems.

These influential cases set a moderately liberal tone. A further movement toward the liberal interpretation of Title VII came with the Supreme Court's decision in *Griggs* v. *Duke Power Co.* in 1971.[106] Although this case did not concern seniority systems or layoffs, it established the validity of the disparate impact theory, which holds that facially neutral practices with a disparate negative effect on protected groups violate Title VII. These cases set out the primary issues in this area: Is the law violated by a facially neutral seniority system that has a disparate impact on women and minorities, thereby perpetuating the effects of prior discrimination?

Subsequent to *Griggs,* the disparate impact theory became a significant issue in cases involving seniority and layoffs. There were several cases involving plantwide last-hired, first-fired systems. A conservative decision was rendered by the Fifth Circuit in 1975 in *Watkins* v. *Steelworkers Local 2369.*[107] Here, it was ruled that irrespective of the previous history of discrimination, the last-hired, first-fired system in question was lawful despite its disparate impact. In 1975, in *Jersey Central Power and Light* v. *Electrical Workers Locals 327 et al.,* the Third Circuit ruled that Congress intended for facially neutral seniority systems that resulted in disparate impact in terms of layoffs to enjoy protection under 703(h). These systems, the court held, may be bona fide irrespective of their perpetuation of the effects of past discrimination. The only valid grounds for challenge would be that the system was discriminatorily applied or formulated with the intent to discriminate.[108] In 1974, in *Waters* v. *Watkins Steel Works,* the Seventh Circuit ruled that the employer's last-hired, first-fired system was facially neutral, despite its disparate impact.[109]

On the other hand, at the District Court level, one can find liberal decisions on this issue. (In fact, many of the decisions of the Courts of Appeals reversed District Court decisions.) In *Delay* v. *Carling Brewing Co.,* a Georgia District Court in 1974 ruled that a plantwide seniority system, although facially neutral, was a violation of the act insofar as it perpetuated the effects of prior discrimination.[110] In *Schaefer* v. *Tannian,* a Michigan District Court in 1975 held that a last-hired, first-fired layoff that had a disparate impact on women was a violation, since their inability to accumulate sufficient seniority was the result of prior discrimination.[111]

However, in the early- to mid-1970s, departmental or line-of-progression seniority systems were not viewed with favor by either the District Courts or the Courts of Appeals. The cases against these systems focused on their effect of segregating women and minorities into less desirable jobs. With respect to layoffs, departmental systems often put an employee at the bottom of the seniority list when that employee transferred into the department. This can result in a minority employee with many years of company service who has recently taken advantage of new opportunities to transfer into a previously all-white department being laid off before a white employee with less company service. The early- to mid-1970s cases involving departmental systems generally cite *Quarles* and *Papermakers* in support of the contention that departmental systems that segregate black and female employees into less desirable jobs and/or perpetuate the effects of prior discrimination are not bona fide and thus not protected by 703(h), irrespective of whether they are currently administered neutrally.[112]

In general, while the decisions concerning seniority systems at the District Court level were liberal through the mid-1970s, the decisions of the Circuit Courts of Appeals through this period were conservative with respect to layoffs made pursuant to a plantwide last-hired, first-fired system, yet liberal with respect to segregation into lower paying jobs resulting from a departmental seniority system.[113] Although this can be explained on purely technical legal grounds, there are two additional substantive explanations. (1) The plantwide last-hired, first-fired system represents the strongest embodiment of the prior contribution ethic. Judges are very favorably disposed toward this ethic. In fact, in some of the cases involving departmental systems it was noted that such systems do not always reward long company service.[114] (2) Cases involving promotions and transfers are perceived differently from cases involving layoffs. Ruling against a departmental seniority system in a case involving promotions and transfers merely denies the white males an opportunity for gain, whereas ruling against a plantwide last-hired, first-fired system in a case involving layoffs can impose the severe cost of job loss upon them. (Any ruling modifying a seniority system will have future consequences for layoffs, but layoffs were not the immediate issue in the departmental cases.)

Starting in the mid-1970s, the Supreme Court began to hear cases concerning the conflict between seniority systems and Title VII. In terms of the routine application of bona fide systems, the Supreme Court in 1977, in *Teamsters* v. *U.S.*, held that 703(h) in effect immunized the routine application of such a system.[115] This case involved a segregated departmental system of the type that had previously been viewed with almost universal disfavor by the Courts of Appeals. The Court ruled that a seniority system can be bona fide even if it perpetuates the effects of pre-Act discrimination. The majority emphasized the seniority rights of innocent white male employees.[116] The majority opinion noted that "were it not for 703(h), the seniority system in this case would seem to fall under the *Griggs* rationale," but also noted that "both the literal terms of Section 703(h) and the legislative history of Title VII" indicate that Congress considered the disparate impact and perpetuation of prior discrimination of many seniority systems but immunized them nonetheless.[117]

In 1980, in *California Brewers Association* v. *Bryant*, the Supreme Court ruled that a seniority system that had an extreme disparate impact on blacks in terms of layoffs enjoyed 703(h) protection.[118] The disparate impact theory was ruled out as a means of calling into question virtually any aspect of a seniority system, even ancillary rules and provisions, with respect to its operation during layoffs. In 1982, in *Patterson* v. *American Tobacco Co.,* 703(h) protection was further extended to seniority systems created after the date of the Act, as long as they were established without discriminatory intent.[119] A seniority system had to be shown to be created with intent to discriminate in order to be overturned. So, both post-Act and pre-Act seniority systems were effectively immunized from disparate impact claims, as long as they were bona fide.

The most recent Supreme Court decision directly concerning seniority systems extended de facto protection to systems whose bona fide nature is highly questionable. The protection was later revoked in the Civil Rights Act of 1991.[120] In *Lorance et al.* v. *AT&T Technologies,* the Court ruled that employees must file any complaint against the system within a time frame directly after the agreement is signed.[121] They cannot wait until the negative effects of the system are felt. According to the liberal dissent, however, such an agreement represents a continuing violation upon which a complaint may be filed as long as it is in effect. In this pithy dissent, Justice Marshall wrote that Congress' goals in enacting Title VII "surely never included conferring absolute immunity on discriminatorily adopted seniority systems that survive their first 300 days."[122] Once again, there was a conflict concerning whether the current neutral application of a system originally adopted with discriminatory purpose constitutes ongoing intentional discrimination. Congress' reversal of *Lorance* was in accordance with the "ongoing discrimination" thesis.

These cases, however, relate to seniority systems embodied in a collective bargaining agreement between an employer and a union. Whether or not a seniority system unilaterally implemented by a nonunion employer enjoys such protection has not been addressed by the Supreme Court.

### Modifications to Seniority and Seniority Relief

The upshot of the cases described above is that it has become difficult to question seniority-based layoff policies agreed to by employer and union absent any showing of discriminatory intent. Different rules apply to employers and/or unions who are participating in a voluntary or court-ordered affirmative action plan. These plans do not necessarily benefit the actual victims of a discriminatory act. Instead, they can be aimed at benefiting members of a protected class.

In 1976, in *Franks* v. *Bowman Transportation Co.*, the Court addressed the question of whether retroactive seniority dating to the time at which an employment application was discriminatorily denied is a legitimate form of relief.[123] In other words, if the company is ordered to offer employment and back pay to aggrieved former applicants, is it legitimate for the courts to order that the victim also be granted a seniority level consistent with what he or she would currently hold had the discrimination never happened? This form of relief avoids a future last-hired, first-fired problem. The majority ruled that retroactive seniority is acceptable even though it impinges on the contractual rights of innocent white male employees in terms of layoff and recall. They contended that purposes of public policy made this burden sharing legitimate. Note, however, that the majority ruled that this was acceptable in part because it benefited actual victims of discrimination by the company, not simply members of the protected class in general.

In 1979, the Court ruled in *Steelworkers* v. *Weber* that it was legitimate for employers to give special preference to female and minority workers to correct a manifest statistical workforce imbalance.[124] Class-based relief in terms of hiring and promotion preference was deemed legitimate. Yet, in the case of class-based relief, the last-hired, first-fired problem may require more than retroactive seniority relief to identifiable victims of discrimination. Can such plans include employment security protection for these recently hired employees? What if only the employer and not the union (or vice versa), agrees to a plan that modifies a preexisting seniority system? The Supreme Court has consistently made conservative decisions on these issues.

In 1983, in *W. R. Grace* v. *Local 759, Int'l Union of the United Rubber Workers*, the Court ruled that the employer could not unilaterally enter into a conciliation agreement with the EEOC that contradicted the seniority-based layoff provisions of the collective bargaining agreement.[125] In a layoff conducted after the conciliation agreement went into effect, newly hired women were retained ahead of men with greater seniority. Male employees brought a grievance under the union contract, and the Court upheld an arbitration award in favor of the union. There is an established doctrine of very limited judicial review of arbitration awards.[126] In addition, according to this ruling, since it was the company, and not the employees or the union, that had brought this dilemma upon itself (both by discrimination in hiring and by entering into two incompatible agreements), it was not proper for the cost of resolving the dilemma to be placed upon the innocent white male employees.

In 1984, in *Firefighters Local Union No. 1784* v. *Stotts,* the Court addressed a conflict between a consent decree that mandated efforts to increase the percentage of black firefighters and a contractual last-hired, first-fired policy.[127] The decree mandated a long-term increase in the number and rank of black employees. When a layoff situation arose, the union sought to obtain adherence to the contractual seniority provisions. The Court ruled that since the consent decree made no mention of layoffs, there were no grounds for overriding the terms of the contract. In addition, it was noted that the union and the nonminority employees were not parties to the consent decree, implying that the contractual seniority privileges could not be considered to have been bargained away. It was also ruled that make-whole relief such as back pay and retroactive seniority could be given only to actual victims of discriminatory acts, not simply to members of a protected class.

Although the Court continued to rule conservatively on cases involving seniority-based layoffs, it also continued to pass down more liberal rulings on class-based affirmative action programs in general.[128] The granting of class-based relief in terms of promotion and hiring to class members that are not actual victims of discriminatory acts is permissible, but grants of retroactive seniority can be given only to identifiable victims.

Recently, in *Martin* v. *Wilks,* the Court ruled that white male employees who were not parties to a consent decree mandating affirmative action could challenge it at any time.[129] The Civil Rights Act of 1991 overturned this, precluding an individual from challenging a previously adopted consent decree if he or she had a prior opportunity to present objections.[130] So, according to Congress, a discriminatory seniority system can be challenged when its effects are felt, but a consent decree containing an affirmative action plan that white male employees may perceive as reverse discrimination must be challenged quickly.

### EEOC Interpretations of the Law

In their day-to-day decision making, employers can refer to the *EEOC Compliance Manual*.[131] This document contains EEOC interpretations of the law, which are not binding legal doctrine. However, if a charge is filed concerning an employment decision that runs contrary to these interpretations, the EEOC may find cause to believe discrimination has occurred and implement conciliation proceedings. If an employer does not run afoul of these interpretations, then the aggrieved employee will be on his or her own—a less costly scenario for the employer. This document details the EEOC's interpretation of what is permissible under Title VII with respect to seniority.[132] The protection against adverse impact and perpetuation of prior discrimination claims in layoff situations established by the courts is reiterated.

It is, however, possible for an employer and union, or an employer alone if there is no union, to implement an affirmative action program that bases employment decisions, including layoffs, in part on race, sex, or national origin. Such an affirmative action plan may be implemented pursuant to an EEOC supervised conciliation agreement or consent decree entered into by the parties to the dispute at hand. Even if the dispute at hand did not arise as a result of a conflict over layoffs, the terms of the agreement entered into by the parties may contain provisions governing the conduct of future layoffs. Once an employer has attracted the attention of the EEOC, the government is not limited to attempting to rectify the discriminatory practice that attracted this attention. In fact, the EEOC's guidelines state that it will attempt to include in all conciliation agreements measures to lessen the effect of reductions-in-force on protected group representation.[133]

An acceptable way of reconciling seniority and affirmative action is for seniority overrides or modifications to be used. Alternatives mentioned include using plant instead of departmental seniority and creating separate seniority lists based on race, sex, and national origin. The first would be useful in a formerly segregated workplace where protected employees have lost accumulated departmental seniority after moving into a formerly all-white, all-male department. The second alternative would be oriented toward solving a last-hired, first-fired problem. One example cited is a policy of laying off two nonprotected group employees for each protected group employee, with all layoff selections made in accordance with the separate seniority lists, until such time as the representation goals of the affirmative action plan have been met. Interviews with managers subject to affirmative action plans confirm that attempts to maintain protected group representation within job categories are common. The EEOC acknowledges that such modifications negatively impact white male employees, and their reverse-discrimination complaints are to be handled the same way as any other.

In terms of seniority systems unilaterally adopted by nonunion employers, it is noted that these "may not fall within the protection of 703(h) and may be subject to challenge as perpetuating the effects of pre- or post-Act discrimination." This issue has not been decisively settled by the Supreme Court. However, it is the commission's position "that section 703(h) applies to seniority systems unilaterally established by employers."[134] Lower court decisions have supported this view.[135]

## Interviews with Corporate Decision Makers

In this section I provide an overview of workforce reduction practices and policies at five companies. This information was obtained in confidential interviews with managers and personnel directors. Interviewees for this phase of the project were recruited by first sending a letter to the chief executives of firms that had recently had large layoffs. This letter requested an interview with the company's personnel director and asked the CEO to pass the letter along to the personal director with the CEO's approval for an interview. In some cases other managers were interviewed as well as the personnel director. Although thirteen companies were studied during the course of this project, these are the only five companies for which I obtained comprehensive enough overviews to write stand-alone case studies.

Five general observations can be derived from the interviews.

First, layoff selections in large- to medium-sized companies that are not constrained by a collective bargaining agreement are made in a decentralized fashion. Managers of the affected departments evaluate their employees and draw up the initial selection list. The personnel department must review these decisions and make sure that they are legitimate and documented, especially when employees protected by antidiscrimination laws are involved. Information processing and control problems are key issues in this regard.

Second, in the nonunion companies studied, seniority is used primarily as a tiebreaker in accordance with the relatively equal logic discussed previously. Seniority in these companies is weighted most heavily when the performance information available for the employees is poor or irrelevant. Although companies may deviate from their own seniority policies in order to achieve equal employment opportunity goals, such deviations typically do not involve eliminating long-service employees in order to retain short-service female and minority employees. In the unionized facilities studied, however, seniority is nearly the sole factor used. Detailing how layoffs are implemented under these systems illustrates the almost mathematical precision with which this criterion is applied in this context.

Third, although seniority systems are ordinarily seen as disadvantageous to female/minority employees due to the last-hired, first-fired problem, the use of seniority as a layoff criterion has benefits for these employees as well. By removing managerial discretion from the layoff process, seniority protects these employees from discriminatory management decisions. Whether or not this benefit outweighs the cost is context-dependent, but the benefit exists.

Fourth, although white male employees may view efforts to combat employment discrimination as contrary to their interests, efforts by employers to protect themselves against discrimination charges have a positive externality for white male employees. By inducing employers who want to conduct performance-based layoffs to document and support their decisions, equal opportunity laws help to ensure that white male employees will have their performance evaluated in the same manner as well. A vague company policy directing managers to retain their best people leaves room for favoritism and nepotism as well as discrimination.

Fifth, attention to statistical representation of women and minorities in the post-layoff workforce does not necessarily result in white male employees with great seniority or excellent performance records being eliminated.[136] Employers who trade seniority and/or performance off against statistical representation evaluate exposure to costly discrimination charges versus the supposed benefit of or seniority rationale for retaining a more able or senior white male employee. If the white male is only slightly more able or senior than the female/minority employee, the exposure outweighs the benefit or seniority rationale. But if the seniority or ability differential is great, the benefit/rationale outweighs the exposure.

The names of these companies and some innocuous details have been changed in the following examples in order to maintain confidentiality. The companies are:

1. Retail Stores of America (RSA)—the umbrella company for a set of retail store chains. There are several operating divisions, each consisting of a chain of retail stores. The company is essentially nonunion.

2. Contemporary Software Solutions (CSS)—a relatively young, medium-sized computer software company. In this company, 4 years of seniority is considered a lot. The company is essentially nonunion.

3. Financial Services Incorporated (FSI)—a large financial services company with facilities across the United States. The company is essentially nonunion.

4. Basic Manufacturing Company (BMC)—a company that manufactures and distributes industrial products; with one large manufacturing plant, which is unionized, and a number of small supplemental facilities, most of which are not.

5. International Products Corporation (IPC)—a manufacturer of a wide variety of technologically sophisticated products, which operates a large number of plants, some of which are unionized while others are not.

### Retail Stores of America (RSA)

Although they have no union, there is an established company policy of using seniority as a criterion for selection for layoff. However, as described below, seniority is used differently for different types of employees. This case highlights the degree to which the use of seniority is seen as a solution to the "principal-agent problem" involved in allowing lower-level managers wide discretion in making selections for layoff.

The stores operated by RSA's operating divisions experience both seasonal fluctuations and permanent market shifts which result in permanent restructurings. Seasonal fluctuations are routinely handled on the store level. However, permanent restructurings involve a process of planning and consultation across several levels of the organization. The degree to which seniority is used as a criterion depends on the quality and quantity of performance data on the employees being reviewed. When good data are lacking, seniority is the primary criterion for selection. When there are relevant performance data, a relatively equal logic is used. A senior employee will be retained over a junior employee as long as the performance of the senior person is no more than slightly worse than that of the junior person.

Data on performance are often very thin or lacking for the lower-level employees working relatively unskilled jobs in the stores. (About 75 to 85 percent of the store employees are female. They are nonunion.) Selections for layoff from these jobs will generally be done by straight seniority. However, there are situations in which performance can be incorporated. For example, one of the departments of the retail stores sells an expensive item that generates repeat customers if they are satisfied with the initial purchase experience. Selling these expensive items involves personal interaction with the customers. Management can evaluate employees by examining the repeat business generated by each salesperson. Since a relevant performance measure is available, the "relatively equal" logic would be used to make selections among these employees. However, in other departments that sell less expensive items it is difficult to evaluate employee performance. These jobs essentially consist of standing behind a cash register and ringing up sales of items that customers bring to the counter.

Other reasons mentioned for using seniority as a criterion include the sunk costs of invested training and rewarding employee loyalty. In addition, at the store level, simply having been there a long time is itself a form of qualification in certain areas. As described above, employees can form relationships with regular buyers of certain items. The salespeople in this department who have been in the store the longest are likely to have the largest number of such ongoing relationships, which generate repeat business.

The use of seniority for making selections among these employees also helps the company avoid potential discrimination problems. (Approximately 25 percent of the company's employees are minority group members.) While seniority systems are ordinarily seen as bad for protected group employees due to the last-hired, first-fired problem, the use of seniority can prevent discrimination by removing discretion from lower-level managers who might otherwise make questionable decisions. In the absence of any real performance measure, allowing the lower-level managers to make selections based on their subjective judgments of employee quality could cause trouble.

In particular, it was stated that lower-level supervisors had to be prevented from using layoffs as an opportunity to eliminate minority employees they consider troublesome. A minority employee who vigorously asserts his or her rights or who has criticized the performance of the supervisor would be highly vulnerable under a system that gave lower-level supervisors much discretion. Although supervisors should in theory be similarly ill-disposed toward nonminority employees who pose such challenges to the supervisor, this problem was noted with particular reference to minority employees. Typically, if there is such a minority employee in a store, district managers or even headquarters people will know about this employee. If this employee is on the list of initial selections of people to be laid off, the upper-level people reviewing the initial plan will raise serious questions about this selection. There are two reasons for this close scrutiny. One is that this might be a very good employee who is simply too "uppity" in the perception of the supervisor. The other is that an assertive personality type may be more likely to file discrimination charges.

In terms of managerial and professional employees at higher levels, performance and ability are the primary criteria in making selections for layoff, with seniority being used as a tiebreaker. When the need for a reduction becomes apparent, there are two planning tasks: (1) redesigning the organization, in effect creating a new organization chart with fewer slots than the old one, and (2) determining which employees would be able to perform the duties associated with the available slots in the redesigned organization. Specific experience in specific tasks is considered more important than generalized ability. However, versatility is also considered. When many jobs are being combined into one, as is often the case in organizational restructurings, someone who performs many tasks adequately is often more valuable than someone who is excellent at one thing but unable to do anything else.

Sometimes, when Job A and Job B are being combined into one, an evaluation is made as to what percentage of the combined job will be tasks formerly performed in Job A and what percentage will be those associated with Job B. If 80 percent of the new job consists of Job A tasks, the Job A occupant will most likely be the one retained in the new job. However, at the higher levels of the corporate hierarchy, jobs become highly specialized. Thus, selection for reduction among several occupants of similar slots is less of a problem.

In workforce reductions, the company attempts to minimize race and age discrimination problems among both lower- and upper-level employees. There is a formal review process aimed at minimizing the disparate impact of a workforce reduction on protected group employees in the affected unit. After an initial round of selections under the criteria described above, the composition of the workforce that would remain under these initial selections is evaluated against the pre-reduction workforce composition. Plus or minus 1 percent for any given protected group is seen as an acceptable impact. If these bounds are exceeded, the managers responsible for making the initial selections will have to make some revisions. In general, however, decision makers at each level are aware of this policy and try to achieve an acceptable impact in their initial selections. When revisions are needed, retained nonprotected group employees marginal under the relevant criteria will be switched with protected group employees who just missed making the initial cut. For low-skill jobs, the people switched will generally be employees close in seniority; for high-skill positions, they will be employees close in ability.

In terms of layoff alternatives, special early retirement incentives have been offered to both store employees and upper-level managerial/professional employees. Three problems associated with such programs were noted. The first problem is uncertainty about how many or which employees will take the incentives. In one of RSA's operating divisions, too many people took an early retirement package, which was very expensive. The second problem is that the employees who take the incentives may come from areas in which the need for reductions is not so pressing. The third problem is the difficulty of keeping supervisors from committing potential age discrimination violations by putting subtle pressure on older employees they do not like to take the early retirement incentives. Acceptance of such offers must be completely voluntary in order not to run afoul of ADEA. It is difficult for upper-level management to monitor such activity.

It was also emphasized that separations are expensive. Both store employees and upper-level managers and professionals receive special separations benefits. These benefits are primarily based on length of service and level of position. If an employee is eligible for pension and is involuntarily terminated, he or she receives an extra boost in benefits beyond what would have been obtained by taking retirement under the regular terms of the benefit plan.

### Contemporary Software Solutions

CSS is a case in which there is an informal corporate culture that uses seniority as a tiebreaker in situations where some people must be selected for a workforce reduction, the primary criterion being performance. If the reorganization involves eliminating an entire department or function, the people occupying the jobs in that department or function are ordinarily eliminated along with their slots. However, when the restructuring involves reducing the number of people performing a given function or combining jobs, selections of employees to be retained must be made. When two employees are considered relatively equal in terms of performance or ability, the more senior employee will be retained.

The company utilizes a formal 5-category performance evaluation scale, with category 3 being "fulfills job specification." However, specific skill mixes or areas of strength and information not captured in a summary rating are also examined. When selections for layoff must be made, managers of the affected units prepare a list of selections for layoff, which in effect generates two lists: a "save" list (employees the manager wants to retain) and a complementary "not save" list of employees initially selected for layoff. There is an informal norm of using the relatively equal logic in preparing these lists. Then, those on the "save" list are compared to those on the "not save" list by people in the personnel department. The performance ratings and seniority dates of those on the "not save" list are compared to the performance ratings and seniority dates of those employees initially slated to be saved.

If an employee with what is considered great seniority by CSS standards is on the "not save" list, this selection will be examined closely, even if the senior person has received a low summary performance rating. The performance ratings are not seen as communicating all relevant performance information. If a previously satisfactory and highly senior (by CSS standards) employee is selected for layoff on the basis of the manager's assertion of a sudden deterioration in performance, the manager is told to save the senior employee and to work with him or her to foster improvement and a return to previous performance. In the future, if performance cannot be improved, a discharge for cause may be necessary. A placement of a highly senior employee on the "not save" list that the personnel department feels is unjustified is referred to as a "seniority inequity."

If someone with a low performance rating (say, 4 on a scale of 1 to 5) is being saved while a 2 is on the "not save" list, the manager who draws up the initial list will also be questioned. It could be the case that the 2 does not have a specific skill that the 4 has. However, if the initial selection cannot be justified in these terms, it is referred to as a "performance inequity." Although the manager may subjectively believe that the person with the low rating should be retained, unless some concrete justification or documentation is available, this decision may be reversed, especially if a protected group employee is being eliminated. As a young company, CSS does not confront problems of potential age discrimination; most employees are not in the over-40 group protected by the ADEA. Title VII concerns, pertaining to potential race and sex discrimination, are of primary importance in CSS's decision making. The personnel department will press for selection revisions which they feel are needed to avoid such problems. There is much concern with documenting decisions affecting protected employees.

The company also keeps track of the statistical impact of workforce reductions on protected groups. The data from the initial round of selections are examined and a judgment made about the disparate impact of these selections. If the impact is seen as excessive, reversals may be made. The most marginal of the "saved" non-protected group employees will then be switched with the "not saved" protected employees who missed the initial cut by the narrowest margin. However, there is no set formula.

When an entire facility is closing, data on workforce composition from that facility will be examined to determine if the closing facility is dominated by a particular protected group. If there is another facility or department close by and the workforce in the closing facility is dominated by a protected group, there could be a discrimination charge contending that transfers should have been offered. When jobs that are predominantly occupied by protected group members are eliminated, the functions associated with those jobs should ideally be gone from the company. The continued performance of those tasks by nonprotected employees would diminish the company's ability to defend itself against charges that the protected employees were eliminated in order to be replaced by nonprotected employees.

### Financial Services Incorporated (FSI)

FSI is an example of a nonunion company with a formal and clearly specified layoff selection procedure. Performance evaluation data are used in a systematic way to implement a relatively equal logic in selecting employees for reduction. Because performance evaluations are used in the selection procedure in a somewhat stricter way than at CSS, much effort is devoted to ensuring that managers are careful in preparing such evaluations.

There are 5 categories in the performance evaluation system. Managers assign employees to a category based on both objective and subjective factors, and employees are evaluated yearly. Examples of objective factors include customer complaints (if the employee's job involves dealing with clients or customers) and the employee's record in meeting deadlines. An example of a subjective judgment is the manager's estimation of the employee's "ability to work with others." It was noted that employees were hardly ever placed in the lowest category by their managers, resulting in a de facto 4-category system.

When an entire department or function is eliminated, the employees in those jobs are eliminated. There is no "bumping." When a department or function is not being eliminated but simply reduced, employees are selected in accordance with a "relatively equal" logic. Again, there is no "bumping." The procedure used in implementing the "relatively equal" logic is as follows: First, the number of people to be eliminated from a department or job category is determined. This is part of the organizational redesign process that must precede the making of any actual selections. The selection procedure begins by eliminating the employees in the department or function who are in the lowest performance category. If there are more employees in this category than the number that must be eliminated, seniority is used to decide which of the employees in this category to eliminate. If the number of employees that must be eliminated is greater than the number of employees in the lowest performance category, all of the employees in the lowest category will be eliminated. The next step then is to examine the employees in the next-to-lowest performance category by a similar procedure, and so on until the first-order target has been reached. However, the selections made under this procedure are not set in stone. Questions are raised to the managers during the selection process, especially if long-service employees are being eliminated. Much attention is given to documenting the performance ratings upon which the selections are based.

In particular, the personnel staff at FSI closely scrutinizes decisions made on the basis of performance ratings that involve a substantial deviation from past performance on the part of the affected employee. In order to isolate these cases, the personnel staff examines the affected employee's 3-year performance rating history. This prevents managers from "playing games" immediately before a layoff is scheduled to take place. For example, if a yearly performance evaluation is scheduled for June and the manager knows or thinks selections for layoff will be made in July, the manager may give inaccurate ratings to some employees.

If the ratings over the last 3 years are consistent, the use of the most recent rating in the selection process described above is seen as legitimate, and a selection made on the basis of this rating will stand. If a decision is made on the basis of a performance evaluation that represents a sudden drop or increase from previous evaluations, a red flag is raised. People from the personnel department will talk to the manager who assigned this rating to determine the strength of the relevant documentation. A consistent history is particularly important with respect to ratings made largely on the basis of subjective managerial judgments.

One problem involved in relying on performance evaluations is the reluctance or inability of managers to assign accurate ratings. Some managers rarely assign negative ratings, and some managers tend to lump all employees together in the "average" category. However, as a result of the policy of relying heavily (although not completely) on the manager's performance evaluations, managers are learning that they have to be careful in assigning and documenting ratings. Under this policy, they cannot give a bad employee a good rating (to avoid a confrontation or for some other reason) and then get rid of that employee in a reduction. The personnel department may tell the manager that the previously adequate ratings given this employee preclude him or her being eliminated on the basis of the manager's sudden change of opinion. If managers lump all employees together in the average category, then there will be no one in the lower categories and selections for reduction will begin within the average category, seniority being used to decide among the employees in this category in accordance with the "relatively equal" logic. This might result in laying off a junior employee that the manager really wants to retain while a less-qualified senior employee is kept.

The personnel department is most aggressive in questioning sudden changes in performance evaluations involving long-service employees. In fact, whenever a highly senior employee is selected for layoff while a much less senior employee is retained, the personnel department questions this selection aggressively, even if no sudden changes in performance ratings are involved. Only if the documentation for the performance evaluations used in this decision is in order will the decision stand.

In cases involving sudden changes in evaluations of long-service employees, ADEA concerns motivate the extra attention given to documentation. It is difficult to go into court and contend that the previous satisfactory ratings were inflated and that the manager's sudden shift to a negative evaluation is justified. Sudden drops in ratings must in general be documented with hard evidence detailing a drop in quality and quantity of work.

"Corporate culture" is also a factor in focusing extra attention on layoff decisions involving long-service employees. FSI is traditionally a long-service company. All employees with over 20 years of service receive special recognition, creating a symbolic seniority breakpoint at 20 years of service. In general, the trigger for aggressive questioning comes when an employee with 20 or more years of service is selected for layoff while an employee about 10 years or more junior is retained. However, if the seniority gap is small, the decision is not questioned so aggressively. The size of the gap between the senior employee selected for layoff and the most junior employee retained is key in this regard. If this gap is only 1 or 2 years, aggressive questioning is not triggered, even if the two employees have 30 and 31 years of seniority, respectively.

FSI has also used both early retirement and voluntary separations programs to reduce the workforce. However, the executive I spoke with on this issue expressed reservations about the "abdication of control" involved in voluntary programs, citing FSI's experience with early retirement incentive programs. The first such program, which gave already retirement-eligible employees an extra cash incentive to retire, went smoothly. Many mediocre long-service employees retired. The personnel department emphasized to the managers the importance of allowing all employees to make their decisions free of pressure, thus avoiding ADEA problems, and the managers generally followed the direction of the personnel department in this regard.

The second time an early retirement incentive program was implemented, things did not go as smoothly. This second program added years of age and service to employees' existing levels of age and service in order to determine retirement eligibility and benefits. However, even with years of age and service added, there were not enough people in the category of those who would be eligible for the targeted number of employees to leave. Furthermore, the demographics of the company had changed. Most of the mediocre long-service employees had already left as a result of the first program. In addition, this time some managers tried to give "hints" to employees they wanted to leave, posing a potential ADEA problem.

Managers may also decide to offer a severance package, based on length of service and salary, to employees who leave voluntarily. But the executive I spoke with on this issue was unenthusiastic about such programs, especially if succeeding "waves" of such offers are made. As is also the case with early retirement incentives, good employees with outside opportunities, having observed ongoing waves of workforce reductions, may be motivated to look elsewhere.

### Basic Manufacturing Company (BMC)

BMC illustrates the different ways in which seniority is used in union and nonunion manufacturing facilities. In BMC's main plant, which is unionized, seniority is the primary criterion. In the nonunion supplemental facilities, however, seniority is usually combined with ability criteria in accordance with the relatively equal logic. Workforce reductions in the unionized plant initiate a complex process of "chain bumping," which can be played out with an almost mathematical precision. In the nonunion facilities, however, reductions are conducted somewhat more flexibly.

The unionized plant is organized by the Manufacturing Workers of America (MWA). The collective bargaining agreement between BMC and the MWA formally specifies a minimum qualifications criterion for selection for layoff. However, in practice, layoffs are almost always done by seniority, although ability considerations may occasionally come into play for highly skilled and craft positions. The MWA typically argues against the use of ability as a criterion during contract negotiations. Attempts by the company to invoke the minimum qualifications criterion are ordinarily countered by a union contention that the senior worker could achieve minimum qualifications for the relevant position with a little training.

In order for the company to permanently eliminate positions specified in the collective bargaining agreement, some discussion with the union will ordinarily be needed, resulting in ad hoc agreements with the union. However, there are situations in which there is no permanent reorganization of the plant, only a cutback in production.

Here is an overview of the operation of the layoff system in the production cutback scenario. Jobs within departments at the plant are arranged in a hierarchical sequence. For example, there could be a progression of seven or eight job levels within a department, forming a sequential job ladder. There may also be workers classified as "laborer" or "janitor" associated with the department, although these jobs are not formally in the sequence. The jobs in the sequence are typically mid- to upper-level skilled positions. There are also craft jobs, such as "electrician" or "mechanic." For the sake of brevity, I shall limit attention to sequence rather than craft jobs.

Plantwide seniority is used to make initial layoff selections from the classifications within a sequence. Then, there are a series of intrasequence "chain bumps" in which those reduced from the top category exercise their plantwide seniority to displace juniors in the next category down. The displaced juniors then use their plantwide seniority to displace employees to whom they are superior in the third level down, and so on, until the lowest level in the sequence is reached. The employees who fall out the bottom of the sequence can then displace people who are laborers or janitors associated with the department. These are "unprotected" jobs—their occupants can be bumped onto the street on the basis of plantwide seniority. However, if an employee who falls out the bottom of the sequence is not senior to anyone in the "unprotected" group, then this employee is on the street. Similarly, if there are only a small number of laborer or janitor jobs in the department, there may be more people falling out of the bottom of the sequence than there are bumpable positions.

An employee on layoff accumulates seniority for the purposes of benefits and recall for 2 years. It is not uncommon for employees on layoff to become retirement eligible during the 2 years after the layoff due to the accumulation of seniority and then to take retirement. After 2 years seniority no longer accrues, but an employee is eligible for recall indefinitely, although the seniority level that is used to determine whether or not the employee is recalled will be the level as of the end of the accrual period.

Procedures are different in the nonunion supplemental facilities operated by BMC. Temporary employees are ordinarily the first to go. These are contract employees who have been hired for specific time periods. Permanent part-time employees will then go, although there are some part-time employees who "fill cracks" that cannot be filled otherwise and are therefore not eliminated. Then, permanent full-time employees will be selected for reduction.

Among permanent full-time hourly employees in the nonunion supplemental facilities, seniority is used primarily as a tiebreaker in accordance with the relatively equal logic. The top 10–15 percent of the employees in terms of performance and ability will be retained irrespective of seniority. The bottom 10–15 percent will be eliminated irrespective of their seniority. Many of the people in the bottom 10–15 percent are put in this category due to attitude and discipline problems as well as inadequate job skills.

For the employees in the middle 70 percent, seniority will act as a tiebreaker when two employees are regarded as relatively equal. However, the way in which "relatively equal" is defined differs somewhat between high-skill and low-skill jobs. For high-skill jobs, two employees have to be fairly close in terms of performance and/or ability in order for seniority to govern. In low-skill jobs, seniority can govern when the two employees are somewhat further apart in terms of performance and/or ability. Thus, seniority plays a greater role in the low-skill positions. Management emphasizes an ability to learn and interpersonal skills rather than knowledge of specific tasks in evaluating ability.

Although procedures are formally the same in temporary and permanent workforce reductions, there are some differences in implementation. If the number of employees to be reduced is such that one must get into the middle 70 percent, seniority will usually be weighted more heavily within this group for temporary as opposed to permanent or indefinite reductions. When employees are being recalled from temporary layoff, the facility will usually try to find a way not to bring the poor performers back, instead recalling employees from the middle 70 percent.

Middle- and upper-level managers in the nonunion facilities find some use of seniority attractive because they regard information from the lower-level supervisors on performance and attitude as imperfectly reliable. For example, if there is a lower-level supervisor who does not do a very good job, an employee who has complained about this will usually be evaluated negatively. If systematic written performance documentation for the hourly employees was available, this would be less of a problem. But management expressed some dissatisfaction with the performance evaluations available for the nonunion hourly employees. Given this fact, using seniority for the middle 70 percent makes life easier for the middle- and upper-level managers. The worst employees are obviously bad; the very good are obviously very good. But in the absence of performance data sufficient to draw distinctions between someone at the top of the middle 70 percent and someone at the bottom, seniority will be used.

In general, seniority will be more important in a more mature facility. Middle- and upper-level managers are often reluctant to eliminate very long service employees even if they are less-than-stellar performers. First-level supervisors are usually more willing to eliminate these employees, since their primary concern is their department's performance. But middle- and upper-level managers are concerned with employee morale and the risk associated with getting rid of highly senior employees, in particular, the risk of charges of age discrimination. So middle- and upper-level managers will sometimes reverse decisions made by first-level supervisors to eliminate poor-performing highly senior employees.

However, the presence of highly senior employees who are poor performers may be due to the first-level supervisors' loose management. Upper management feels that sometimes supervisors are not attentive enough to getting the poor performers to work efficiently during good times. After there has been such inadequate supervision for an extended period, it is simply not feasible to improve the employee's performance in the middle of a crunch.

Another scenario in which revisions to initial selections may be made by middle- and upper-level managers is when the initial selections result in a disparate impact on protected employees. In the union facilities, the legal protection enjoyed by seniority systems specified in collective bargaining agreements renders adjustments unnecessary. However, management believes that the lack of such a protected seniority system in the nonunion facilities makes some level of adjustment desirable. After selections for reduction have been made in accordance with the relatively equal logic outlined above, the aggregate impact of the selections on protected group percentages is examined. If there is no negative impact, the initial selections are maintained. But if there is a negative impact, adjustments in selections may be made.

The first step in making such changes is to examine the performance documentation for each protected group employee selected for layoff. If the employee's inadequate performance is well documented, the decision is maintained. If the documentation is not completely in place, a risk analysis is conducted. Lack of clear documentation results in a higher probability of a successful discrimination charge, which is balanced off against the cost of retaining a supposedly less qualified protected group employee. If a decision to eliminate a protected employee is reversed, then some nonprotected employee will have to go. Such tradeoffs will ordinarily take place in the middle 70 percent group. The protected group employees who barely missed the original cut will replace the most marginal previously retained nonprotected group employees. There is very little bumping in the nonunion facilities, so those who are finally selected are ordinarily gone from the plant.

Workforce reduction procedures and criteria for BMC's nonunion salaried white-collar and technical employees do not in general take seniority into account. Typically, after the number and types of employees that will be needed in the restructured organization have been determined, the next step in reducing the workforce is to eliminate those employees who are on a form of performance probation. Then management determines whether there are any employees in the department(s) affected by the reduction who can fill an open job elsewhere in the organization. If not enough reductions can be made this way, early retirement incentives will be offered to eligible employees. If more people volunteer to take retirement than the number of reductions required, then the most senior of the volunteering employees will be allowed to retire. Only after the voluntary alternatives have been tried does the company select people for involuntary reduction. This is done on the basis of documented performance. An employee selected for layoff in this manner cannot bump less senior employees in positions not eliminated, but the selected employee can move down to a lower-level position if a slot is open on the lower level.

Employee performance is evaluated on the basis of whether the employee has achieved goals that were previously agreed upon by the manager and the employee. Every 6 to 12 months, the manager and the employee each write down what they believe the employee's responsibilities and the timetable for completing them over the next 6 to 12 months should be. They then discuss these plans at a formal meeting. The goal of the meeting is to arrive at a formulation that both the manager and the employee can sign off on. The final agreement is like a contract between manager and employee: progress is reviewed on a periodic basis with the subordinate, and consistent failure to achieve planned objectives is viewed very negatively. The fact that the employee agrees to the plan makes it more difficult for the employee to claim that a subsequent negative evaluation, made on the basis of the failure to achieve specified goals and resulting in some adverse employer action, is unfair. This is particularly important with respect to discrimination charges.[137] Managers who do not devote sufficient attention to documenting performance problems (e.g., by documenting failure to fulfill plans) may end up having to "eat" employees they want to eliminate in a workforce reduction.

Race, age, and sex will sometimes be taken into account when involuntary reductions are taking place. In general, the management committee of the affected department makes its selections to avoid disparate impacts. However, if its initial performance ranking results in too many protected employees being selected for elimination, the most marginal nonprotected employees who were originally supposed to be retained may be switched with the highest ranking among the protected employees slated for layoff. The personnel department is involved in reviewing the percentages and evaluating disparate impact. It will prod the management committee to reconsider selection of protected group employees whose inadequate performance is less than completely documented. This revision process causes much heated debate within management committees.

But when the documentation for the performance ranking is complete, the managers can make selections based purely on the ranking. It is only when the ranking is not so well documented that such switches will take place. This switching will diminish the disparate impact and also reverse decisions whose documentation is weak enough to run the risk of a successful charge of discrimination.

Of the companies studied, BMC is the only one in which need is explictly taken into account as a criterion. Among salaried employees at BMC, need has been used both formally and informally in exempting people from layoff. The frequency of this practice has declined, since the business environment has become very competitive and the company cannot afford well-intentioned policies not aimed at increasing organizational efficiency. But the practice still exists. Need is taken into account only in extreme cases— the hypothetical example discussed was of an employee with a sick spouse and many children. Usually, managers know which employees are in such dire situations and will be more likely to retain them. If the employee is pension-eligible, they will try to find some way for this employee to receive an enhanced pension. Departments usually make such decisions by themselves, but sometimes the personnel department will step in on behalf of such an employee. In addition, there is a formal exception process, which involves approval by an upper-level executive. Sometimes the employee will write a letter to the relevant executive and make his or her case; sometimes the departmental manager will do it for the employee.

### International Products Corp. (IPC)

IPC has both union and nonunion manufacturing facilities. Unlike BMC, IPC is party to many different collective agreements (CBAs). Within the unionized IPC facilities, strict seniority is typically specified in the CBA. In general, the seniority units within which selections for layoff are made are defined quite specifically, being structured by job classification, job family, and geographic location. Performance and/or ability is not usually an issue in the unionized facilities. Since selections for layoff are made within quite specific job and classification definitions, one can use strict seniority while avoiding the problem of retaining a senior employee who is unable to perform the available work. However, along with the benefits of a CBA that specifies strict use of seniority within highly defined job classifications and ladders comes a cost, namely a lack of flexibility in the allocation of manpower due to the very specific task definitions in the CBA.

In some CBAs, employees selected for layoff can elect to bump a junior employee currently working a job that the laid-off employee has previously held. This will ordinarily be a job on a lower rung in the job ladder that the laid-off employee has ascended. However, the degree to which bumping is permitted varies across the company's many CBAs and tends to increase with the length of the relationship between the company and the union. Over time, the contract steadily becomes more and more complex. There is a "ratchet effect"—new clauses and provisions get put into the contract year after year, but old clauses and provisions are not removed. Although the company regards bumping as disruptive and would try to keep provisions permitting bumping out of any new CBA, in a long relationship, sooner or later provisions permitting bumping will get into the agreement, and then it is difficult to remove them.

The degree to which management consults with the union before implementing a reduction varies in accordance with the atmosphere of relations with the union at the facility in question. At facilities where relations are cooperative, the company will sometimes sit down and talk with the union before implementing a planned reduction. For example, at one facility the company informed the union that some reductions would be needed and then negotiated more flexible work assignments and practices that allowed some jobs to be preserved. (Although the IPC executive I spoke with on this issue regarded this as beneficial to the employees, unions regard such negotiations conducted in the shadow of reductions as strong-arm tactic.) At the very least, if relations are good the union will receive some informal advance notice before the time mandated by the CBA. But at facilities where relations are hostile, management basically draws up a list of employees to be laid off and hands it to the union. If the union feels that the layoff selections are violative of the contract, they can activate the grievance procedure, possibly leading to arbitration.

Among the hourly employees in IPC's nonunion facilities, seniority is used as a tiebreaker in accordance with a modified relatively equal logic. There will typically be a group of poor performers who will definitely be eliminated and a group of outstanding performers who will definitely be retained. However, among the employees in the middle group, seniority will be taken into account as a tiebreaker. Some tendency was noted for a choice between a junior and a senior employee to go in favor of the latter in proportion to the magnitude of the seniority difference betweeen them. This implies that there is a tradeoff element as well as a relatively equal (seniority as tiebreaker) element in the way seniority is taken into account. However, throughout the interview the logic was summarized as "tiebreaker" rather than "tradeoff," indicating that tiebreaker is the dominant tendency.

It was stated that, level of seniority difference aside, deciding to eliminate someone with long service is always difficult. However, it was also stated that someone who has been with the company a long time is probably an adequate employee. Truly inadequate employees would either have had their problems corrected or have been discharged at some point during the years of their service. In fact, if someone with a high absolute level of seniority appears on the initial list of those to be reduced within a facility, this initial selection may be reversed by upper management if there is no strong documentation of a specific justification for this selection.

The strong legal protection given seniority systems arising from a collective bargaining agreement eliminates the need for IPC to worry about discrimination charges resulting from workforce reductions in unionized facilities as long as strict seniority is used. However, in the nonunion facilities, there is no CBA, and ability and/or performance as well as seniority are used to make selections. Thus, IPC is concerned with documenting decisions adversely affecting protected group employees within these facilities. The selections are not made or revised to achieve specific numerical goals aimed at minimizing disparate impact. Instead, the emphasis is on documenting individual decisions. Although many charges have been filed against IPC, the company has been successful in fighting almost all of them.

However, evaluation of numerical impact data does play a role in activating a closer review of decisions affecting protected group hourly employees. For example, if there is a small number of women working in a large facility and they are all selected for layoff, the decisions will be closely reviewed by an upper level of management. But if the women are all low in seniority or have well-documented performance problems, the decisions will stand.

For lower-level white-collar employees, the logic of "keep the outstanding employees, eliminate the poor employees, use seniority to decide among the rest" is implemented. However, there must be some sort of significant performance history in order for ability to be a criterion. Thus, if one was selecting employees for layoff within a group of short-service employees, seniority would be weighted heavily, given the absence of significant performance differences documented over some length of time.

In general, performance is weighted more heavily for professional and technical white-collar employees than for lower-level white-collar employees. In some business units, the technical and professional population is rated via a process known as *2D ranking*, which stands for "two-dimensional ranking." This involves a unit-wide ranking of professional personnel by department, by function, and by function within department.[138] The ranking is done periodically as part of ongoing personnel administration, being worked out by the relevant managers as a group. Very specific, formalized procedures are used to create these rankings. They are used to determine bonuses and to give employees continuous feedback on their performances. But these rankings will be also available for use in a reduction situation, although they would not be used as the sole factor. Evaluations done by only one manager are difficult to use, because managers vary in their strictness of evaluation. But the formalized 2D ranking process involves all the managers.

Earlier, IPC used early retirement programs to implement voluntary workforce reductions. The company now uses voluntary separations incentives that are not age-targeted and thus are not covered by ADEA. The executive with whom I spoke on this issue expressed the opinion that under current law early retirement incentives could not be targeted very specifically. Thus, once the early retirement incentives have been offered on a unit- or facility-wide basis, the company cannot stop crucial or talented employees from leaving. However, under a program that is not age-targeted, the company has the right to refuse an employee's request to be given the severance offer. (Typically, such incentive programs offer employees a lump sum based on their years of service if they resign.) So high-quality employees who might otherwise easily be able to find a new job after taking the severance offer can be denied the incentive, thus making leaving the company less attractive.

## Conclusion

One of the main themes of the above review is the information problem that employers encounter in making workforce reduction decisions. Information from foremen and supervisors is not always reliable. Even if they attempt to pass along correct information, it is not always possible to measure individual performance in any meaningful way. Quantifiable measures are not always available. It is not always possible to measure the individual contributions of employees who work together in teams. The seniority criterion avoids these problems. Sometimes an employee's seniority date is the only certain thing a manager knows about him or her.

The information problems encountered in the layoff arena differ from those found in transplantation and college admissions. In the latter two arenas, there are easily available quantitative measures of criteria predictive of "success" somehow defined. Medical tests reveal an individual's antigen patterns. College applicants provide colleges with GPAs and SATs. Debates in these arenas focus on whether prediction of success should really be the relevant criterion.

In the layoff arena, however, there are often no easily available quantitative measures that directly measure past performance and directly predict future job performance. Instead, there is a quantitative measure—seniority—which incorporates nonperformance criteria (such as prior contribution) and which is at best indirectly related to performance (accumulated experience may make a worker more able). In transplantation, there is a similar quantitative measure—time on the waiting list. But there is no such measure in college admissions. While membership in historically aggrieved groups can be used as a criterion in this area, this does not directly measure anything an individual has done or experienced. (It may be an indirect measure in that minority group members are likely to have experienced racism.) Although college admissions officers may consider an individual's particular non-academic accomplishments, the goal is to produce a class that is somehow a "well-rounded" group. This then becomes an essentially group-based rather than individual criterion.

Once one takes into account employers' information problems in conducting layoffs, one acquires some skepticism concerning the view that employment discrimination laws are unnecessary because they impose rigid guidelines on decisions that, if left to the market, would eventually result in equitable outcomes anyway. This view is based on the contention that employers who discriminate will be less efficient that those who do not, and will eventually lose to their non-discriminating competitors.[139] Below, I describe particular problems with this view with respect to the issue of layoffs.

First, note that the argument against employment discrimination laws assumes that if protected employees on average are as qualified as the unprotected, companies will eventually hire and retain them in equal numbers to their representation in the relevant labor market in order to compete effectively. But lower-level managers who are predisposed to view female/minority/older employees as less able may be psychologically unable to provide higher-level decision makers with accurate performance information. In theory, provision of such inaccurate information in the event of a workforce reduction will result in bad selections and lower post-layoff efficiency. In practice, however, higher-level managers operate in a noisy environment with many conflicting signals. Since business was already bad before the layoff, there must be a variety of possible reasons why the company is continuing to perform poorly. It is therefore unlikely that higher-level managers who are not predisposed to focus on employment discrimination issues will extract from this morass of chronic problems the conclusion that better representation of protected groups in the workforce is the key to regaining competitiveness.

Second, note that if all companies are afflicted with such decision-making problems then there is no competitive disadvantage associated with such irrational employment decisions. An evolutionary selection model in which companies that do not make efficient employment decisions are weeded out works only if there are other companies that—perhaps randomly, perhaps by design—make better employment decisions. But sufficiently deep-rooted and pervasive problems of conscious or unconscious discrimination will preclude such design or variation.

Finally, as the above study indicates, managers are often unable to make fine distinctions between employees on the basis of their ability, in part due to the usual information-processing problems but also due to the fact that many employees in the middle group really are pretty much the same on this dimension. A department manager who does not want to work with certain types of people (blacks, let us say) can therefore eliminate all the blacks in the middle group during a layoff without anticipating or experiencing any decline in the post-layoff efficiency of his department. Nor, for that matter, would retaining them instead of the roughly equivalent white males bring any real gain in efficiency. Ironically, the market may be unable to eliminate discrimination on the basis of age, race, and sex because decision makers within the market are unable to discriminate on the basis of ability.

## NOTES

1. The two most important laws for the purposes of this study are Title VII of the Civil Rights Act of 1964 and the Age Discrimination in Employment Act. Title VII prohibits discrimination on the basis of race, color, sex, religion, or national origin. Most Title VII cases involve race and/or sex, although national origin cases are becoming more prominent with the increasing role of Hispanics in the labor market. The Age Discrimination in Employment Act prohibits discrimination against workers aged 40 or over. In 1992, the Americans with Disabilities Act extended protection similar to that provided by Title VII to disabled people. Most states have their own fair employment practice laws providing essentially the same coverage for these groups, as well as incorporating other groups. The prohibition of discrimination on the basis of physical or mental handicap has been a feature of many of these laws for some time.

2. D. S. Hammermesh, "What Do We Know About Worker Displacement in the U.S.?," *Industrial Relations* 28, no. 1 (1989).

3. "Companies Plan More Job Cutbacks, Survey Indicates," *Wall Street Journal*, 24 September 1993, p. A2.

4. M. Podgursky and P. Swaim, "Duration of Joblessness Following Displacement," *Industrial Relations* 26, no. 3 (1987): 221. For an analysis of the effects of duration of displacement on wages in the subsequent job, see J. T. Addison and P. Portugal, "Job Displacement, Relative Wage

Changes, and Duration of Unemployment," *Journal of Labor Economics* 7, no. 3 (1989).

5. "In Latest Recession, Only Blacks Suffered Net Employment Loss," *Wall Street Journal,* 14 September 1993, p. A1.

6. "Layoff Fever Spreads To Robust Firms," *Chicago Tribune,* 12 September 1993, Section 7, p. 1.

7. "Survivors of Layoffs Battle Angst, Anger, Hurting Productivity," *Wall Street Journal,* 6 December 1993, p. A1.

8. The following discussion draws from M. Golden, "A Comparative Inquiry into Systems for the Allocation of Job Loss," paper presented at the 1990 Annual Meeting of the American Political Science Association.

9. For a slightly different argument with basically the same flavor, see J. L. Medoff, "Layoffs and Alternatives under Trade Unions in U.S. Manufacturing," *American Economic Review* 69, no. 3 (1979).

10. P. Kuhn and J. Robert, "Seniority and Distribution in a Two-Worker Trade Union," *Quarterly Journal of Economics* 104, no. 3 (1989).

11. See the data presented in R. B. Freeman and J. L. Medoff, *What Do Unions Do?* New York: Basic Books 1984, p. 209.

12. See J. Pencavel, *Labor Markets Under Trade Unionism: Employment, Wages, and Hours,* London: Basil Blackwell 1991, p. 72. He notes that highly senior employees are more willing than junior workers to accept wage reductions in concession bargaining, given a risk of massive layoffs affecting even them if wage concessions are not made. He attributes senior workers' concern with job security to the difficulties they are likely to face in finding new employment.

13. S. H. Slichter, *Union Policies and Industrial Management,* Washington, DC: The Brookings Institution 1941, p. 99.

14. Ibid., p. 99.

15. R. I. Abrams and D. R. Nolan, "Seniority Rights Under The Collective Agreement," *The Labor Lawyer* 2, no. 1 (1986): 103.

16. Ibid., p. 103.

17. See Pencavel, *Labor Markets Under Trade Unionism,* pp. 79, 81–92.

18. See G. Becker, *Human Capital,* 2d ed., New York: National Bureau of Economic Research 1982; also P. Doeringer and M. Piore, *Internal Labor Markets and Manpower Analysis,* Armonk, NY: M.E. Sharpe, Inc. 1985.

19. See A. Rees, *The Economics of Trade Unions,* 3d ed., Chicago: University of Chicago Press 1989, pp. 142–144.

20. For other examples of the use of seniority for this purpose in nonunion companies see F. K. Foulkes, *Personnel Policies in Non-Union Companies,* Englewood Cliffs, NJ: Prentice Hall 1980.

21. J. Fiorito, C. Lowman, and F. D. Nelson, "The Impact of Human

Resource Policies on Union Organizing," *Industrial Relations* 26, no. 2 (1987).

22. In fact, one of the original case studies in this chapter, since dropped, was of a company that had never had layoffs. Management expressed a strong belief in this policy. Not too long after our interview, the company, in serious trouble, began layoffs.

23. See F. Blau and L. Kahn, "Race and Sex Differences in Quits by Young Workers," *Industrial and Labor Relations Review* 34 (July 1981); W. K. Viscusi, "Sex Differences in Worker Quitting," *Review of Economics and Statistics* 62 (August 1980); "Differences in Male and Female Job Quitting Behavior," *Journal of Labor Economics* 4, no. 2 (1986).

24. Unemployment insurance is administered on a state-by-state basis. See *Highlights of State Unemployment Compensation Laws,* Washington, D.C.: National Foundation for Unemployment Compensation and Workers Compensation 1992. The states where unemployment insurance benefits consider the number of a worker's dependents are Alaska, Connecticut, District of Columbia, Illinois, Indiana, Iowa, Maine, Maryland, Massachusetts, Michigan, New Jersey, Ohio, Pennsylvania, and Rhode Island.

25. F. Elkouri and E. A. Elkouri, *How Arbitration Works,* 4th ed., Washington, D.C.: Bureau of National Affairs 1985.

26. Data from *Collective Bargaining Negotiations and Contracts,* Washington, D.C.: Bureau of National Affairs 1992, p. 60:1.

27. See Freeman and Medoff, *What Do Unions Do?* pp. 112–114 for documentation and discussion of this phenomenon.

28. Bureau of Labor Statistics, *Layoff, Recall, and Worksharing Procedures,* Bulletin 1425-13, 1972.

29. K. G. Abraham and J. L. Medoff, "Length of Service and Layoffs in Union and Nonunion Work Groups," *Industrial and Labor Relations Review* 38, no. 4 (1984).

30. Data from Ibid., p. 90.

31. Data from Ibid., p. 92.

32. For a review of the developing state law on this topic, see *Employment-At-Will: A 1986 State-by-State Survey,* Larkspur, CA: National Employment Law Institute 1987.

33. J. L. Medoff, "Layoffs and Alternatives under Trade Unions in U.S. Manufacturing," *American Economic Review* 69, no. 3 (1979).

34. F. D. Blau and L. M. Kahn, "Unionism, Seniority, and Turnover," *Industrial Relations* 22, no. 3 (1983).

35. See J. S. Heywood, "Do Union Members Receive Compensating Wage Differentials? The Case of Employment Security," *Journal of Labor Research* 10, no. 3 (1989).

36. S. M. Jacoby, *Employing Bureaucracy: Managers, Unions, and the Transformation of Work in American Industry, 1900–1945,* New York: Columbia University Press 1985, p. 14.

37. J. Buttrick, "The Inside Contract System," *The Journal of Economic History* 12, no. 2 (1952); E. J. Englander, "The Inside Contract System of Production and Organization," *Labor History* 28, no. 4 (1987).

38. Jacoby, *Employing Bureaucracy,* p. 15. Although skilled workers shared power with the foreman in controlling the pace and direction of production, employment decisions fell entirely within the purview of the foreman.

39. Ibid., p. 16.

40. Ibid., pp. 21–22.

41. Ibid., p. 23.

42. C. Gersuny, "Origins of Seniority Provisions in Collective Bargaining," *Labor Law Journal,* August 1982, p. 522.

43. Ibid.

44. Jacoby, *Employing Bureaucracy,* p. 24.

45. Ibid., pp. 27–28.

46. Ibid., p. 28.

47. Ibid., pp. 31–32.

48. Ibid., pp. 39–44.

49. Inexperienced workers were more likely to damage equipment and to cause accidents, and the steep drop in immigration after 1907 reduced the supply of cheap, compliant labor. See C. Gersuny, "Employment Seniority: Cases From Iago to Weber," *Journal of Labor Research* 3, no. 1 (1982): 112.

50. For a Marxist perspective on these developments, see D. M. Gordon, R. Edwards, and M. Reich, *Segmented Work, Divided Workers: The Historical Transformation of Labor in the United States,* Cambridge: Cambridge University Press, 1982: 127–148. They see innovations in personnel management as motivated not by changes in the technical requirements of production but instead by capitalists' desire to forestall the radicalization and organization of the working class.

51. Jacoby, *Employing Bureaucracy,* p. 123.

52. Ibid., pp. 17–18. See also Mackie's chapter in the present volume.

53. For an overview see A. Kessler-Harris, "Stratifying by Sex: Understanding the History of Working Women," in R. C. Edwards, M. Reich, and D. M. Gordon (eds.), *Labor Market Segmentation,* Lexington: D.C. Heath 1975.

54. For an overview see R. Higgs, *Competition and Coercion: Blacks in the American Economy, 1865–1914,* Chicago: University of Chicago Press 1980.

55. Jacoby, *Employing Bureaucracy,* pp. 133–165.

56. M. Dubovsky, "Industrial Relations: Comparing the 1980's with the 1920's," paper presented at the 38th annual meeting of the Industrial Relations Research Association.

57. S. M. Jacoby, "Norms and Cycles: The Dynamics of Nonunion Industrial Relations in the United States 1897–1987," in K. Abraham and R. McKersie (eds.), *New Developments in the Labor Market: Toward a New Institutional Paradigm,* Cambridge: The MIT Press 1990.

58. National Industrial Conference Board, *Lay-Off and Its Prevention,* New York: NICB 1930, p. 53.

59. Ibid., pp. 38–39.

60. Jacoby, *Employing Bureaucracy,* pp. 208–215.

61. Data from "Hiring and Separation Methods in American Factories," *Monthly Labor Review,* November 1932, p. 1013.

62. Disaggregating the data by industry reveals that the use of need was particularly common in Southern textile mills, perhaps reflecting the effect of paternalistic agrarian Southern culture. Excluding Southern textile mills does not change the overall distribution that much, however, although the use of seniority becomes more common than the use of family responsibility (19.9 percent seniority, 14.3 percent family responsibility).

63. National Industrial Conference Board, *What Employers Are Doing For Employees,* New York: NICB 1936, p. 59.

64. Jacoby, *Employing Bureaucracy,* p. 218.

65. Ibid., p. 219. Liberal groups strongly criticized this practice. In fact, the average age of workers employed in manufacturing declined between 1930 and 1940.

66. Also known as the Wagner Act, found at 42 U.S.C. Sections 151–169.

67. Jacoby, *Employing Bureaucracy,* pp. 242, 244–245.

68. Data from National Industrial Conference Board, *Curtailment, Layoff Policy, and Seniority,* NICB Studies in Personnel Policy No. 5, New York: 1938.

69. Even firms that at least partially pursued the union substitution strategy tried to evade the NLRA's protections for labor. See H. J. Harris, *The Right to Manage: Industrial Relations Policies of American Business in the 1940's,* Madison: University of Wisconsin Press 1982, pp. 23–26.

70. Ibid., pp. 47–60.

71. Ibid., p. 43.

72. Jacoby, *Employing Bureaucracy,* p. 269. Although dismissals for alleged cause are distinct from economically motivated layoffs, this indicates a general decline in the authority of the foreman.

73. Bureau of Labor Statistics data reported in T. A. Kochan, H. C. Katz, and R. B. McKersie, *The Transformation of American Industrial Relations,* New York: Basic Books 1986, p. 31.

74. Jacoby, "Norms and Cycles," p. 43.

75. National Industrial Conference Board, *Seniority Systems in Non-unionized Companies,* NICB Studies in Personnel Policies No. 110, New York: 1950.

76. Title VII of the Civil Rights Act is found in 42 U.S.C. Sections 2000e–17.

77. See L. B. Edelman, "Legal Ambiguity and Symbolic Structures: Organizational Mediation of Civil Rights Law," Institute for Legal Studies Working Paper DPRP 10-7, pp. 6–10.

78. See the many studies cited in Ibid., p. 4.

79. Data from various sources collected and summarized in Jacoby, *Employing Bureaucracy*, p. 246.

80. The ADEA is found in 29 U.S.C. Sections 621–624.

81. *Lapeer Foundry and Machine, Inc.*, 289 NLRB 952 (1988).

82. See S. A. Williams, "Distinguishing Protected From Unprotected Campaign Speech," *Labor Law Journal,* May 1982, for a general discussion. The issue of permissible employer conduct in countering unionization drives raises complex First Amendment concerns. The Supreme Court addressed this issue, and set down some rather murky guidelines, in *NLRB* v. *Gissel Packing Co.*, 395 US 575 (1969).

83. The Board is staffed via presidential appointment, and its composition changes as the presidency changes hands. Pro-union people believe that the current Board tends to decide against labor.

84. The authority of Congress to regulate private employment in this fashion is based on their right to regulate interstate commerce. An employer must have 15 or more employees to be covered by Title VII. Labor unions and employment agencies are also covered. In fact, many suits name both employer and union as respondents. For a concise summary, see M. D. Levin-Epstein, *Primer of Equal Employment Opportunity,* Washington, D.C.: Bureau of National Affairs 1987, pp. 13–18. For a more detailed discussion, see L. M. Modjeska, *Employment Discrimination Law,* Rochester: The Lawyers Co-operative Publishing Co. 1988, pp. 1–307.

85. 42 U.S.C. Section 2000e-(2)(h).

86. For a colorful description of the legislative history of this and other aspects of the act written by a Congressman involved in civil rights issues, see C. Whalen, *The Longest Debate: A Legislative History of the 1964 Civil Rights Act,* Washington, D.C.: Seven Locks Press 1985.

87. The Americans with Disabilities Act is found at 42 U.S.C. Sections 12111–12117.

88. Conservatives opposing the act were afraid that an agency or board with the power to decide cases would be staffed by civil rights activists who would tend to rule against employers.

89. See Executive Order 11246, as amended by E.O. 11375 and E.O. 12086 (401 FEP Manual 601), E.O. 11141 (401 FEP Manual 615), and E.O. 12250 (401 FEP Manual 2401).

90. Any employer doing more than $10,000 worth of business with the government is subject to this regulation. See 38 U.S.C. Section 2011.

91. Any employer doing more than $2,500 worth of business with the government is covered. See 29 U.S.C. Section 791 *et seq.*

92. See Edelman, "Legal Ambiguity and Symbolic Structures," p. 11.

93. 29 U.S.C. Section 623(f)(2).

94. The ADEA states that it is permissible for executives and high-level policy makers to be involuntarily retired at age 65 under certain specified pension conditions, but other employees cannot be involuntarily retired. However, even executives cannot be involuntarily retired prior to age 65.

95. For a summary of federal laws, see Levin-Epstein, *Primer of Equal Employment Opportunity*, 120–134. For a more detailed discussion, see Modjeska, *Employment Discrimination Law*, pp. 193–307.

96. The EEOC is very overburdened, receiving about 100,000 charges a year, and not all charges can be investigated properly. A study by the General Accounting Office found that of the cases closed by six of the Commission's district offices in 1987 with "no cause to believe discrimination occurred" findings, 41 to 82 percent were not fully investigated according to the GAO's criteria. Also, in examining the operations of the state agencies of Georgia, Michigan, New York, Northern California, and Tennessee, the GAO found that 40 to 87 percent of these were not fully investigated. The EEOC and four of the five state agencies took exception to the study, disagreeing with the criteria used to judge the adequacy of investigation. See "Congressional Study Says Job Bias Cases are Poorly Handled," *New York Times*, 12 October 1988.

97. Levin-Epstein, *Primer of Equal Employment Opportunity*, pp. 135–137.

98. Section 1981 of the Civil Rights Act of 1866 specifies that both blacks and whites shall have the freedom to make and enforce contracts. See 42 U.S.C. Section 1981.

99. The 1991 act modified Section 1981 to allow this.

100. See, for example, the Tenth Circuit's 1981 decision in *Sears* v. *Atchinson*, 645 F.2d 1365.

101. See, for example, the 1981 decision of a Georgia District Court in *Miller* v. *Continental Can Co.*, 544 F.Supp. 210.

102. See, for example, the 1981 decision of a Wisconsin District Court in *Wattleton* v. *Ladish Co.*, 520 F.Supp. 1329.

103. See B. E. Hernandez, "Title VII v. Seniority: The Supreme Court Giveth and the Supreme Court Taketh Away," *American University Law Review* 35, no. 2 (1986), for more discussion of the inclusion of this amendment.

104. 279 F.Supp. 505.

105. 416 F.2d 980.

106. 401 U.S. 424.

107. 516 F.2d 41. This overturned a District Court decision, even

though the layoff had nearly eliminated blacks from the company. It was noted that even though the employer had discriminated in the past, hiring practices had been nondiscriminatory for over 10 years; that the layoff victims had not themselves been victims of discrimination (this was a class action); and that the seniority system had not been adopted with intent to discriminate.

108. 508 F.2d 687. This case presaged a problem that the Supreme Court would later address: what is to be done when a conciliation agreement conflicts with the terms of a collective bargaining agreement? The company, the union, and the EEOC had entered into an agreement specifying goals for minority and female representation. In a layoff situation, the company sought guidance on whether to follow the last-hired, first-fired provisions in the union contract. A District Court ruled that the contract could not be construed in such a way as to frustrate the terms of the conciliation agreement. But the Third Circuit reversed, noting that the conciliation agreement only mentioned hiring and promotions and citing 703(h) protection of seniority systems.

109. 502 F.2d 1309. This case also involved a reversal of a lower court decision. The Seventh Circuit noted the problems of a last-hired, first-fired system and urged caution in the design of seniority systems.

110. This case is unreported in F.Supp., but see 10 FEP Cases 164.

111. 394 F.Supp. 1136. The court pointed to aspects of the legislative history of the act that indicated that Congress anticipated the possible need to modify seniority systems.

112. See e.g., *Robinson* v. *P. Lorillard Co.*, 444 F.2d 719 (Fourth Circuit, 1971); *Nance* v. *Union Carbide Corp.*, 540 F.2d 718 (Fourth Circuit, 1976); *Russell* v. *American Tobacco Co.*, 528 F.2d 357 (Fourth Circuit, 1975); *Hairston* v. *McLean Trucking Co.*, 520 F.2d 226 (Fourth Circuit, 1975); *Carey* v. *Greyhound Lines Inc.*, 500 F.2d 1372 (Fifth Circuit, 1974); *Swint* v. *Pullman-Standard*, 539 F.2d 1977 (Fifth Circuit, 1976); *Sabala* v. *Western Gillette, Inc.*, 514 F.2d 678 (Fifth Circuit, 1975); *EEOC* v. *Detroit-Edison Co.*, 515 F.2d 301 (Sixth Circuit, 1975); *Head* v. *Timken Roller Bearing Co.*, 486 F.2d 870 (Sixth Circuit, 1973); *Rogers* v. *International Paper Co.*, 510 F.2d 1340 (Eighth Circuit, 1974).

113. A similar point is made in Michael Pritchett, "No Retrenchment in Affirmative Action: The Tension Between Civil Rights Laws and Layoffs," *Missouri Law Review* 50, no. 3 (1985): 678–679. He notes that "most Courts of Appeals have reached the same result that the Supreme Court reached in *Stotts,* i.e., that it is generally improper for a court to issue orders which result in nonminority employees being laid off before less senior minority employees in order to maintain a particular proportion of minority employees. . . . The District Courts that have addressed the issue have, more often than not, found that orders which result in layoffs of nonminority employees before less senior minority employees can

be an appropriate remedy, even where no actual victims of discrimination have been determined. The District Courts, though, have often been reversed."

114. See e.g. *Russell* v. *American Tobacco Co.,* 528 F.2d 357, at 363; *Gamble* v. *Birmingham Southern Railroad,* 514 F.2d 678 (Fifth Circuit, 1975), at 683.

115. 431 U.S. 324. In this case the Court laid down criteria for determinining if a system is in fact bona fide. The system must be "rational and consistent," it must apply equally to all race and ethnic groups, it must not have had its genesis in racial discrimination, and it must have been negotiated and maintained free from any illegal discriminatory purpose. Note the emphasis on intent. For an interesting, albeit not entirely successful, effort to show how statistical data concerning the impact of a seniority system might be used to establish that a system is not bona fide, see M. R. Kelley, "Discrimination in Seniority Systems—A Case Study," *Industrial and Labor Relations Review* 36, no. 1 (1982).

116. 431 U.S. at 353.

117. Ibid. at 349–350.

118. 444 U.S. 598.

119. 456 U.S. 63.

120. See the 1991 amendments to Title VII at 2000e-5(e)(2).

121. 490 U.S. 900 (1989).

122. Ibid. at 914.

123. 424 U.S. 747.

124. 443 U.S. 193.

125. 461 U.S. 757.

126. For a good discussion of this topic, as well as of *W. R. Grace,* see D. L. Gregory, "Conflict Between Seniority and Affirmative Action Principles in Labor Arbitration, and Consequent Problems of Judicial Review," *Temple Law Quarterly* 57, no. 1 (1984).

127. 467 US 561.

128. See *Sheet Metal Workers Local 28* v. *EEOC,* 478 US 421 (1986). In *Sheet Metal Workers* the Court upheld efforts to increase minority membership in a union that had been ordered by a lower court. (The union, apparently, was a particularly egregious violator.) Note also that in 1987, in *United States* v. *Paradise,* 480 US 149, the Court held that a class-based plan relating to minority hiring did not conflict with the equal protection clause of the Fourteenth Amendment.

129. See 490 U.S. 755 (1989).

130. See the amendations to Title VII at 42 U.S.C. Section 2000e-(2)(n).

131. Reprinted in Commerce Clearing House's *Employment Practices Guide.*

132. See Section 616.

133. *EEOC Compliance Manual,* Section 1152.7, reprinted in *Employment Practices Guide.*

134. See *EEOC Compliance Manual,* Appendix 616-C.

135. See, for example, the Fifth Circuit's 1982 decision in *Williams* v. *New Orleans Steamship Association,* 673 F.2d 742. For a case on the District Court level holding that a nonunion employer could have a bona fide seniority system, see *EEOC* v. *E.I. du Pont,* 445 F.Supp. 223 (D. Delaware, 1978).

136. It is increasingly common for companies to evaluate the quantitative impact of proposed layoff selections on the representation of legally protected groups in the company's workforce, and to make revisions in these selections if there is a disparate impact. See "Statistics Used to Deter Suits After Layoff," *Wall Street Journal,* 10 May 1994, p. B5.

137. However, the BMC manager I spoke with concerning salaried workforce reductions stated that insulation from discrimination suits is not the most important factor leading to the adoption of this practice. It is simply good management, in the opinion of this BMC manager, to know what everyone is supposed to be doing and whether or not they are doing it.

138. Since there is a departmental and a functional dimension to the ranking, it is called a *2D ranking.*

139. For a recent exposition of this view, see R. A. Epstein, *Forbidden Grounds: The Case Against Employment Discrimination Laws,* Cambridge and London: Harvard University Press 1992, Chapter 2. Epstein also contends that some discrimination may be rational and efficient, due to the lower "governance costs" associated with homogenous employees. The roots of the "inefficient discrimination" view are found in Gary S. Becker, *The Economics of Discrimination,* 2d ed., Chicago: University of Chicago Press 1971.

# CHAPTER FIVE

# U.S. Immigration Policy and Local Justice

## *Gerry Mackie*

I MMIGRATION POLICY is a matter of local justice. In the United States, both the first-order determination of how many to admit and the second-order determination of whom to admit are governed by Congress. In this respect, immigration differs from other central issues of local justice. In similar countries, such as Canada and Australia, second-order determinations are delegated to relatively autonomous cabinet-level agencies. Even in the United States, however, immigration principles differ from policies that aim at global justice in that, practically, they are not compensatory, except with respect to refugees. Also, immigration policy does not involve cash transfers, but rather the allocation of an in-kind good; admission and membership in the society. As with other local justice problems, the first-order determination is generally regulated by efficiency considerations, the second-order determination by equity considerations, and the third-order determination by various self-interests.

Allocative issues may be classified "according to the presence or absence of scarcity, indivisibility, and homogeneity."[1] Immigration is a good of weak natural scarcity ("there is nothing anyone could do to increase the supply to the point of satiating everybody") or perhaps of artificial scarcity ("the government could, if it so decided, make the good available to everyone to the level of satiation"). Immigration rights, although essentially indivisible, can be bunched in different ways: The right can be granted to an individual or to an individual with derivative rights to certain family members. Finally, immigration rights need not be homogeneous: One can receive a grant to visit, work temporarily, settle, or become a citizen.

Immigration policy, like other local justice topics, is a "messy business . . . made up of compromises, exceptions, and idiosyncratic features that can be understood only by reference to historical accidents."[2] This chapter proceeds historically because of the strong path-dependence of immigration policy choices. The rate of immigration to population (I shall always use the term *rate* to refer to the ratio of immigration to population and the term *level* for absolute figures) was high in the pre-Revolutionary decades, very low from 1776 to 1819, high again from about 1830 to about 1920, and very low from 1930 to 1980. From 1787 to 1874, immigration to the United States was allocated by the market on the noninterventionist principle that immigration should neither be discouraged nor encouraged. During the era of qualitative restriction, from 1875 to 1916, the principle of nonintervention evolved into a principle of neutrality: The problems of a high rate of entry were attributed to artificial or subsidized immigration, and restrictions were justified as prohibitions on subsidized immigration. Qualitative restrictions multiplied and insensibly became more illiberal, but the problems of immigration remained. Immigration rates reached record levels and rates in the decade prior to World War I, when diverging interests converged on the literacy test as a new admissions procedure, breaking the norm of free immigration.

The literacy test, imposed in 1917, immediately failed to reduce numbers. Public opinion demanded an end or a limit to immigration. A low limit was easily agreed to, but allocation within the limit was bitterly contested. The general idea was to allocate positions proportional to the existing population. A scheme proportional to the existing immigrant population would facilitate immigration of Central, Southern, and Eastern (CSE) Europeans, whence was greatest demand. A scheme proportional to both the native and immigrant populations would disfavor CSE Europeans, whom patrician nativists disdained as racially inferior. The latter scheme of nationality quotas was adopted pursuant to 1924 legislation, and by 1930 immigration came to a comparative halt.

The Immigration Act of 1952 substituted culture for race as the rationale for exclusion. Conservative anti-Communists, who prevailed, associated the immigrant and Communist threats; liberal anti-Communists argued that the nationality exclusions offended America's allies in the Cold War. The liberal camp, including maturing CSE European constituencies, prevailed in the 1965 Immigration Act. Overall immigration was not intended to increase, nationality quotas and other racial criteria were eliminated, and the principle of kin-based immigration was adopted. The new principle removed the offense to foreign-policy allies, appealed to CSE European immigrants with close relatives in Europe, and satisfied the nativists by promising to maintain the ethnic balance.

Refugees were neither popularly nor legally distinguished from immigrants until after World War II. The refugee category emerged as presidents conducting Cold War foreign policy sought means to circumvent the tight restrictions on immigration. Illegal immigration largely originated in a wartime foreign agricultural worker program, which formally ended in 1965 but was informally extended by agricultural employers. The resultant question of legally prohibiting employers from hiring illegal aliens divided standard political coalitions, but the prohibition was finally enacted in 1986, linked to legalization of the clandestine population. The 1965 immigration reform had the unintended effect by 1978 of concentrating immigration in a handful of source countries in Central America and Asia. The 1990 legal-immigration reform sought to open immigration to other regions, especially to already illegally immigrating Europeans such as Irish and Poles, and did so by, for the first time, an explicit increase in immigration levels. If present trends extend, American immigration rates will approach historic highs by the end of the century.

## The Era of Market Allocation: 1787–1874[3]

The early colonies welcomed immigration and occasionally promoted it. Item Seven of the indictment of the King in the Declaration of Independence, 1776, reads:

> he has endeavored to prevent the population of these states; for that purpose obstructing the Laws of Naturalization of Foreigners;

refusing to pass others to encourage their migrations hither, and raising the conditions of new Appropriations of Lands.

However, colonial charters frequently excluded Catholics and other peculiarly disfavored religions, and various measures were devised to deter the landing of paupers and convicts.[4] In the period before the Revolution, immigration was proportionally as high as later peaks, so that perhaps up to 10 percent of the population was foreign-born. The Constitution gave the power to regulate naturalization to Congress and, in ambiguous language relating to the slave trade, reserved immigration matters to the states until the year 1808. Following the Jacobin excesses in France, and perhaps in an effort to embarrass Jefferson (who enjoyed the support of some wealthy émigrés), in 1798 the Federalists passed the Alien and Sedition Acts, permitting the deportation of enemy aliens. Popular disapproval was overwhelming, fatally weakening the Federalists, and removing immigration regulation from the national agenda for two generations. From 1776 to 1819 immigration dropped to a trickle due to war in America and Europe.

Immigration in the period 1787 to 1874 was allocated by the pure market, "the price was the cost of the ticket."[5] However, this was not "the avoidance of self-conscious choice," as Calabresi and Bobbitt might have it.[6] The pure-market immigration policy was publicly discussed and was the intentional policy choice of the revolutionary generation. It was supported by several principles. First, by the republican ideals of liberty and natural rights (which linger as immigration norms to the present day). Second, the policy of neither encouraging nor discouraging immigration had a natural focal-point quality.[7] Third, the need for enhanced national power spoke for some immigration, while the need for national integration spoke against too much of it; nonintervention was the simplest balance point. Fourth, the cost of the ticket was enormous, and by itself assured positive self-selection of individual immigrants, that is, those who could afford passage would be good citizens; that this was understood is illustrated by the special animus against encouraging (subsidizing) immigration and by the outrage against subsidized exportation of convicts and paupers from Europe.

Immigration was never "free" in the sense that aspirants would have their way paid. The pure-market immigration policy was a mechanism based on purchasing power, as opposed to discretionary principles that require the assessment of status, individual welfare, or other properties of the applicants. Immigration resumed after peace in Europe, coincident with a financial panic in 1819, when Congress passed "steerage legislation," which set minimum standards on transatlantic vessels and required ship captains to report on immigrant deliveries.[8] Some states, notably Massachusetts and New York, continued colonial traditions on paupers, convicts, and ship-captain reporting, but attempts to enact immigrant head taxes to defray indigent relief led the Supreme Court in 1849 to void such state taxation of immigrants.[9]

In the 1830s, immigrant composition shifted toward the Irish and German, peaking with the potato famine in 1845 and the refugee outflows after the revolutions in 1848. They were followed by Chinese on the West Coast who were attracted by the Gold Rush of 1849 and construction of the intercontinental railroad, and by Scandinavians who settled into the new agricultural lands of the Midwest. The nativist American Party ("Know-Nothings"), founded in 1849, catapulted to prominence but collapsed over slavery in 1855.[10] Then came the Civil War.

In the wartime emergency, under a new Republican Party dominated by business interests, the first departure from pure-market allocation was undertaken. The Act to Encourage Immigration (Contract Labor Act) was adopted in 1863, over organized labor's objection, and worked to subsidize unskilled immigration. The government subsidized advertisement in Europe, and private recruiting firms collected fees from steamship companies and from employers who were permitted to bind the services of imported workers for one year. The new National Labor Union won repeal of the Contract Labor Act in 1868, but the lucrative practice of contract-labor importation continued nonetheless.[11]

## The Era of Qualitative Restriction: 1875–1916

Immigration history dubs this the period of *qualitative restriction,* as compared to the later imposition of quantitative limits to immigration. In local justice terms, following the distinctions of

Hofstee, "admission procedures" were instituted which compare "individuals against an absolute threshold, and offer the good to all those and only those who exceed the threshold."[12] Selection procedures, by contrast, rank individuals and select from the top of the list until the good is exhausted.

After the Civil War, immigration boomed with industrial expansion, growing through the 1870s and peaking in 1882 at 789,000 (a number not surpassed until 1903). Labor unrest ran in the coal fields from 1865 to 1875, and mine owners imported European laborers in response. Financial panic hit in 1873, followed by a few years of depression. The Immigration Act of 1875, which barred the immigration of convicts and prostitutes, was the first federal regulation of immigration since the detested Alien and Sedition Acts of 1798, and in 1876 the Supreme Court voided all remaining state immigration laws. With larger and faster vessels, the steamship companies considerably lowered the cost of crossing the Atlantic and Pacific.

Following anti-Chinese violence and the political agitation calling for their exclusion, a new principle was weakly applied—that of foreign-policy interest as declared by the president and his diplomats. The Burlingame Treaty of 1868 between the United States and China assured Chinese of the right to immigration, though not to naturalization. In 1879 Congress passed a bill requiring abrogation of the immigration provisions of the Burlingame Treaty, but it was vetoed on the grounds of presidential prerogative and the need for initial diplomatic effort. The treaty was revised in 1880 to permit reasonable regulation of labor immigration. In 1881 a suspension of Chinese immigration for 20 years was passed, but vetoed; finally in 1882, a 10-year suspension, the Chinese Exclusion Act, was enacted. This was periodically extended to 1904, when it became a permanent measure.[13]

Also in 1882 Congress added idiots, lunatics, and paupers to the restricted classes. Contract-labor abuses worsened. The Knights of Labor pleaded inconsistency, as industry enjoyed protective tariffs, while workers were subject to unprotected competition from immigration. In 1885 Congress adopted the Alien Contract Labor Law (amended in 1887 and 1888), which imposed the stiff penalty of $1,000 per violation against any person or business financially or otherwise encouraging the immigration of aliens under terms of contract. The new restrictions on contract labor and Chinese entry were justified as consistent with early republican ideals: Organized labor, for example, praised voluntary immigration but opposed "induced" immigration. The Chinese, it was claimed, were "forcibly" imported (although some were in fact self-initiating immigrants). Contract labor was subsidized. "If not imported under contract, such labor had at least been induced, tempted, or persuaded to go to the United States by business interests, steamship lines, or labor agents."[14] In 1888 the first deportation law authorized deportation of contract laborers.[15]

In the 1880s a third wave of mass immigration began, this time including Central, Southern, and Eastern (CSE) Europeans, who dominated the flow from the 1890s to the restriction of 1924.[16] On the Pacific Coast, employers turned to willing Japanese immigrants. These third-wave immigrants were more distant from the Anglo-Americans in language, religion, customs, and appearance than were their Irish, German, and Scandinavian predecessors of the second wave, who were advancing and gaining acceptance. The new "social science" began to consider and to worry about assimilation. The new immigrants were believed to be less skilled than the old, with higher rates of crime, pauperism, and insanity (although properly controlled data comparisons show no such unfavorable differences).[17] "Scientific" racism was born among some intellectuals, supported by influential Anglo-American patricians fearful of losing their way of life. (Immigration-inspired American racialism later provided early intellectual, and sometimes political, support to Hitlerism.)[18] Organized labor blamed the depressions of 1891 and 1893 on high immigration, and the downturn lowered immigrant numbers (until 1900).[19] Labor's gains were stagnating, and mechanization was associated with the addition of unskilled immigrants.[20] The head of the American Federation of Labor (AFL), Samuel Gompers, argued that voluntary immigration was good but subsidized immigration bad, and that proper enforcement of the contract labor law would end subsidized immigration.

In 1887 an economist proposed a new admissions procedure, for the first time intended to limit immigration numbers: a literacy test in one's native language.[21] Patrician nativists made its secondary consequence their primary consequence: exclusion of CSE Europeans. The procedure had a broad appeal in selecting on the basis of individual merit (liberal tradition), discouraging CSE European immigration (ethnocentrism), and, it was believed, sharply lowering immigration numbers (labor welfare). Literacy-test legislation passed Congress in 1895 but was vetoed. Organized labor increasingly debated "the immigration problem." One side celebrated natural rights, human brotherhood, and labor solidarity. The other side exhibited increasing distress over labor standards, alongside reasonable to unreasonable concerns over American political culture and social customs, although the latter were just as often instrumental appeals to the prejudices of sections of the owning class.[22]

In 1896 labor endorsed the literacy test but lost interest upon the economic recovery of 1898 (immigration in that year numbered 229,000). "Union membership rose from 447,000 in 1897 to almost two million in 1903."[23] Employers launched a militant counteroffensive, and union membership declined through 1906. Meanwhile, immigration climbed to record levels and rates of 1,000,000 in 1905; 1,100,000 in 1906; and 1,300,000 in 1907; and kept up at near those numbers through 1915. Both owners and workers were aware that a reduction in the volume of immigration would increase labor's bargaining power and assist it to enforce the closed shop. The employers openly declared that the upsurge in immigration after 1900 was a "possible counterpoise to the harm" being done through the growth and domination of unionism."[24]

Labor supported renewal of Chinese exclusion in 1902. The endorsement was justified on the explicit grounds of culture, not race, setting an uneasy precedent for group exclusion on cultural grounds.[25] The literacy test gained in its appeal to unionists because it proposed selection by acquired individual traits. The manufacturing interests opposed the literacy test, a fact that organized labor took as additional evidence of its virtue. In 1903 Congress added epileptics, the insane, beggars, anarchists, and white slavers to the list of inadmissible classes; and in 1906 added imbeciles, the feeble-minded, the tubercular, women coming for immoral purposes, unaccompanied minors under 16, and several other classes.[26] Labor endorsed the literacy test again in 1906 and never again lost interest in it.

The literacy test was kept off the congressional agenda by

House Speaker Cannon from 1902 to 1910. With President Theodore Roosevelt, Cannon feared splitting the Republican Party but agreed to the establishment of the so-called Dillingham Immigration Commission in 1906. (Presidential vetoes and appointments of commissions are unusually frequent in the evolution of immigration legislation, probably because the issues cleave the standard political coalitions, with right-wing ethnocentrists and racists and left-wing laborites advocating restriction, and right-wing business interests and left-wing liberals and humanitarians advocating expansion: commissions both investigate and delay, vetoes are either for foreign-policy purposes or to preserve the legislative coalition for the president's broader purposes.) The Dillingham Commission's 42-volume report, issued in 1911, presented both economic and ethnic arguments, coalescing on the literacy test as a solution that would decrease immigration by a quarter, especially, it was believed, of CSE Europeans. The literacy test passed Congress again in 1912 and in 1915, but it was vetoed by two presidents.[27]

Immigration dropped off with World War I, and employment was high because of wartime production. But fear that both returning soldiers and immigrants from war-torn Europe would swamp the economy led labor to mobilize for the adoption of the literacy test, over President Wilson's second veto, in the Immigration Act of 1917. The socialists, who had earlier split from the labor federation, were now seeking reconciliation and were in no position to demand an internationalist position. Their internationalism was muted, but they also, while rejecting the literacy test, had become troubled by the labor-welfare consequences of unrestricted immigration and feebly proposed "proletarian" solutions (such as no immigration without a job guarantee at a decent wage).[28] The Immigration Act of 1917 also added constitutional psychopathic inferiority, men entering for immoral purposes, chronic alcoholics, stowaways, vagrants, and others to the inadmissible classes.[29]

The full policy detail of the era of qualitative restriction is exceedingly tedious. Summarizing, Hutchinson wrote:

> we can see the development of more and more excludable classes; reinforcement through deportation provisions that extended longer

and longer after entry; greater and greater elaboration of the wording of the laws in an attempt to cover every conceivable case and aspect of the labor contract, the immoral classes, the anarchist or subversive classes, and others; provision after provision for penalties; attempts to put the burdens of advance screening and responsibility on the steamship companies; steps to close the open land borders; and much more to the same purpose. An unhappy fact that must have been more-or-less apparent . . . was that the regulatory system was not working.[30]

The era of qualitative restriction began with modifications to the pure-market principle that were at first intended as consistent with that principle. The first restrictive departure from nonintervention was the exclusion of forcibly imported convicts and prostitutes; barring involuntary immigration did not violate the revolutionary era ideal of free immigration. This was followed by federalization of voided state law against artificial immigration of idiots, lunatics, and paupers, commonly exported to America by the European states. Then the Chinese were barred, on an imprecise analogy of the coolie trade with the slave trade, a measure that departed from individual selection and set a precedent for group exclusion. Immigration was an indubitable good, labor argued, so any harm from it must come from artifice; but the Contract Labor Acts, intended to remove the artifice, did not work in preventing harm. The norm of free immigration was powerful, and departures from it justifiable only in admissions procedures targeted against identifiable evils, and such departures multiplied and became more illiberal. Finally, the ambiguous nature of the literacy test broke the norm. For one set of actors, organized labor, the literacy test was a principle of individual admission whose primary consequence was to reduce numbers and unskilled entrants, although the secondary happenstance consequence of reducing CSE European immigration was not denied. For another set of actors, the ethnocentrists and racists, the intended primary consequence of the literacy test was group exclusion. Thus, the literacy test was the convergent solution from quite different principles.

## The Great Restriction and Its Aftermath: 1917–1949

The immediate problem with the literacy test of 1917, as with the contract labor law, was that it did not work as hoped to reduce immigration, partly because CSE Europeans had become more literate in the 30 years since the notion was first entertained. Immigration went from 141,000 in 1919 to 430,000 in the postwar depression of 1920, to 805,000 in 1921. Regulation by admissions procedure was about to be abandoned, because the good of immigration right was seen as about to be exhausted.

National crisis and nativist impulse form the standard explanation for the rise and success of restrictionist movements in American history. World War I and its aftermath as national crisis is familiar ground and needs no elaboration: urbanization, industrialization, monopolization, war, dual loyalties, Bolshevik Revolution, Wilsonian disillusion, postwar recession and nationalism, Americanization, and red scare. What had changed from revolutionary times? The imagery of "a nation of immigrants" is somewhat misleading: the foreign-born have rarely exceeded 10 percent of the population. "Natural" regulation of entry by purchasing power had been violated by subsidy but, more importantly, the cost of the ticket had dropped qualitatively. As a result, the rate of immigration per population increased eightfold from 1820–1830 to 1901–1910. There were late attempts to restore selection by cost of passage by imposing a head tax on immigrants arriving by vessel, starting at 50 cents in 1882 and increasing in four increments to $5 by 1912, but to push this too far was thought unfairly discriminatory to those from poorer countries.[31]

In contrast, say, to Polish anti-Semitism, which abided despite the absence of its object, restrictionist movements and legislation rise and fall with the rate of new immigration. An annual immigration rate greater than 8 per 1,000 of U.S. population, as averaged over a decade, results in restrictionist agitation and significant new legislation. In addition to the impulsive or irrational ethnocentrist or racist objections to immigration, I believe that there is a purely economic component as well. Unequal distribution of costs and benefits certainly accounts for the diverging positions of organized business and organized labor on the question. From an aggregate viewpoint, the costs of immigration are short term and the benefits long term. As the rate of immigration increases, so do costs. At some point a crisis occurs, when labor markets, settlements, and public goods become congested and private and public investment is diluted by the increase in labor. Just prior to the great restriction, some believed that the American capacity to manage

## Table 5.1

**IMMIGRATION NUMBERS (in thousands)**
**AND ANNUAL IMMIGRATION RATE**
**(per thousand of U.S. population), BY DECADE**[32]

| Period | Number | Rate |
|--------|--------|------|
| 1820–1830 | 152 | 1.2 |
| 1831–1840 | 599 | 3.9 |
| 1841–1850 | 1,713 | 8.4 |
| 1851–1860 | 2,598 | 9.3 |
| 1861–1870 | 2,315 | 6.4 |
| 1871–1880 | 2,812 | 6.2 |
| 1881–1890 | 5,247 | 9.2 |
| 1891–1900 | 3,688 | 5.3 |
| 1901–1910 | 8,795 | 10.4 |
| 1911–1920 | 5,736 | 5.7 |
| 1921–1930 | 4,107 | 3.5 |
| 1931–1940 | 528 | 0.4 |
| 1941–1950 | 1,035 | 0.7 |
| 1951–1960 | 2,515 | 1.5 |
| 1961–1970 | 3,322 | 1.7 |
| 1971–1980 | 4,493 | 2.1 |
| 1981–1990 | 7,338 | 3.1 |
| 1991 | 1,827 | 7.2 |

cultural assimilation was depleted (the desirability of assimilation—"Americanization"—was unquestioned). Jeffersonian fears as to political assimilation were also voiced. All this was described after World War I as "alien indigestion."

Other factors offered in the literature as explanations for the great restriction are: the closing of the frontier in 1890; urbanization (concentration of immigrants and dense proximity of groups); industrialization (fewer unskilled farm jobs); technological change, that is, less need for unskilled labor in manufacture; developing nationalism; and state-building.

Calls for suspending immigration began and increased in frequency in the twentieth century. Liberal opinion either avoided the issue or surrendered. The leading progressive journal, *The New Republic*, declared in 1916:

Freedom of migration from one country to another appears to be one of the elements in nineteenth-century liberalism fated to disappear. The responsibility of the state for the welfare of its individual members is progressively increasing.[33]

In 1919 a bill to suspend immigration for 4 years was reported out of House committee, but not acted on. Similar bills proliferated in 1920, and in December the House unexpectedly passed a bill to suspend immigration for 14 months, by a vote of 296 to 42.[34] Suspension was opposed by business interests, and the Senate responded with a substitute to adopt country-quota limits on European immigration, based on "3 percent of the number of natives of the given country enumerated in the 1910 census, the quota number so obtained to be the limit in any fiscal year."[35] The bill passed but was vetoed by President Wilson. Largely identical legislation was passed and signed by President Harding in 1921. This was the first numerical limit on immigration, as well as being the universalization of overt group selection previously directed only at the Chinese, and then the Japanese.

Politically, there were only two options left: to end immigration or somehow to limit it. Most imaginable individual standards, up to the literacy test, had been tried and found wanting, either because they were hard to administer or because they did not have the intended effects. The "percentage-quota principle" originated in 1914 as the responsible liberal alternative to immigration suspension. Dr. Sidney Gulick, a former missionary to Asia, sought to justify Asian immigration. His argument was empirical:

The proved capacity for genuine Americanization on the part of those already here from any land should be the measure for the further immigration of that people.[36]

If numerical limitation was given, then his proposal had an egalitarian ring. Each nationality would be "assigned a quota proportionate to the number of naturalized citizens and their U.S.-born children already drawn from that nationality."[37] The proposal also enjoyed a certain focal point appeal.

Public opinion was nearly unanimous in supporting a much lower first-order allocation (affecting the total amount of the good), and such was the main interest of the economic actors. The second-order question (of how to allocate within the total) was difficult and divisive. After the limitation and quota principles were confirmed in the 1921 Act, there were 8 years of jockeying among business and labor actors over numbers, and much more intensely among recipient ethnic actors, native and foreign-born, over group allocations. The temporary 1921 Act proposed allocation on the basis of 3 percent of the immigrants from any given country enumerated in the 1910 census. The ethnocentrists and racists thought this unfair to the "pioneer stock," and proposed 2 percent of the immigrants of any given country enumerated in the 1890 census, thus effectively shutting out the CSE Europeans, who thought that unfair. The choice was presented in neutral terms, but all evidence is that the debate was over the secondary consequences of the competing principles. The permanent Immigration Act of 1924 settled on 2 percent of 1890 as an interim measure, pending statistical elaboration of the proposed new national-origins system.

The racist appeal, though frequent, was not acceptable to the majority of the population. Thus, the nativists could not long defend the "undemocratic" 2-percent-of-1890 principle. But they discovered a ploy with more convincing surface egalitarian and focal point appeal, which would still allow them to achieve their intended secondary consequences. Rather than base quotas on percentage of immigrants present at a certain date and then fall into dispute over an indefensible date, they believed that the quotas should be based on the national origins of the entire American population, native and immigrant, as of the most recent 1920 census. This procedure was presented as "more equal" than basing quotas only on immigrants.[38]

An administrative quota board set about determining the national origins of the American population. The task was inherently difficult, and disagreement remains as to whether the quota board's results were imprecise or manipulative. The process split the restrictionist movement. The quota board's first report in 1927 would have discouraged further immigration of Irish, Germans, and Scandinavians, in contrast to the 2-percent-of-1890 principle, thus offending an essential component of the restrictionist coalition. Under conflicting political pressures the board tried again in

1928, and again in 1929, but quota proposals differed little. The quota principle lost ground as Congress was whipsawed by opposing ethnic groups. Individual-selection principles were mentioned as an alternative and were supported by many social scientists, but the nativists attacked them on the grounds of impracticality: The literacy test had failed to limit numbers.[39] "A majority of the American people appeared to be unconcerned over how the quotas were distributed as long as the principle of restriction was maintained."[40] In 1929 the National Origins Act was adopted and quotas were made permanent.[41]

The first numerical restriction in 1921 created an immediate problem, the solution to which became a permanent principle of U.S. immigration policy: kin-based immigration. The 1921 Act gave "nonquota status" to children under age 18 of U.S. citizens—that is, such persons would be allowed to immigrate outside the numerical and ethnic limits. As the restrictions first took effect, natives and naturalized immigrants became unable to bring in their wives and infant children, which was abhorrent to public opinion. People would go to the boats to greet their off-loading kin, only to have them turned back as outside the quotas, after enormous expenditure of time and funds. A major public scandal ensued, probably instigated by the powerful steamship companies. The 1924 Act responded in two ways. First, the initial screening

*Table 5.2*

**COMPARISON OF QUOTAS ALLOTTED TO REGIONS UNDER THREE DIFFERENT VERSIONS OF THE QUOTA SYSTEM**[42]

| Region | 1921 Act 3%-1910 | 1924 Act 2%-1890 | 1929 Nat'l Origins Plan |
|---|---|---|---|
| Asia | 492 | 1,424 | 1,423 |
| Africa/Oceania | 359 | 1,821 | 1,800 |
| NW Europe | 197,630 | 140,999 | 127,266 |
| SE Europe | 155,585 | 20,423 | 23,235 |
| Total | 354,066 | 164,667 | 153,724 |

of immigrants would no longer be done on the American shore, but rather in the emigrant's home country through the American consuls, and the burden of proof was shifted from the United States to the immigrant. The primary intended consequences were to prevent waste of the emigrant's funds and to bring administrative order to the country waiting lists. Second, and more importantly, the Act expanded the category of nonquota immigrants (not subject to numerical or ethnic limit) to include wives and unmarried children under age 18 of U.S. citizens.[43] This was both a first-order and second-order allocation: Nonquota immigrants did not require numerical restriction, since eligibles were by definition linked to numerically limited immigrants or to citizens marrying overseas. Over the years, nonquota family immigration brought in as many numbers as quota immigration.

The principle of family immigration was never the subject of controversy or debate, at least not concerning close relatives. Whatever the speculative costs and benefits of a quantity of immigrants, family immigration delivered a large and incontestable benefit to individual citizens. Moreover, there was an explicit calculation of benefit to social welfare. Two concerns over the immigration flow were the preponderance of young males and the related issue of "birds of passage" who came to work temporarily and not to partake in national life. An immigrant with family was more likely to stay and join in economic and cultural life.[44]

Preferences within the quota allocations became a permanent feature of policy. These were mentioned in the 1921 Act, institutionalized in the landmark 1924 Act, and refined to byzantine regulatory complexity thereafter. The 1924 Act established a first preference, dedicated to up to one-half of each nationality quota. The first preference was made available to two classes, without priority between them: the class of parents and husbands of U.S. citizens, and the class of skilled agricultural workers and their families (it was believed that urbanization had made such labor scarce). The remaining half of the nationality quota, and any spaces remaining unused from the first preference, were dedicated to the second preference: wives and unmarried children under age 18 of legally resident immigrants. The third preference was that any remaining slots unused by the first two preferences were available to other qualified quota immigrants.[45] Unused slots in an annual nationality quota could not be carried over to the next year. For oversubscribed nationality quotas, a waiting list formed, ranked by date of visa application. In 1929 aliens with unrecorded entry were permitted to register—in other words, those who had previously entered illegally were forgiven.[46]

To move back some years, racial violence and protests and memorials from the Western states for restriction of Japanese immigration were seen as an insult by the Japanese government, with a distinct possibility of war.[47] This issue was resolved in a secret understanding between the United States and Japan that the latter country would continue to discourage the migration of its subjects to the United States, the "Gentleman's Agreement" of 1907. The Immigration Act of 1917 established the so-called Asiatic Barred Zone, defined by longitude and latitude, prohibiting immigration of laborers from a huge area, from Saudi Arabia to the Pacific Islands. The boundaries of the Asiatic Barred Zone did not include China and Japan, only because the natives of those lands were already excluded by older provisions of immigration law. The 1924 Act included a provision that no alien ineligible for citizenship would be permitted admission (with minor exceptions), an effective bar against Japanese immigration given the provisions of the Gentleman's Agreement.[48] In 1924 the Japanese Ambassador threatened "grave consequences," and the effective date of the 1924 Act was declared a day of national mourning in Japan.[49] The 1924 Act also established the U.S. Border Patrol, for the initial purpose of preventing the illegal importation of Chinese over the southern border.

Under the national-origins system, whose outline was proposed in the 1924 Act, immigrants were to be "charged" against quotas, not by their country of birth but by their respective national origins. Thus, a Polish ethnic born in German territory was charged to Poland, an Asian born in France charged to Asian quotas. Not content with the almost total exclusion of Asians, the baseline against which nationality quotas would be allocated would count all those peoples who had voluntarily immigrated to the United States and not the "descendants of involuntary immigrants." This meant no quotas for Chinese and, notice, Negroes. The secondary consequences were intended and in fact the whole purpose. After excluding the whole world, except for Northwestern Europe, it may seem as if the framers had blundered in giving residents of the Western Hemisphere nonquota status; that is, immigration without numerical restriction. This was dealt with by other methods.

Except from Canada, immigration from other Western Hemisphere countries was quite infrequent. Their populations were small and impoverished, and transportation and communication costs were still formidable. The deserts of northern Mexico and the Southwestern United States, barely populated and with the first rail just under construction, were like a Chinese Wall. Many Mexicans fled across the border during the Mexican Revolution (1911–1920), but many returned to that weakly populated land. Contrary to a common impression, Mexican labor was not significant until World War I, 1920 being known as the year of the "Mexican harvest" (and was not striking again until the early 1950s, and then again in the 1970s to present). In 1924, the year of peak Mexican entry, there was alarm among the reigning nativists and Southwest organized labor. However, there was no national effect, and Southwestern farm and business interests were able to block rapid legislative action.

The restrictionists were stymied by an equality problem. They could not single out Mexico, as such a provision would be too unfair to win passage. Their only resort would be to impose quotas on the entire Western Hemisphere, but that lost the sympathy of states bordering on Canada and risked offending all the countries in Latin America, whence there was minuscule immigration. The United States had strong foreign-policy interests in Latin America, and the State Department came down hard against Western-Hemisphere quotas. Coolidge's secretary of state wrote in 1927 that

> It seems to me inconceivable, that for the sake of preventing a relatively insignificant migration from Mexico, the undesirability of which is at least questionable, we should endanger our good relations with Canada and Latin America.[50]

In the place of embarrassing legislation, the State Department acted administratively in 1929 to ensure stringent application of literacy tests, and contract-labor and public-charge[51] provisions against visa applicants in Mexico, and Mexican immigration dropped. Debate raged in Congress and a quota nearly passed, but the fact of informal Mexican restriction, the equality problem, and foreign-policy interest robbed the issue of clarity, and it faded away with the Depression.

That left only one major potential source of immigration: the Philippines, then an American colony. Filipino immigration was small, but Filipinos were U.S. subjects and free to enter, and the mighty California growers were eager to recruit replacements for the excluded Chinese and Mexicans. Filipino politicians waged a purely moral campaign, with great savvy. First, they told Congress in 1930 that they had been taught that the United States was a great country and they wished to come and study its methods so as to improve conditions at home. Roxas, Speaker of the Philippines Legislature, told Congress that the proposed Philippines restriction

> has no precedent in the annals of colonization since the birth of time. No country, however imperialistic, however commercialistic its policy in its dealing with its colonies, has ever prohibited the citizens of its colonies from migrating to the mother country.[52]

The appeal to fair play to a colonial dependency won over public opinion. The nativists in Congress, who also tended to be imperialists, dropped the matter, choking on the suggestion that independence for the Philippines would solve the immigration problem. Next, in 1932 the Philippines Independence Commission took "a practical view of the immigration question and . . . reached an understanding with the American Federation of Labor and its political supporters in Congress." The understanding was that

> In case Congress should enact a law fixing a date for independence, the Filipino representatives would accept a provision restricting Filipino immigration to the United States during the transition period, provided that the restriction was based not on racial but on economic grounds.[53]

Independence was granted in 1934.

The legislative restrictions were followed by the Great Depression and World War II, and immigration fell to almost nothing, an average of 22,000 a year. Many analysts credit the Depression and the war, although past periods of depression and war did not see such drastic reductions. Also, immigration continued to be inconsequential through the prosperous 1950s and 1960s, suggesting to me that the legislation was decisive. The first-order goal of low immigration was achieved. The second-order goal of ethnic composition did not work exactly as intended. From 1932 to 1950 half as many immigrants came from NW Europe as permitted by quota, and twice as many from CSE Europe. The nationality quotas for NW Europe were typically undersubscribed, while the quotas for CSE Europe were typically oversubscribed, with backlogs. Earlier immigrants from NW Europe had usually come with family, while the later lone-male immigrants from CSE Europe became naturalized and began bringing in wives and children outside quotas. In some years the major portions of immigrants were outside the quotas: relatives of U.S. citizens and natives of the Western Hemisphere. There was a shift to higher-skilled immigration, resulting from the same numbers of skilled immigrants but reduced numbers of unskilled immigrants. The restriction was certainly a factor contributing to the northward migration of blacks in the period.

## The National Security Era: 1950–1964

Before World War II the 1924 immigration system was adhered to with dogmatic tenacity, particularly because of the joblessness of the Depression years. Efforts to ease admission of refugees from Europe were vigorously opposed by the restrictionist lobby, with the passive support of public opinion. The most notorious incident was the defeat of 1939 legislation that would have rescued 20,000 children, under private sponsorship, from Nazi Germany. Their admission would have exceeded the German quota. Some of the restrictionist leaders made anti-Semitic remarks at the hearings, and that leadership tended to coincide with the America First isolationists. Even some German refugees eligible under the quota were excluded on public-charge grounds.

In 1943 Congress repealed the Chinese Exclusion Laws and established a minimal immigration quota for Chinese, in recognition of wartime alliance.[54] This was the first abolition of a racial exclusion, and it was due mainly to foreign-policy considerations. The same was done for India and the Philippines in 1946. All subsequent reform and repeal of racial provisions of immigration law cited foreign-policy concerns. Special refugee legislations were enacted in 1946, 1948, 1950, and 1951 (discussed in detail below), the first numerical departures from the 1924 system.

The world was in ruins and the United States was now the triumphant power, with global responsibilities. "Scientific" racism was utterly discredited with the defeat of Hitler. The fate of the excluded German refugees was horrifying, a public scandal. American foreign-policy interest opposed the maintenance of racial laws and also wished to embarrass Communism. The once less-developed CSE countries were urbanizing and industrializing. CSE European immigrants had proven themselves and moved into the political system. Some nationality quotas were barely used, whereas others accumulated backlogs for years. The need for exceptional refugee acts revealed the further decrepitude of the immigration system. Just as in the years preceding restriction, new demands led to absurd complexification of the law. The Cold War began. The principle of national security dominated the 1952 revision of immigration laws in two divergent interpretations.

From 1947 to 1952 the Senate Judiciary Committee undertook a comprehensive review of immigration policy. On one matter the Committee could not wait. The Internal Security Act of 1950, dealing with communist subversion, added Communists and totalitarians to the list of inadmissible classes. Some Committee witnesses proposed abolishing national origins, going to individual standards and a point system, or aligning immigration with labor-market needs. What happened instead was codification of existing law and court decisions, and retention of national-origins allocation with minor changes. The primary thrust of the reform was ideological: Race was banished as an argument, and culture substituted. The conservative anti-communists in control of the legislation declared:

> Without giving credence to any theory of Nordic superiority, the subcommittee believes that the adoption of the national origins quota formula was a rational and logical method of numerically restricting immigration in such a manner as to best preserve the sociological and cultural balance of the United States.[55]

The sponsors also stated that the 1952 Act "made all races eligible for naturalization and eliminated race as a bar to immigration."[56] This was formally true, but the method for allocating country quotas ensured minuscule numbers for Asian countries. The 1929 formula was revised so as to set an annual area quota "at 1/6 of 1 percent of the number of inhabitants in the continental United States in 1920 whose ancestry or national origin was attributable to that area"; all countries outside the Western Hemisphere were given a minimum quota of 100, but those in the Asian-Pacific triangle (most of Asia and Oceania) had a special aggregate ceiling of 2,000.[57] Removing the bar to Asian immigration would make some 600,000 persons of Asian ancestry residing in the Western Hemisphere eligible for immediate entry because immigration from the Western Hemisphere was unrestricted. Therefore, a special provision made clear that Asians would be charged against their country of ancestry rather than their country of birth. Another facially progressive change was to establish new colonial quotas of 100 per unit, as a matter of fairness; the secondary intended consequence was to choke off the flow of Anglo-Caribbean blacks, who had been coming in under the underutilized British national quota. Otherwise, Western Hemisphere policy went unchanged, with explicit references to foreign-policy considerations and to the continuing practice of administrative exclusion by means of the public-charge provision.[58]

Within each country quota, preferences would be allocated as seen below. The largest change was in the new first preference for skilled immigrants, a slight concession to those who had argued for principles of individual selection or economic welfare. The sponsors explicitly rejected the alternative of individual standards in order to preserve "the sociological and cultural balance." Otherwise the major principle was family immigration. Quotas worked as before, unused spaces lapsing each year, and backlogs ranked by order of visa application.

## Preferences Under
## The Immigration and Nationality Act of 1952[59]

Spouses and unmarried children of U.S. citizens are exempt from numerical quotas and preference requirements.

**1. First preference.** Highly skilled immigrants whose services are urgently needed in the United States and the spouses and children of such immigrants—50 percent.

**2. Second preference.** Parents of U.S. citizens over age 21 and unmarried adult children of U.S. citizens—30 percent.

**3. Third preference.** Spouses and unmarried adult children of permanent resident aliens—20 percent.

**4. Fourth preference.** Brothers, sisters, and married children of U.S. citizens and accompanying spouses and children—50 percent of numbers left after satisfying demand in the first three preferences.

Although it appeared politically possible to discard the national-origins system immediately after World War II, matters changed with the onset of the Cold War. National security interests determined immigration policy. Proponents and opponents of liberalizing reform each argued their case in terms of anti-communism. Nativists (who had been largely isolationist) allied with conservative anti-communist sentiment, already fused in the leadership of the two immigration subcommittees. Communism was symbolically alien, and most American Communists were in fact foreign-born from the pre-restriction immigration wave. The Senate Judiciary Committee stated:

> the Communist movement in the United States is an alien movement, sustained, augmented, and controlled by European Communists and the Soviet Union. The severance of this connection and the destruction of the life line of communism becomes, therefore, substantially an immigration problem.[60]

The Communist Party had gone underground, expecting the advent of fascism in the United States. Immigration law was a top Party priority, since, recalling the Palmer Raids and deportation of alien radicals after World War I, the Communists now feared extinction by deportation. The struggle of exposed popular-front organizations against the 1952 Act worked to confirm the beliefs of the nativist and anti-Communist proponents of the legislation and weakened the credibility of liberal opposition.

A different interpretation of national security interests was offered by President Truman and global leadership Cold War liberals. They pointed out the close connection between the theory of national-origin quotas and the racial doctrines of the defeated and loathed Nazis, and they argued that America's new world position required the removal of laws offensively implying the ethnic inferiority of Cold War allies. Truman vetoed the 1952 Act, and made an issue of immigration. His veto message read:

> The basis of this quota system was false and unworthy in 1924. It is even worse now. At the present time this quota system keeps out the very people we want to bring in. . . . Today, we have entered into an alliance, the North Atlantic Treaty, with Italy, Greece, and Turkey, against one of the most terrible threats mankind has ever faced. . . . But through this bill we say to their people: You are less worthy to come to this country than Englishmen or Irishmen.[61]

Truman's veto was overridden. He appointed a commission, which in 1953 recommended abolition of the national-origins system on antidiscrimination and foreign-policy grounds. The Commission Report had no immediate effect, but it influenced the 1965 reforms.

In his unsuccessful veto of the Immigration Act of 1952, President Truman suggested that retention of the national-origins system would result in continued "emergency" immigration legislation. He turned out to be right. Administrative and legislative exceptions to the 1952 Act became commonplace, usually for refugees from Communism who were often CSE Europeans. In winning the Refugee Relief Act of 1953, allocating 214,000 new entries for the first time outside quota limits, President Eisenhower declared the new humanitarian-anti-Communist principles: the refugees "look to traditional American humanitarian concern for the oppressed. International political considerations are also factors which are involved."[62]

In his tenure Eisenhower sent three different messages to Congress urging revision of the 1952 Immigration Act, but only one minor revision passed in 1957. Senator John Kennedy said then that a full revision of immigration policies was required. In 1957, 1959, 1961, and 1962 interminable minor modifications to the 1952 Immigration Act were proposed or enacted, symbolizing political determination on the part of the opponents of national origins but also reflecting political stalemate. The most noteworthy trend was the several temporary programs bestowing nonquota status on far-backlogged cases, in the name of family reunification. The first-order allocation as to general numerical limit was holding, to the relief of those concerned with that allocation. Therefore, with respect to the second-order allocation, interest was shifting from the battered ethnic principle to the kin-based and skills-based principles already present in the preference system.[63] With the several special refugee enactments, based on the dual appeal to principles of humanitarianism and foreign policy, a precedent was developing that refugee admissions could go beyond the first-order immigration allocation.

## The Era of Kin-Based Immigration: 1964–1989

In 1961 John Kennedy, an Irish American Democrat who as a senator had been an active opponent of the national-origins system, became president. He promised major immigration reform but was distracted by the Cuban missile crisis and other international events. In 1961 Congress passed legislation removing the aggregate ceiling of 2,000 on the Asia-Pacific triangle of 1952. In 1961 and 1962 a number of bills were introduced to scrap the national-origins systems. In 1963 President Kennedy proposed a 20 percent a year phase-out of the quota system, with released and unused annual numbers placed in a new pool devoted to the principle of family reunification. Kennedy said the national-origins system "discriminates among applicants for admission into the United States on the basis of accident of birth."[64] Kennedy stressed that there would be no change in the first-order allocation of the number of immigrants.

Kennedy was assassinated in late 1963. This event, along with the relative extremism of the Republican candidate in the 1964 presidential election, resulted in a Democratic landslide and the fecund "Civil Rights" Congress of 1965. Many of the new members represented maturing CSE European constituencies. A flood of reform bills burst loose. President Johnson, who had no particular interest in the matter but who was a renowned vote counter, joined the bandwagon with a serious legislative initiative. The final Immigration and Nationality Act Amendments of 1965 abolished the ethnic-based national-origins system and eliminated all direct and oblique references to race. An overall ceiling of 170,000 annually for Eastern Hemisphere immigration was established (slightly above the 1952 level to include refugees), with an annual limit of 20,000 for any one country (the per-country limit affected Italy, whose enormous backlog would have crowded out other countries). After taking full effect in 1968, immigrants would be selected only under the preference system (previous qualitative exclusions remaining in effect), illustrated below. A prospective immigrant would apply and if thwarted by full subscription of the respective annual preference limit or the country limit, be placed in a waiting line by date of visa application. The act created a new formal refugee category in its seventh preference.

## Preferences Under The 1965 Immigration Act, as Later Modified[65]

Spouses, unmarried children, and parents of U.S. citizens are exempt from numerical quotas and preference requirements. Immigrants are numerically limited to 270,000 a year. The spouse and unmarried children of a visa recipient generally receive visas in the same preference category.

*1. First preference.* Unmarried adult children of U.S. citizens—20 percent (54,000).

*2. Second preference.* Spouses and unmarried adult children of permanent resident aliens—20 percent (26 percent after 1980: 70,000), plus any numbers unused in first-preference allocation.

*3. Third preference.* Members of the professions and scientists and artists of exceptional ability—10 percent (27,000). Requires labor certification.

*4. Fourth preference.* Married children of U.S. citizens—10 percent (27,000).

*5. Fifth preference.* Brothers and sisters of U.S. citizens over age 21—24 percent (64,800), plus any numbers unused in first four preference categories.

**6. Sixth preference.** Skilled and unskilled workers in occupations for which labor is in short supply in the United States—10 percent (27,000). Requires labor certification.

**7. Seventh preference.** Refugees from Communist countries or Communist-dominated countries or the general area of the Middle East—6 percent. Removed with enactment of Refugee Act of 1980, the 6 percent going to the second preference.

**8. Nonpreference.** Applicants not entitled to one of the above preferences. Not used past 1978, because preference applicants took up all available places.

The liberalization lobby, composed of ethnic and religious groups and the "VOLAGs" (the private voluntary agencies that processed refugee resettlement), had gained political strength and maturity since its defeat in 1952. It supported the administration bill, which gave first priority to skills-based immigration and second to family-based immigration, while opposing new restrictions on Western Hemisphere immigration. Organized labor affirmatively supported repeal of national origins, but was distrustful of skills-based immigration because it could give too much power over admissions to the business interest. The nativists organized in the "patriotic societies" who had dominated the debates of the past were relatively silent. Rather than oppose the reform, they sought to shape it. They favored emphasis on kin-based immigration (this also happened to favor Italy, Poland, and Greece, attracting these elements to the liberalization coalition), because it was good for families and good for assimilation. However, in the spirit of consistency and nondiscrimination, the old nativists insisted that the Western Hemisphere be brought under the numerically restricted system governing the Eastern Hemisphere.[66] This was fiercely opposed by the liberalization lobby and its supporters in the Johnson Administration, and the issue became the central topic of debate.

Two powerful senators, Republican Everett Dirksen and Democrat Sam Ervin, opposed ending the national-origins system, but this turned out to be something of a ploy. Latin American immigration was predicted to increase due to booming population growth and plunging transportation costs. Dirksen and Ervin would support the bill only if a ceiling were established on Western Hemisphere immigration. Johnson, treacherously according to the liberalizers, logrolled with his old colleagues Dirksen and Ervin, and also conceded to labor, nativists, Italians, Poles, and Greeks an emphasis on family reunification. A ceiling of 120,000 was arrived at, reflecting recent annual immigration from the Western Hemisphere, and hastily pasted into the final bill to take effect in 1968, pending report of a special commission on such immigration (the commission deadlocked). In the rush of compromise, no preferences or country limits were included under the Western Hemisphere ceiling. After the ceiling took effect in 1968, instant backlogs developed, reaching 300,000 by 1976—a line 2.5 years long. To relieve the backlog through access to a larger pool (which would allow the Western Hemisphere to utilize undersubscribed Eastern Hemisphere quotas) and to attain uniformity, 1976 and 1978 legislation assimilated Western Hemisphere immigration to the Eastern Hemisphere model, combining the two hemispheric ceilings for a world ceiling of 290,000. Just as nativists of the 1920s had been prevented from singling out Mexico for unfavorable treatment on the principle of country equality, advocates of increased Canadian or Mexican immigration from 1976 onward have been defeated on similar grounds at several attempts to give those countries favorable immigration treatment.

The family-preference system, according to the *Wall Street Journal* at the time, "had emotional appeal and, perhaps more to the point, insured that the new immigration would not stray radically from the old one."[67] Vialet[68] offers convincing explanations for the 1965 reforms. First, quoting Bennett,

> Whether by design or circumstance, Congress had, in a 12-year period, by legislative exception to the . . . Act of 1952, abandoned the national-origins quota system without repealing it outright. It was dead. Its obituary was in the statute books, and its life's failures were delineated in the statistics [of immigration] . . . for 36 years.[69]

In the two decades preceding 1965, only one out of three immigrants had come under the national-origins quotas, either because of the refugee enactments and their effects on family immigration or because of formally unlimited Western Hemisphere immigration. The ethnic-composition goal of the national-origins system was already a dead letter.

The prosperous economy and the nominal immigration increases eased any anxieties organized labor might have had, so the AFL-CIO supported the reform. Additionally, "Public support for the repeal of the national origins quota system reflected genuine changes in public attitudes toward race and national origins."[70] The same Congress in 1965 passed the landmark civil rights legislation.

Senator Edward Kennedy, the lead reformer, consulted with the remnants of the old nativist "patriotic" societies. He reported that

> all recognized the unworkability of the national-origins quota system and at the close of the meetings agreed to cooperate in finding a new formula for the selection of immigrants. No significant opposition to eliminating the national-origins quota system was organized by any of their organizations.[71]

The principle of kin-based immigration was expected to have the secondary consequence of maintaining the ethnic composition (an expectation not lost on the old nativists),[72] silently contributing to the diverse appeal of the new principle. Japanese Americans, for instance, complained that

> there are very few of Asian-Pacific origin in this country who are entitled to provide the specified preference priorities to family members and close relatives abroad. . . . although the immigration bill eliminates race as a principle, in actual operation immigration will still be controlled by the now discredited national origins and the general patterns of immigration which exist today will continue for many years to come.[73]

Finally, the legislation passed because political power had accidentally landed in the hands of the reformers with the Democratic landslide of 1964. In Senator Kennedy's words,

> There is little doubt that of key importance was the unusual parliamentary situation in Congress, where the large Democratic majority was generally responsive . . . to the Administration's proposal. Repub-

lican leaders were also ready to act on the issue. Moreover, in the Judiciary Committees of both Houses, the balance of power lay with those who long worked for reform.[74]

The 1965 Act was a vindication of the CSE Europeans, who had for decades been working relatives through long backlogs in the quota system, with boosts through special refugee legislation. Their concentrated interest defined the basis of the new second-order allocation, the principle of kin-based immigration. From 1965 to 1977, Portuguese immigration rose by 382 percent, Soviet immigration by 210 percent, and Greek immigration by 162 percent. Italian immigration rose in the first years then fell, 31 percent over the whole period, because the new system rapidly cleared the CSE European backlogs that had inspired it. United Kingdom immigration fell by 55 percent, Irish by 77 percent, Canadian by 67 percent.[75]

However, the CSE Europeans and their silent and strange bed-fellows, the old nativists, could not know the unintended consequences of the reform. In 1964, Attorney General Robert Kennedy predicted that the proposed reforms would result in no increase in minuscule Asian immigration:

> I would say for the Asia-Pacific Triangle it would be approximately 5,000, Mr. Chairman, after which immigration from that source would virtually disappear; 5,000 immigrants would come in the first year, but we do not expect that there would be any great influx after that.[76]

NW European immigration fell immediately because immigrants from those countries no longer had close relatives in the United States. CSE European immigration fell gradually as backlogs cleared and Europe gained prosperity. Asian immigration was 20,683 in 1965 and 157,759 in 1977, a rise of 663 percent. North American immigration (from Mexico, Central America, and the Caribbean) rose 48 percent; South American immigration only 6 percent.[77] By 1980 the top sending countries had become, in order, Mexico, the Philippines, China-Taiwan-Hong Kong, Korea, Jamaica, India, and the Dominican Republic. In 1965 there were no Asian backlogs, because until 1963 there was an aggregate Asian ceiling of 2,000 and Asians simply did not bother to apply. After the 1965 reforms, talented Asians pioneered in the small wedges remaining for skills-based immigration; then, first as residents, later as naturalized citizens, utilized the various family preferences in extending chains of migration. The apparent high performance of non-refugee Asian immigrants may be an artifact of the selection process.[78] The North Americans (and, notice, not the more distant South Americans) gained because they immigrated outside numerical limits up to 1968, and with no country limits up to 1976, thus seeding future chains. The kin-based system has the unintended second-order effect of favoring the relatives of the most recent members of American society. A first-order effect was a marked increase in immediate-relative immigrants outside the numerical limitation, doubling overall immigration.

By 1978, the "nonpreference" slots that could seed new sources of immigration were absorbed by the preference backlogs, thus intensifying the concentration of immigration source countries. Under the family-reunification system, annual immigration was allocated to relatives of citizens and legal residents and to a very few professionals; other new immigrants would be admitted only if there were no relatives demanding admission. A Brazilian, for instance, probably could not immigrate as a relative of a U.S. resident, as few Brazilians live in the United States, but must enter under the nonpreference category. After 1978 there was no nonpreference immigration because family immigration, mostly from a few source countries in southern North America and in Asia, took all positions. Hence, immigration from the seeded countries, such as Mexico and the Philippines, tended to increase, while legal immigration from countries such as Brazil or Kenya could only decline.

The evolved complexity of the legal-immigration system has the unintended secondary consequence of selecting skilled and foresighted immigrants. The per-country limits make for years-long lines in high-demand countries of southern North America and elsewhere. Getting on the list makes for a psychological feeling of entitlement, thus creating a stimulus for illegal immigration, a topic of dominant concern in the 1980s.

## Postwar Refugee Policy

George Washington declared America an asylum for the oppressed and the needy of the earth. If everyone is admitted, as was largely the case before World War I, there is no need for a refugee policy. Indeed, distinctions between the oppressed and the needy, refugee and immigrant, were not operational until after World War II. During the Depression, when there was net emigration in some years, those fleeing fascism were viewed merely as immigrants, a conceptualization whose flaws were shown up by the Nazi exterminations. Articulation of a refugee category in law and practice arose for a number of reasons: a sense of shame over the fate of refugees denied entry before the war, foreign policy considerations following from America's role as victor in World War II and later as protagonist of the Cold War, the national consensus on limited immigration, second-generation ethnic pressures, and the development of international efforts and standards.

Until 1962, refugee admissions were accomplished by temporary legislation or extraordinary Presidential action. At the end of 1945, President Truman ordered admission of an eventual 80,000 persons from Eastern and Southern Europe, on the argument that their country quotas had been underused before the war; the entrants came under the quotas, but at U.S. government expense. The War Brides Act of 1946 speeded admission of 175,000 alien spouses, fiancees and children of members of the armed forces.[79] The Displaced Persons Act of 1948 and its extensions permitted the extraordinary admission of some 400,000 Europeans by the novel method of quota-mortgaging: entrants were charged against the present annual quota and then against up to one-half of each future year's quota (Estonia, Latvia, and Lithuania were mortgaged more than 60 years into the future).[80] The general European policy of homeland resettlement was not applied against those fearing persecution from the new Communist regimes in Eastern Europe, nor against minorities loathing the notion of living in German territory. The Refugee Relief Act of 1953 resulted in 189,000 visas over 3 years for European and notably Palestinians and Chinese refugees from Communism, the first major departure from national-origin quotas.

The 1948 and 1953 Acts were opposed by traditional restrictionists and loaded with specific national provisions that evidence a lobbying contest both among ethnic groups and between such groups and nativists, with the final provisions often effectively biased against Catholics and Jews. Under the 1948 Act, for example, displaced-person preferences, subpreferences, and priorities were inscrutably complex, altogether amounting to 15 categories, for example, the third preference: blood relatives of citizens and residents "within the third degree of consanguinity computed according to the rules of common law."[81] However, the Acts were presented and understood by the executive as volleys in the Cold War. After the failed uprising of 1956, President Eisenhower admitted some 38,000 Hungarian refugees, most of them through the "parole authority" of the attorney general established by the Immigration and Nationality Act of 1952. Although the parole authority was intended as a minor expedient to permit the admission of individuals on a temporary basis, Eisenhower's expansive interpretation set a precedent for future extraordinary presidential admissions. The Hungarian parolees were given normal resident status by special legislation in 1958. A 1957 Act canceled the quota mortgages imposed under the Displaced Person and related Acts.

The Fair Share Refugee Act of 1960 was enacted in honor of World Refugee Year and was intended to empty and close the European refugee camps. At that time the mandate of the U.N. High Commissioner for Refugees extended only to Europe. The fair-share program would, for two years, admit to the United States, under the so-called parole authority, refugees under the commissioner's mandate. Its interesting feature was that the number admitted would be up to one-fourth the total number of refugees resettled by other countries. One problem of refugee resettlement is that a country willing to help with some of the burden may not want to be saddled with the whole burden. A fair-share agreement commits to generous entry conditional on parallel generosity by other countries. The fair-share mechanism was decried as mean-spirited by American refugee advocates, and has not been used since. If a present obstacle to refugee resettlement is the fear by many possible receiving countries that their initial generosity would be inundated, then some kind of fair-share agreement might increase global refugee resettlement.

In 1959 Castro gained power in Cuba, and in over 2 years some 120,000 Cubans came to the United States, the majority on regular visas. Following the break in diplomatic relations at the start of 1961, the newly elected President Kennedy established the Cuban Refugee Program and directed routine admission of Cubans under the parole authority. With the spectacle of famine in the People's Republic of China, the United States in 1962 moved to admit 15,000 Chinese refugees through Hong Kong, a policy theme that has not since been repeated. Kennedy's Migration and Refugee Assistance Act of 1962 formalized expansive parole authority and established permanent administration and budget for U.S. participation in developing international refugee assistance programs. Kennedy declared that refugee resettlement was "importantly related to free world political objectives," including

> the extension of hope and encouragement to the victims of communism and other forms of despotism, and the promotion of faith among the captive populations in the purposes and processes of freedom and democracy.[82]

The 1965 immigration reform limited the president's parole authority to "emergency, individual, and isolated situations,"[83] and placed refugees as the seventh preference entitled to 6 percent of the annual numerical immigration limit, far below the annual average admitted under parole in previous years. Persecuted persons fleeing Communist countries or Communist-dominated areas, or anyone fleeing the Middle East, could apply abroad and would be admitted on conditional entry for 2 years before requesting adjustment to permanent resident status. Weeks after enactment Castro permitted free emigration from Cuba, and the Johnson administration responded that all were welcome in the United States, to be admitted under parole authority, thus immediately undermining the attempted congressional restraint on executive discretion. The 1966 Cuban Refugee Adjustment Act allowed such entrants to adjust to permanent residence status after 2 years. Initially, the Cubans were charged against the new overall Western Hemisphere limit, a provision later voided by the courts. Up to 1973, when Castro again banned emigration, another 270,000 Cubans were admitted.

Following North Vietnam's victory over South Vietnam in 1975, President Ford admitted 130,000 Indochinese refugees to the United States under the parole authority. Most were related to U.S. citizens or allied with the U.S. war effort. A more general outflow from Vietnam, Laos, and Kampuchea began, some 1.2 million from 1975 to its peak in 1979. International refugee policy prefers harboring or resettling refugees in neighboring countries of "first asylum." However, Thailand, Malaysia, Indonesia, and Hong Kong were not willing to resettle large numbers, and they would tolerate temporary resettlement only if other countries would assume the burden of permanent resettlement. Thus, President Carter in 1979 ordered admission of 250,000 Indochinese under parole authority. Indochinese admissions were premised on a sense of humanitarian responsibility, on America's credibility as an ally, and as propaganda against the victorious Communist regimes. As with previous extraordinary admissions, those admitted under parole were later adjusted to permanent resident status by special legislation.

In some years the number of paroled refugees exceeded the number of legal immigrants, under dubious executive authority. This was meant to be rectified by the Refugee Act of 1980, the major refugee legislation of the postwar period. The Act was responsive to foreign policy aims, including President Carter's human rights campaign. After May 15, 1980, the president's parole authority was statutorily limited to compelling individual cases. *Refugee* was redefined to incorporate into U.S. law the international definition contained in the United Nations convention and protocol on refugees. Specifically, in part,

> any person who is outside any country of such person's nationality . . . and who is unable to unwilling to avail himself or herself of the protection of that country because of persecution on account of race, religion, nationality, membership in a particular group or political opinion.

Under the new law, *refugee* was no longer limited to those fleeing Communist domination or the geographical Middle East. Also, the president can on discretion recognize as refugees persecuted persons remaining in their country of nationality (in conformance with the practice of interviewing refugee applicants in Vietnam, Cuba, and so on). Applicants are subject to the qualitative exclusions governing immigrant admissions, and those who have assisted in the persecution of others are ineligible for refugee status.

Next, how many? The seventh preference for refugees was abolished, reducing the world immigration ceiling from 290,000 to 270,000. The average of those admitted under parole authority between 1956 and 1979 was 44,670; excepting the Indochinese admissions, a limit of 50,000 would have accommodated entries in each of those years. Therefore, the annual "normal flow" of refugees under the Act would be 50,000 a year, and thus there would be no net increase in immigration and refugee flow resulting from the Act, supporters said.[84] The 50,000 ceiling was stipulated for 1981 and 1982; then and thereafter, a larger annual ceiling could be specified by the president in advance of a year, in consultation and hearings with the Immigration Subcommittees of Congress. Moreover, the president is required to make geographic allocations within his annual proposal so as to discourage any one region from dominating the flow. The overall and geographic allocations are ceilings, not goals. Recently, any unused annual regional allocation could be administratively transferred to another region. Any unused overall allocation is not carried to the next year. In September, 1980, President Carter notified Congress that he wished to admit 217,000 refugees in the next fiscal year, 168,000 from Indochina. The Reagan Administration admitted 99,200 in 1982, narrowing Indochinese admissions to those with family or other ties to the United States. Thereafter admissions ran at about 70,000 a year until greater Soviet admissions in 1989, and have been running at around 130,000 a year in the 1990s.

The refugee admissions program admits particular individuals (with derivative status to immediate family members) from abroad after application, within numerical and geographical allocations. The following priorities are defined by regulation. First, those in immediate danger of loss of life for whom there appears to be no alternative to resettlement in the United States; also, those of compelling concern to the United States, such as celebrated political prisoners. Second, those employed by the U.S. Government for at least 1 year before their refugee claim. Third, spouses, un-

*Table 5.3*

**PROPOSED REFUGEE ADMISSIONS IN 1991**

| Area of Origin | Number |
| --- | --- |
| Africa | 4,900 |
| East Asia | 52,000 |
| Eastern Europe | 5,000 |
| Latin America and Caribbean | 3,100 |
| Near East and South Asia | 6,000 |
| Soviet Union | 50,000 |
| Unallocated, Privately Funded | 10,000 |
| Total | 131,000 |

married children, or parents of legal residents of the United States. Fourth, those with other ties to the United States, such as former employees of U.S. organizations or those educated in the United States. Fifth, more distant relatives of U.S. residents. Sixth, from regional groups (basically Indochina), where admission is in the national interest. The president's annual report also declares changing specific priorities, such as in 1991, Cuban political prisoners among others, or Albanians, Bulgarians, and Romanians in the Eastern European region. This system is a mix of discretion and objective criteria, in that the executive has discretion to devise annual criteria subject to congressional review, differences resolved usually by informal bargaining. The annual ceiling is a flexible first-order allocation, constrained by the budget and legislative-executive negotiation.

If accepted, 1 year after resettlement such refugees may apply for permanent residence status. They are granted 90 days of federal assistance through 12 private resettlement services (and are immediately eligible for all federal benefits). Moreover, in fiscal year 1989, $732 million was obligated to reimburse states for refugee-resettlement expenses. Unlike legal immigrants, refugees have a direct budget impact. This acts as a strong institutional constraint on refugee admissions.

The Refugee Act also established a new procedure for recognizing and adjudicating asylum claims, allowing up to 5,000 approvals per year (from 1952 to 1980 the few such claims were handled by administrative stay of deportation). Individuals physically present in the United States or at its borders may apply for asylum with the Immigration and Naturalization Service (formally advised by the State Department on country conditions), regardless of legal status, i.e., whether they are visitors, visa overstayers, or illegal entrants. The applicant has the burden of proving that he or she meets the definition of refugee under the Act. Applicants are given work authorization but no government assistance. If the application is approved, the asylee's immediate family gains derivative status whether present or abroad. After 1 year, the asylee may adjust to permanent resident status, and after another 4 years, may become naturalized. Asylum claims increased from 26,107 in 1987 to 101,679 in 1989, due to Central American claims. Asylum admissions create two incentive problems. First, the desire of the authorities to give the benefit of the doubt to distressed asylum claimants invites dubious or fraudulent claims from less distressed individuals seeking to circumvent immigration restrictions. Second, the American insistence on due process, together with the administrative practice of granting legal status on equity grounds to those in long residence, creates a potent incentive to pursue dubious claims. In response, asylum administration becomes narrowly legalistic in denying claims so as to avoid precedent.

In 1980, within weeks of congressional restraint of the president's parole authority, Castro opened the door for a mass exodus to the United States—the Mariel boatlift—amounting to some 130,000 individuals. President Carter at first welcomed the refugees from Communism with "open arms," but within a week was openly seeking to halt the process. In the same period a smaller number of Haitians were landing in Florida. The Carter Administration created a new immigration category, "Cuban-Haitian Entrant (Status Pending)," and issued 6-month parole to eligible entrants. This parole was regularly extended, and the 1986 immigration reform bill adjusted those 1980 entrants to permanent resident status as a component of its larger amnesty program.

The Mariel Cuban entrants did not fit the precise refugee definition of individuals persecuted by virtue of attribute or political opinion. However, there was no question of returning them because of foreign-policy considerations, Miami Cuban political sentiment, and sheer impracticality since Castro refused return. The policy adopted was to declare them quasi-asylees as a group. Haitians, who came in smaller numbers around the Mariel period and were fleeing one of the poorest countries on earth, also did not fit the precise refugee definition, but they were initially required to apply for asylum as individuals. The Reagan Administration originally proposed permanent admission for the Cubans but not the Haitians, and in 1981 executed a deterrence program that involved interdicting and returning Haitian smuggling boats on the high seas so as to prevent their ability to initiate asylum claims on landing in the United States. Also, Haitian asylum claimants (and later asylum claimants in illegal status of all nationalities) were detained. This led to charges of foreign policy hypocrisy and racism and to complaints that the treatment was wrongly inconsistent compared to the Cuban case, resulting in major cause litigation. On final appeal, the court adopted the traditional judicial position on immigration questions and deferred to executive and congressional prerogative in defending the borders.

The sanctuary movement that emerged in 1982 alleged that the United States was returning Salvadoran refugees to face persecution by the Salvadoran government and garnered great publicity through civil disobedience. The basic charge was that U.S. asylum decisions were improperly determined by foreign policy rather than humanitarian concerns, in that asylum applicants from pro-Soviet regimes such as Nicaragua were approved at a greater rate than applicants from pro-American regimes such as El Salvador. This was true, but the contrast was not as stark as painted by the sanctuary activists. El Salvador was the second largest source of illegal immigration to the United States from before its civil war. The United States did sometimes grant asylum to claimants from countries friendly to U.S. foreign policy. Yet the sanctuary activists' argument of inconsistent treatment had powerful appeal to liberal and humanitarian audiences. Legislation to provide "extended voluntary departure," a form of temporary legal status, to Salvadorans in the United States eventually passed the House four times in the late 1980s, but it languished due to filibuster and veto threat driven by general objections to alien amnesties and by the foreign policy concerns of the administration. In order to depoliticize and broaden support for the Salvadoran safe haven legislation, sponsors eventually added Nicaraguans.

In 1990 Nicaraguans were dropped from the proposal for temporary safe haven for Salvadorans, but Kuwaitis, Lebanese, and Liberians were added, again so that the measure could not be construed as an embarrassment to foreign policy. The motive of some proponents was humanitarian, but the motive of others was clearly to embarrass U.S. foreign policy: Asylum relief to Salvadorans would be a formal admission of the brutality of the U.S.-supported Salvadoran regime. The latter proponents opposed adding Nicaraguans, etc. to the legislation, as that would dilute their agitational message. The former proponents wanted, more pragmatically, to add nationalities so as to gain the acquiescence of the administration. Also, the Cold War ended. Because the Salvadoran civil war was no longer a contest of the superpowers, in the 1990 legal immigration bill Republicans acceded to the demand of the powerful House Rules Committee Chair for 18 months of "Temporary Protected Status" to the estimated half million Salvadorans illegally present in the United States, beginning on January 1, 1991 (the other nationalities were shunted to the attorney general for determination).

## Illegal Immigration[85]

Industrial agriculture was born in California and south Texas which, in their huge landholdings and political access to cheap labor, differed from the more typical American pattern of small farms and family labor. California growers first recruited Mexicans legally during World War I and informally thereafter, ending with voluntary and forced repatriations in the Great Depression and the arrival of the internal Dust Bowl emigrants. Farm wages then improved relative to industrial wages until, in 1942, the California growers won a U.S.-Mexico agreement for the regulated importation of Mexican nationals, the so-called Bracero program. Mexico refused cooperation with Texas, due to the latter's explicitly anti-Mexican laws, but U.S. officials turned a blind eye to cross-border recruitment by Texas cotton growers, who had lost their native sharecroppers to emigration and wartime mobilization. The bilateral agreement expired in 1948 but was continued by the United States unilaterally until the Korean War in 1951. Although the initial program was small, involving 73,000 Braceros at its height in 1945, it established networks of employment, communication, and transportation so that by 1951 apprehension of illegal Mexican crossers had increased from a few thousand to a half million.[86]

The entry of so many illegal and exploited workers aroused the ire of organized labor, displaced Mexican-Americans, and their liberal political allies, and was thought a national disgrace. The growers used the Korean War to obtain an expanded Bracero program, which first attained large proportions in 1951 with 200,000 workers. In return, Mexico and liberal American politicians demanded enactment of penalties against importing illegal aliens. It was made a felony to harbor illegal aliens, but the bill arrived on the floor with a change inserted by the Immigration Subcommittee Chair Senator Eastland of Mississippi, himself a cotton plantationist later revealed as a regular employer of Mexican illegal aliens. This so-called Texas proviso declared that employment and any incident practices thereto would not constitute such harboring. Congressional liberals objected heatedly but lost to agricultural bloc logrolling. McCarran and Walter, whose parallel codification of the Immigration and Nationality Act in 1952 continued restriction of legal immigration from CSE Europe, sided with the Southwestern growers promoting illegal immigration from Mexico. A 1952 political cartoon portrayed a congressman declaring, "I don't want any legal immigration around here."[87] By 1953, apprehensions of Mexican crossers reached a record high of near 900,000, and national media were awash with reports of a "wetback crisis." Liberal forces were appalled by the labor-standards and welfare implications. The Eisenhower Administration responded with a massive quasi-military deportation drive dubbed "Operation Wetback" in 1954, and with extension and expansion of the emergency wartime Bracero program, the former deterring and the latter regulating migration. Operation Wetback was mostly uncontroversial at the time and was a successful deterrent (retrospective judgment is that it was illiberal and racist). Illegal immigration was insignificant from 1955 to 1965. The Bracero program was always controversial because the entrant was bound not only to an occupation, agriculture, but also to a particular employer.

The bound labor of the Bracero program was contrary to American principles, and survived only because the intense interests of the Southwest growers outweighed the dispersed interests of the more numerous opponents. Labor and reform interests regularly mobilized to oppose legislative renewal of imported contract labor in agriculture. Bracero conditions became a major national scandal, typified by Edward R. Murrow's prize-winning television documentary, "Harvest of Shame." Eisenhower's secretary of labor published compromise remedial regulations in 1959, and growers responded with a law stripping him of authority. Opponents of the program, led by Senator Eugene McCarthy, then served notice that they would no longer seek compromise but abolition. With the election of Kennedy as president in 1960, Southwest growers lost support and labor won support in key lower echelons of the executive branch. After several close and dramatic legislative battles, the program closed in 1965, its congressional supporters conceding moral exhaustion on the issue: The growers' demands were not publicly justifiable.

Reformers expected farm labor conditions to improve as a result. It was no coincidence that the United Farm Workers Union (UFW) formed in 1965 and thrived for a few years thereafter. But as the farm labor movement loudly advanced, so, quietly, did illegal immigration, apprehensions roughly quadrupling from 1965 to 1969. (Apprehensions are only a crude approximation for illegal entry, but the latter is difficult to measure. Apprehension figures vary according to changes in law-enforcement budgets and techniques but are still useful in indicating major changes in immigration flows.) For the growers, the exploitation of illegal entrants was even better than the relatively more-regulated Bracero program. In response, liberals in Congress called for repeal of the Texas proviso. In 1971 the AFL-CIO called for prohibition of the knowing employment of illegal aliens, so-called employer sanctions. Representative Peter Rodino, who chaired the House Immigration Subcommittee, held field hearings on the topic in 1971 and 1972. Again, labor, farmworker, and Mexican American organizations supported punishing knowing employers of illegal aliens, while a few marginal elements of the old left and new left took up the growers' old claim that employer sanctions would amount to undue discrimination against those of "foreign" appearance.

Rodino's legislation passed the House without objection in 1972, but it was thwarted by the reactionary grower Eastland's chairmanship of the Senate Immigration Subcommittee. Eastland killed the measure again in 1974. Meanwhile, dramatically increasing annual apprehensions, a politically active Border Patrol union, and a new commissioner of the Immigration and Naturalization Service spotlighted illegal immigration as a major national issue. When Rodino began he opposed suggestions that employer sanctions be coupled with an amnesty for illegal aliens already present in the country. Liberal Democrats, such as the Italian American Rodino who had fought for the 1965 abolition of the national-origins system, were responding to overlapping labor constituencies concerned by threatened labor standards and old ethnic constituencies wanting eased legal immigration for relatives. Rodino worried that tolerance of illegal immigration would erode public support for legal immigration and that amnesty of illegal entrants would be unfair to applicants in the legal-immigration stream. More conservative parties argued that amnesty would create an incentive for future illegal immigration, or would reward law-breaking.

Rodino, and his Senate counterpart Ted Kennedy, slowly came to accept the argument that amnesty was justified because the illegals were present due to deliberate policies of nonenforcement, and because immigration practice already forgave long-resident illegal entrants on equity grounds. Moreover, mass expulsion would be politically unacceptable, while failure to legalize a considerable population might perpetuate the very conditions of exploitation that the employer sanctions were intended to rectify. Finally, sanctions coupled with amnesty were presented as a tradeoff intended to build a winning coalition through the center.

Until 1975 UFW, which remained morally influential although practically defeated in the fields by 1973, and the major Mexican American organizations supported employer sanctions, arguing that their members suffered most from competition by employers of exploited illegals. But, precisely as the amnesty proposal came seriously on the table, such organizations went to strongly opposing employer sanctions, arguing that the prohibition on employing illegal aliens would exacerbate employment discrimination. There is no obvious explanation for the rapid and passionate reversal of position among the Mexican American leaders, especially given the enduring majority support for employer sanctions among Mexican Americans, as measured by opinion polls into the present. (The illegal population was composed of dozens of nationalities but most were Mexican, and policy was clearly driven by the size of the southern flow.) Rodino's judiciary committee reported an employer sanctions bill in 1975, but for the first time part of the congressional left opposed it. Eastland blocked action in the Senate. The outgoing Republican Ford Administration supported sanctions, and, more importantly, endorsed amnesty.

In August 1977 the newly elected President Carter unveiled a major legislative proposal crafted by his prestigious Texan Secretary of Labor Ray Marshall: employer sanctions, temporary resident status for those present since January 1, 1977, and improved labor law and border immigration enforcement. The proposal was a political disaster. Rather than unite a winning coalition, it fragmented historical coalitions. First, there was almost no support in public opinion for the broad amnesty; the right appealed to public sentiment, while Democrats had nothing to gain by supporting the novel demand of the emerging Mexican American leadership. Second, the powerful Southwest growers had an intense interest in maintaining cheap labor and demanded either no employer sanctions or a new Bracero program. Third, enacting sanctions was an old priority for organized labor, while defeating sanctions became a new priority for the Hispanic organizations, splitting the Democrats; but both labor and Hispanics opposed any new Bracero program that would be demanded by the growers. The Carter proposal remobilized the maturing Chicano New Left, previously exhausted by success on civil rights and failure in labor organizing, around the issue of free immigration.

The 1978 legal immigration bill reconciling Western and Eastern Hemisphere admissions also contained a provision establishing a Select Commission on Immigration and Refugee Policy to study immigration policy, including the questions of illegal immigration. The Commission would report in 1981, after the next presidential election, burying the issue, to the relief of politicians of all stripes.

In 1978 and 1979 apprehensions passed the million mark, just below the record set in 1954 during the "crisis" conditions of Operation Wetback. Meanwhile, the second oil shock, the Iranian crisis, and the Soviet invasion of Afghanistan made access to Mexican oil a foreign policy priority; the nationalist administration in Mexico explicitly linked oil access to the issue of free immigration; and in 1980 Carter suspended interior immigration enforcement, ostensibly for census purposes. However, annually increasing illegal immigration, changing composition of legal immigration, the admission of Indochinese refugees from 1975, and especially the spectacle of the Mariel Cuban boatlift of 1980 kept the immigration issue alive. Carter's disastrous equivocation during the Mariel episode symbolized his larger political problem and certainly contributed to his defeat.

The blue-ribbon Select Commission (SCIRP) was headed by Fr. Theodore Hesburgh, President of Notre Dame University, a civil rights leader, moderate liberal, and importantly, given American immigration history, a Catholic. The Commission recommended employer sanctions, a national identification system to prevent undue discrimination by employers, a qualified amnesty, and the easing of little-used guestworker provisions to accommodate growers, followed by moderate expansion of legal immigration. This was called "closing the back door so as to open wider the front door." The new Reagan Administration, surprisingly, endorsed most of the Commission's recommendations. A major illegal immigration bill was introduced by Rep. Mazzoli, the Democratic chair of the House Immigration Subcommittee, and Sen. Alan Simpson, the Republican chair of the Senate Immigration Subcommittee. The Simpson-Mazzoli bill was supported in its broad contours by Hesburgh, the AFL-CIO, the NAACP, environmental and population control advocates such as Zero Population Growth and Federation for American Immigration Reform, and by most of the nation's editorialists, who in following years consistently championed the cause as a case of the general interest against the special interests. Organized labor, importantly, endorsed amnesty coupled with sanctions. Public opinion supported employer sanctions and opposed amnesty. The Simpson-Mazzoli bill was opposed by Hispanic organizations, the civil-liberties organizations, parts of the civil rights coalition, and the internationalist left. These parties opposed employer sanctions on the argument that employers would be led to discriminate against the "foreign"-appearing, and generally criticized amnesty as insufficient. Supporters of employer sanctions often stated that "our borders are out of control," and appealed to a sovereign right to control immigration. Sanctions were defended as a more acceptable method of controlling illegal immigration than sweeps and deportations, on the argument that previous law punished the illegal immigrant but not the exploiting employer, and as a defense of labor standards. Opponents of sanctions said that undocumented aliens were scapegoats for failings of the capitalist economy, that the sanctions proposal divided the working class, or that free immigration was due as reparations for imperialism.

The legislation followed a tortuous path, appearing in numerous incarnations. It overwhelmingly passed the Senate in 1982, but it was blocked by late-session parliamentary maneuvers in the House by Mexican American Representative Edward Roybal. It again passed the Senate in 1984 and the House by a narrow margin after a week of debate, but it died late in Conference Committee, rather mysteriously over the peripheral point of compensation to state governments for services to newly legalized aliens. This was probably due to the Democratic leadership's unstated wish to avoid the issue in upcoming national elections, and to the powerful growers' failure to win their maximum program. While other forces loudly debated the principles of the legislation and universally opposed a temporary-worker program in agriculture, the growers were always the quiet obstacle to any final compromise.

In 1985 Simpson announced that, given public opinion, he would push for employer sanctions alone, absent compromise from the various interests. He won Senate passage of a bill with an amnesty 3 years distant contingent on the success of improved immigration enforcement—although if enforcement worked, few would be eligible for amnesty. This loosened the political deadlock in the House. Meanwhile, labor, Hispanics, and the liberals opposed to the growers' demand for a broad, bound-labor guestworker program assumed that the conservative Simpson's vehement and sincere opposition to Bracero-type programs would prevail, and they failed to mobilize on the issue. However, over the years the growers' PACs had targeted key House members of both parties on the priority issue of cheap labor. Their objective was not to compromise but to maintain the status quo of exploitable illegal immigration. So, their leaders calculated, even if sanctions and amnesty could be made the subject of compromise, the Democratic leadership would be split between labor and growers on the irreconcilable issue of bound labor. However, a novel and independent solution to the farm-labor question emerged that cleared the way for enactment in late 1986.

As with most compromises, no interest could claim victory. The central provisions of the Immigration Reform and Control Act of 1986 were employer sanctions, new prohibitions against employment discrimination, a legalization program, and a "Special Agricultural Worker" (SAW) program. The Texas proviso was repealed and all employers subjected to penalties for knowingly hiring an alien not authorized to work in the United States. The Select Commission's prominent insistence on reliable national identification as a deterrent to employer discrimination and fraud, even though "essential," had been dropped early in the legislative deliberation because it attracted strong additional opposition to an already delicate proposal. To prevent discrimination, all new hires would be subject to verification of work authorization, which would be established through existing documents such as drivers' licenses and social security cards. It became illegal for employers to discriminate on the basis of citizenship status, legal aliens were granted standing, and an anti-discrimination enforcement unit was established. Moreover, the neutral General Accounting Office was tasked with reporting whether a widespread pattern of discrimination resulted from employer sanctions. If after 3 years this proved to be the case, the issue of repeal would by statute be forced on the congressional agenda.

Aliens who entered the United States illegally before January 1, 1982, and who resided continuously since (with minor interruptions) could apply for temporary resident status and then apply for permanent resident status after 18 months, and, like everyone else, for citizenship after another 5 years (with citizenship, one can more easily bring in close relatives). However, the newly legalized aliens would not be eligible for most federally funded programs, including welfare benefits, for 5 years (legalization advocates had so strenuously denied the stereotype of the alien on welfare that they were left defenseless to the conservative floor amendment prohibiting federal benefits). Only individuals would qualify; there would be no derivative status to immediate family members, from concern over chain effects. The amnesty was justified on the grounds of improving immigration enforcement, the costliness of mass deportation, the need to eliminate a fearful illegal subclass that undercut labor standards, and to reward those who had made some contribution to the society. The cutoff date for legalization was a trading chip to the very end. A recent date would have the incentive effects of increased fraud in applications (proving 5 years' residence is harder than proving 6 months') as well as increased illegal crossings, and result in larger numbers of applicants. A distant date would prevent the enforcement or fairness objectives of the legalization from being attained because too many of the relatively settled aliens would remain in illegal status. A poorly subscribed program would invite future amnesty proposals and thus perhaps a precedential chain of legalizations that would erode the goal of limitation.

The literacy test of 1917 neatly appealed to a coalition of different interests. The Special Agricultural Worker (SAW) farm labor compromise in the 1986 illegal immigration bill succeeded by not sufficiently offending the different interests that were committed to the legislation as a package. The growers' lobby was not fooled by the cleverly limited transition guestworker programs offered in earlier versions of the legislation. A quiet offer to exempt fruit and vegetable growers from employer sanctions was rejected by the canny growers, who recognized that exemption from a controversial new obligation imposed on everyone else would quickly backfire. Realizing that the growers would again block enactment of the long-suffering legislation, a Brooklyn Congress member on the House Immigration Subcommittee got together with two California liberal Democrats, one a former lawyer for the United Farm Workers, the other a leading advocate of growers in his district. The growers were too interested to budge, while organized labor would never accede to the bound labor necessary to any expanded guestworker program. The three privately arrived at the solution of legalizing any alien who worked in the fields so long as he or she kept working in the fields for a time.

This solution would satisfy the growers' ostensible complaint of disastrous future labor shortages, while avoiding a permanent program of bound labor that was repugnant to organized labor. The three authors of the solution secretly canvassed the idea to interest-group leaders, who found the proposal odious. The growers privately feared losing tractable low-cost labor, although their publicly expressed fear of labor shortage was accommodated; organized labor disliked the temporary binding of workers to agriculture; Hispanic farmworkers would benefit, but the special program would reduce political pressure for a more recent cut-off date on a general amnesty; restrictionists worried about unknown numbers and fraud; finally, the plan was plainly unfair, a fact that its authors freely admitted, justifying it only by political expediency. House Democratic leaders, caught between labor, growers, and public opinion, endorsed the proposal with a rule forbidding floor amendment and even debate on the agricultural compromise. This almost lost the House vote, which was delivered by whip. The Senate's delegates refused to accede because of the SAW program, but national headlines and thousands of phone calls from sanction or amnesty supporters revived the conference and ensured final compromise legislation.

The resultant Special Agricultural Worker Program permitted those illegally present who worked 60 days in the fruit and vegetable industry from May 1985 to May 1986 to apply directly for permanent resident status. Moreover, such applicants would not be denied federally funded benefits. However, such workers would need to work 60 days in the fields in each of the first 2 years to avoid deportation, and for each of 5 years to attain naturalization. If by 1989 the Secretaries of Agriculture and Labor determined presence of an agricultural labor shortage, further Replenishment Agricultural Workers would be admitted from abroad for permanent residence under similar conditions.

The new law seemed to work to deter illegal immigration in its first years. However, apprehensions have since returned to pre-enactment levels. The temporary decline in apprehensions is probably attributable to the mere legalization of flow by the one-time amnesty programs. The employer sanctions are ineffective due to the ease of document fraud, whereas more secure identification systems are opposed by the civil liberties lobby. Whether the sanctions led to a pattern of widespread discrimination against foreign-appearing persons remains a contested issue, although Congress declined to make such a finding. By the end of the application periods, 1.7 million people had applied for the general program and 1.3 million workers for the SAW program, and nearly all applications were approved. In 1990 derivative status was granted to immediate family members, probably because the size of that eligible population was known. Because of the easy documentary requirements, far more than expected applied for the SAW program and application fraud was enormous; however, no administrative finding of agricultural labor shortage occurred. Legislation in 1988 to extend the amnesty application period for 7 months but not otherwise expand eligibility was brought to vote and failed, demonstrating the fragility of support for the amnesty component of the reform.

## Expansion of Principles and of Admissions: 1990[88]

The increasing concentration of source countries, their difference from older source countries, and the near impossibility of any immigration other than by relatives led to increasing complaints against the 1965 system, especially from the American Irish but also from CSE European ethnic groups. The family-reunification system had also come to exclude any significant immigration from South America and Africa. In 1990, 79 percent of all immigration hailed from Asia and North America (mostly Mexico, Central America, and the Caribbean). A late-night rider was attached to the 1986 illegal-immigration bill, defining a class of countries "disadvantaged" by the 1965 reforms, with the intended secondary consequence of admitting the Irish. Its 10,000 visas were made available on a first-come, first-served basis; over 1 million applications resulted. Later, the same advocates offered 20,000 such visas on a lottery, and 3.2 million entered.[89] The intense Irish lobby pressure cleared the path for less-interested European ethnic groups, represented by Northeastern Democrats, to seek change.

Although the family-reunification system was facially neutral at its inception, its intended secondary consequence was the admission of relatives of the most recent immigrants, the CSE Europeans in 1965, in some minds as compensation for past discrimination.

By 1990 the unintended consequence was to limit immigration to two regions of the world, southern North America and parts of Asia. Therefore, in addition to the European interest, there was a weak cosmopolitan interest in devising neutral criteria with a neutral effect across regions of the world. Another problem was the crowding out of skills-based immigration (the Canadian immigration system, by contrast, is primarily oriented to labor-force considerations) as the business interest became concerned with skill decline, with predicted future labor shortages, and with lagging American competitiveness. Finally, the influential 1981 report of the Select Commission on Immigration and Refugee Policy had recommended a moderate increase in legal immigration following the enactment of illegal-immigration reform. So, in 1988, the liberal Senator Kennedy and the conservative Senator Simpson, both of whom had sat on the Select Commission, rapidly negotiated a legal-immigration compromise, which overwhelmingly passed the Senate due to their prestige on the issue. The incoming Bush Administration indicated that it would accept any congressional compromise, barring direct budgetary impact.

Under the 1965 system, immediate relatives of U.S. citizens were not included in the numerical limitations. Simpson's objective was to "cap," place a numerical limit on all immigration, excluding refugees, by increasing the limit from 270,000 excluding the immediate relatives of citizens to 590,000 including them, which would comfortably accommodate historical levels of total preference and nonpreference immigration. Kennedy's secondary objective was to liberalize immigration, and his primary objective to satisfy the new illegal Irish lobby. Both Kennedy and Simpson wished to establish a category of "independent immigrants" who would "seed" the family-reunification system with more diverse source countries and to satisfy organized-business demand for skilled immigration. The independent-immigrant category of 55,000 visas per year would admit applicants according to a point system with credit for such things as youth, education, English-language skills, work experience related to U.S. labor-force need, and pre-arranged employment. Eighty percent of the visas would be allocated by lottery to those scoring beyond a threshold of points and 20 percent to those scoring the highest points, again to promote diversity. (Just as with per-country limits, diversity is not only an ideal goal, it maximizes potential congressional support.) Kennedy wanted increases in the second preference—spouses and unmarried children of permanent residents—due to an enormous backlog; Simpson agreed, providing the numbers came by narrowing the fifth preference from "adult siblings of U.S. citizens and their spouses and children" to "never-married siblings."

Points for English skills would satisfy business-skill demands and those concerned by multilingualism and assimilation, and also increase immigration from Ireland and the rest of Europe where English is common. Hispanics and Asian Americans, among Kennedy's traditional national constituency, disliked his Irish gambit, and successfully lobbied for removal of language points. Hispanic and Asian lobbyists also denounced the reduction in the fifth preference as "cultural discrimination," claiming that their groups, unlike Europeans, honored the extended family. Hispanic, Chinese, and Jewish groups objected to the immigration cap. Business mobilized for more flexibility in temporary visas. Libertarian economists favored open borders, or, as an alternative, visa auctions, but their proposals were not seriously entertained. The final Senate bill resolved the difficulties by increasing the overall visa level to 630,000 per year—480,000 for family immigration and 150,000 for independent immigrants. Admission of immediate relatives of U.S. citizens was unrestricted within the 480,000 family cap; the preferences for less immediate relatives of citizens and all relatives of residents were increased from 216,000 to 260,000; but from fear that immediate relatives of citizens might "eat up" the 480,000 ceiling, a floor of 216,000 was guaranteed for the other relative family preferences, thus the cap was "porous." The fifth preference for siblings was restored. Within the 150,000 independent immigrant allocation, the third preference for individuals of exceptional ability was increased, as was the sixth preference for skilled workers to fill positions lacking qualified workers in the United States; new visas were established for rural medical personnel and investors, and 54,000 for new immigrants under the proposed point system. Of those 54,000, 10,000 were reserved for natives of the 36 countries adversely affected by the 1965 reforms, practically, that is, the Irish. Independent immigrants could apply with spouses and children, except for those coming under the point system.

The chairs of the House Judiciary Committee and Immigration Subcommittee were still smarting from the bloody House fight over illegal immigration and failed to act on the Senate bill, but a small Irish lottery bill passed. However, in 1990, Judiciary Chair Rodino had retired, and Immigration Subcommittee Chair Mazzoli was replaced, over his objection, by Representative Bruce Morrison of Connecticut, due to several related and unrelated disputes Mazzoli had with House Democratic leadership. Morrison was also running for governor of his state and aggressively solicited contributions from national ethnic, labor, and business organizations. Morrison proposed legislation that would about double legal immigration; for example, removing the numerical limit on the second preference of immediate relatives of residents, increasing business immigration, increasing visas for Europeans, and legalizing relatives of amnestied aliens. His proposal was scaled back in subcommittee and full committee, and came off the House floor as follows: no limit on immediate relatives of U.S. citizens; family preferences increased from 216,000 to 300,000; business immigration increased from 54,000 to 65,000; for the first three years, 25,000 a year for natives of the "adversely-affected countries" living illegally in the United States (mostly the Irish), 15,000 for Eastern Europeans, 15,000 for Africans; after 3 years 50,000 annual "diversity visas" for countries with low numbers under family and employment admissions criteria; temporary status for Salvadorans and other nationalities; and so on. The House rejected the Kennedy-Simpson point system for independent immigrants as elitist and ethnically divisive. The annual legal immigration level would increase to about 800,000. The general pattern of the process was that second-order conflicts were resolved by expanding the first-order allocation.

On the Senate side, Kennedy leaned toward the House approach, while Simpson stuck to the contours of the 1988 Kennedy-Simpson bill. Simpson had two objectives: improving control of illegal immigration and stabilizing legal immigration with a ceiling, but he was somewhat indifferent over the level of stabilization. He introduced a bill to reduce document fraud among illegal aliens, improve border enforcement, and educate employers on the anti-discrimination provisions of the employer-sanctions law. He also opposed legalizing relatives of amnestied aliens and temporary status for Salvadorans and others, on the grounds that the 1986 amnesty was sold as a one-time-only affair. He demanded a firm, "nonporous" cap on immigration at 630,000 visas annually. Simpson had been politically compelling in previous immigration legislation, but the controversial House bill had mobilized ethnic and business interests. They prevailed on Simpson's Republican colleagues in the Senate, who urged him to "split the difference" with the House, which is roughly what happened.

The Immigration Act of 1990 was the first major revision of the legal-immigration system since 1965. The amended system is monstrously complex, suggesting that, as was the case prior to 1924 and to 1965, the basic principles are coming under strain. Legal immigration would increase from 500,000 to 700,000 annually during the first 3 years, and 675,000 thereafter. For the first 3 years, 520,000 of the visas would go to family immigration, 480,000 thereafter. Immediate relatives of U.S. citizens would remain numerically unrestricted but would be subtracted from the overall family-immigration limit, the remainder going to the family preferences, so the immigration cap was "piercable." If the remainder was below 226,000 visas, the family preferences would nevertheless be guaranteed at 226,000, thus the cap was "porous." Some skill-based and, for the first time, investment-based, immigration was added.

## The 1990 System

### Family Preference

**First preference.** Unmarried adult sons and daughters of U.S. citizens, 23,400 visas a year, plus any visas left over from the fourth preference. This was 54,000 in the superseded law, but that figure was never reached, numbers falling to the second preference.

**Second preference.** Spouses and children of permanent residents, 114,200 visas a year. This was 70,200 in the superseded law. The second preference is further subdivided into 87,900 visas for spouses and minor children of permanent residents, and 26,300 for the unmarried adult children of permanent residents. Of the 87,900 visas available for spouses and minor children, 75 percent will be allocated without regard to per-country limits, and 25 percent allocated within per-country limits. This is designed so that high-demand countries such as Mexico and the Philippines will continue to enjoy the bulk of visas while not squeezing out low-demand countries. If subtracting immediate-relative immigration from the family-visa total of 465,000 does not hit the 226,000 floor, then the extra visas are added to the second preference. Additionally, second preference gets any leftover numbers from the first preference, as before.

*Third preference.* Married sons and daughters of U.S. citizens, 23,400 visas a year. This was 27,000 in the superseded law. Third preference gets any leftover numbers from first and second preference.

*Fourth preference.* Brothers and sisters of U.S. citizens, 5,000 visas a year, about the same as under the previous law. This class was called the fifth preference under the superseded system.

### Other

Per-country limits are raised from 20,000 a year to 7 percent of the total of family-preference and employment-based visas, about 25,600 a year.

For three years beginning October 1991, 40,000 visas a year are made available to persons from states adversely affected by the 1965 reforms, available to those with a firm offer of U.S. employment for at least a year and not denied to those illegally present. This is implicitly intended to benefit Irish and Poles. The visas are awarded by a mail-in lottery, first-come, first-served by order of mail receipt. Multiple entries are permitted, but the applicant has limited control over mail-arrival time, so that both pluck and luck contribute to the selection.

Beginning October 1995, there will be 55,000 visas a year for "diversity immigrants" to benefit countries that currently experience little family-based immigration. Such immigrants must have the equivalent of high school or 2 years of job experience. Visas will again be awarded by lottery.

### New Employment Preference System

The previous employment-based third and sixth preferences, totaling 54,000 a year, are abolished and replaced with 140,000 visas in a new employment-preference system.

*Priority workers.* Persons of extraordinary ability, such as outstanding professors and researchers or multinational executives, 40,000 visas a year. Another 40,000 visas a year for degreed professionals and others of exceptional ability. Another 40,000 visas a year for skilled workers, professionals, and other workers (2 years' experience), subject to labor certification (application to the Department of Labor that there are not sufficient U.S. workers available), and notice to the union of jurisdiction.
*Religious workers.* 10,000 visas a year.
*Investors.* 10,000 visas a year available for those who will invest a million dollars or more in a job-creating enterprise employing at least 10 U.S. workers. Resident status revocable for failure to meet conditions.

Hong Kong visas were increased from 5,000 a year to 10,000 for each of the first 3 years and to 20,000 annually therafter, with an additional 12,000 allocated to employees of U.S. companies in Hong Kong; considerable lobbying and political action accompanied this proposal. The complicated diversity-immigrant lottery is basically an amnesty for the Irish, its facially neutral criteria designed to evade objections against ethnic-specific legislation and against any new legalization program, since there is something of a norm of no new amnesties following from promises made in the 1986 legalization legislation. There is a full Christmas tree of minor provisions not reported here.

Senator Kennedy stated the following rationale in presenting the bill for final enactment:

> By redressing the imbalances which have inadvertently developed in recent years, we will again open our doors to those who no longer have immediate family ties to the United States. By placing more emphasis on the particular skills and qualities that independent im-

migrants possess, we will bring our present laws more in line with the Nation's economic needs. These reforms will be achieved without reducing our traditional priorities for family reunification. The visas currently reserved for family members of recent immigrants, as established in the 1965 reforms, will not be reduced. This compromise bill will add visas; it does not subtract visas.[90]

The new law triggers review of immigration levels every 3 years, a first. This ensures allocative dispute into the foreseeable future. Congress answers intense immigration demand with increased visas, constrained by negative but relatively diffuse opinion.

## Conclusion

It may seem as though immigration allocation mechanisms and their rationales have been presented in crushing detail but, in fact, this was but a brief, surface tour. A phenomenological feel for the detailed complexity of immigration principles allows for insights otherwise unavailable. Why the complexity? Part of the answer is as follows. If America decided to admit all aspiring immigrants, then there would be no need to choose among categories or individuals. The same freedom from choice would result if the country closed its borders to immigration. This illustrates the principle that at very high or very low rates of first-order allocation, second-order allocations are relatively easy, while at intermediate rates of first-order allocation, second-order allocations are relatively hard.[91] Philosophical theories of justice tend to find an obligation to admit usually all immigrants or none, depending on whether the standpoint is cosmopolitan or national, overlooking the real rights and wrongs of intermediate rates of immigration.[92]

The evolution of U.S. immigration policy is discontinuous. This is due to the divisive nature of immigration questions, the internal logic of allocation principles, and changing conditions of immigration demand. Immigration questions split standard political coalitions, so politicians prefer to avoid the issue until forced to act by some crisis. Once a broad allocation principle is selected, it will persist and will respond to increasing pressures with epicyclical elaborations. This is exacerbated by the American system of divided government and the easy access of concentrated interests to any of the three branches, more reasons for the particular complexity of U.S. immigration policy. Problems accumulate to the point where the issue is forced on the political agenda, where it lingers until a new allocation mechanism is discovered. A new mechanism is one that simultaneously appeals not merely to the interests but especially to the principles of divergent groups; a sort of normative coalition forms on an innovative allocation mechanism that is at least a principled "second-best" for the major actors.[93]

To illustrate, immigration was hotly debated in the Revolutionary era: The principle of nonintervention satisfied proponents of immigration that the federal government would not discourage immigration and opponents that it would not encourage it; this was followed by an unrelated cessation of immigration demand to 1820. Immigration rates returned to historic highs, yet the principle of nonintervention dominated until about 1875. The principle of neutrality emerged from the principle of nonintervention following the ambiguous precedent of Republican subsidization of immigration in the Civil War: The new principle of prohibiting subsidized immigration was portrayed as a return to the norm of free immigration. The principle of neutrality held, becoming ever more intricate, even as the frontier closed, the cost of passage dropped, and immigration rates reached annual and cumulative highs. Immigration was near the top of the public agenda from 1900 to 1920, but a new principle of allocation was lacking.

The literacy test of 1917 satisfied liberal, labor, and ethnocentric principles, broke the norm of free immigration, and established a first-order norm of limited immigration. The ambiguity of the literacy test as both an individual and a group standard led rapidly to the new second-order principle of immigration allocated in proportion to the national origins of the population. In one version—proportional to the immigrants in the population—the principle would address fears about assimilation. In another version—proportional to the whole population—the principle would surrender to fears about assimilation. The latter version prevailed, and in 1924 racial exclusion became the basis of immigration law. Even as the United States later assumed Cold War responsibilities, its immigration laws denigrated and denied admission to needed allies. The decrepit immigration system became ever more complex, while presidents conducting foreign policy sidestepped it entirely.

Kin-based immigration moved from the background to the foreground in 1965, as the principle that simultaneously appealed to U.S. foreign-policy allies, to the excluded CSE Europeans as a rectification of past injustice, and to the nativist patriotic societies as maintaining the ethnic balance. The kin-based system had the eventual unintended effect of excluding immigration from Europe, an issue not addressed until 1990 because of the rigidity of immigration enactments. Meanwhile, illegal immigration began to sidestep the legal immigration system, and the ratio of the populations of sending countries to the American population began increasing. The 1986 illegal-immigration reform and the 1990 legal-immigration reform were unimaginably convoluted, an indication that the kin-based system of 1965 may be exhausting its political logic.

Immigration policy is affected by foreign policy, ethnonationalist, and economic factors. The relations of foreign policy and immigration policy, apparent from 1787 onward and particularly during the Cold War, deserve more thorough investigation. How will the end of the Cold War affect U.S. immigration and refugee policy? Textbook immigration historiography, inspired by Higham, explains restrictionist policy as a consequence of nativist impulses.[94] Although irrational xenophobia is unmistakably present in U.S. immigration history, as is unvarnished altruism, a supplementary approach would look at immigration to America as an interaction among millions of individual natives and immigrants, with different individuals experiencing different benefits and costs as a result. Benefits and costs of high immigration were jaggedly distributed, and key partisans in the restrictionist debates around World War I poorly concealed their respective self-interests; business, for example, praised cheap labor and feared labor shortages, while organized labor praised wage growth and feared labor surpluses. Higham charts the ebb and flow of nativism, relating it to macro-variables, such as national crisis or intellectual currents, while neglecting its much stronger relation to the rate of immigration. Nativist movements collapsed after the restrictions of 1924, says Higham, from increased national self-confidence and "slackening of . . . impulse," failing to notice that they subsided along with immigration, even though millions of the feared immigrants remained.[95]

I am not aware of any scholarly research on the micro-links between high immigration rates and restrictionist political action. Why does a particular threshold seem to trigger agitation and a higher threshold legislation? American immigration rates were near historic lows from 1930 to 1980. In the 1990s they appear to be climbing toward historic highs. If past patterns are predictive, then immigration restriction would climb back up the public agenda before the end of the decade, but divided political parties would not act effectively on the issue until moved by some sense of national panic.

## NOTES

1. Elster, *Local Justice*, p. 21.

2. Elster, *Local Justice*, p. 15.

3. The account relies on J. Higham, *Strangers in the Land: Patterns of American Nativism 1860–1925*, New York: Atheneum 1969 (first published in 1955); A. T. Lane, *Solidarity or Survival? American Labor and European Immigrants, 1830–1924*, New York: Greenwood Press 1987; V. Briggs, Jr., *Immigration Policy and the American Labor Force*, Baltimore: Johns Hopkins University Press 1984; E. P. Hutchinson, *Legislative History of American Immigration Policy, 1798–1965*, Philadelphia: University of Pennsylvania Press 1981; M. C. LeMay, *From Open Door to Dutch Door: An Analysis of U.S. Immigration Policy Since 1820*, New York: Praeger 1987; Select Commission on Immigration and Refugee Policy, U.S. Immigration Policy and the National Interest, Staff Report, Washington, DC: U.S. Government 1981 (timeline at pp. 33–42, Chapters 5, 7); M. T. Bennett, *American Immigration Policies: A History*, Washington, DC: Public Affairs Press 1963; and R. A. Divine, *American Immigration Policy, 1924–1952*, New Haven: Yale University Press 1957.

4. Hutchinson, *Legislative History of American Immigration Policy*, pp. 388–396.

5. G. Calabresi and P. Bobbitt, *Tragic Choices*, New York: Norton 1978, p. 171.

6. Calabresi and Bobbitt, p. 44.

7. T. Schelling, *The Strategy of Conflict*, Cambridge, MA: Harvard University Press 1960, points out that in indeterminate bargaining situations

parties may choose a naturally salient outcome, such as fixing a political boundary at a river; such are focal-point solutions.

8. Select Commission, p. 33.
9. Hutchinson, pp. 396–404.
10. LeMay, pp. 30–33.
11. Briggs, p. 24.; LeMay, p. 35.
12. As cited in Elster, *Local Justice,* p. 24.
13. Hutchinson, pp. 71, 73, 76–77, 430–431.
14. Lane, pp. 83–84.
15. Select Commission, p. 36.
16. LeMay, p. 40.
17. Lane, pp. 124–127.
18. LeMay, p. 59.
19. LeMay, pp. 57–58.
20. Lane, pp. 117–120, 137.
21. Select Commission, p. 184.
22. Lane, pp. 147–167.
23. Lane, p. 173.
24. Lane, p. 174.
25. Lane, pp. 174–178.
26. Select Commission, p. 37.
27. Briggs, pp. 36–38; LeMay, p. 69.
28. Lane, pp. 182–184.
29. Select Commission, p. 38.
30. Hutchinson, p. 156.
31. Hutchinson, in passing. Elster says that "it seems to hold quite generally that people are more willing to accept bad outcomes if they are the result of anonymous social processes than if they are the intended result of deliberate intervention." *Local Justice,* p. 224.
32. U.S. Bureau of the Census, *Statistical Abstract of the United States,* 113th edition, Washington, DC; GPO 1993, p. 10, sources and qualifications omitted.
33. Quoted in Higham, p. 302.
34. Hutchinson, p. 175.
35. Hutchinson, p. 176.
36. Quoted in LeMay, p. 80.
37. LeMay, p. 80.
38. Higham, pp. 320–324.
39. In 1917 opinion favored the literacy test over ethnic quotas as a limiting device. Hutchinson, p. 166.
40. Divine, pp. 49, 50–51.
41. LeMay, pp. 86–91.
42. Adapted from LeMay, p. 91, citing Bernard.
43. Bennett, pp. 51, 56.

44. Hutchinson, p. 505.

45. Bennett, p. 57.

46. Briggs, p. 47.

47. Briggs, p. 34.

48. Hutchinson, pp. 38–39.

49. Bennett, pp. 38–39.

50. Divine, pp. 60, 52–66.

51. In 1906 Congress added those likely to become a public charge to the list of inadmissible classes. For those arriving by vessel, a family head had to have $25 in possession. Hutchinson, p. 139.

52. Divine, p. 71.

53. Divine, p. 73.

54. Select Commission, p. 307.

55. J. Vialet, *U.S. Immigration Law and Policy: 1952–79,* Committee Print, Committee on the Judiciary, United States Senate, Ninety-Sixth Congress, First Session, May 1979, p. 8.

56. Vialet, p. 6.

57. Vialet, p. 7.

58. Vialet, p. 9.

59. Copied, with revisions, from L. Bouvier and R. W. Gardner, "Immigration to the U.S.: The Unfinished Story," *Population Bulletin* 41, no. 4 (1986): 14.

60. Vialet, p. 10.

61. Vialet, p. 6.

62. Vialet, p. 16.

63. Vialet, pp. 15–24, 45.

64. Vialet, p. 48. Of course, so would the new system of kin-based immigration.

65. Copied, with revisions, from Bouvier and Gardner, p. 14.

66. Statement of Mrs. Olive Whitman Parsons, Immigration Committee, American Coalition of Patriotic Societies, *Immigration: Hearings before the Subcommittee on Immigration and Naturalization of the Committee on the Judiciary, United States Senate, Eighty-Ninth Congress, First Session, on S. 500,* Part 2, pp. 739–752.

67. 4 October 1965, as cited in Reimers, p. 85, n. 71.

68. This section relies mostly on Vialet, passim, somewhat on Briggs, pp. 61–86, and LeMay, pp. 109–116.

69. Vialet, p. 52.

70. Ibid.

71. D. Reimers, *Still the Golden Door: The Third World Comes to America,* New York: Columbia University Press 1985, p. 71.

72. The American Legion declared this openly, Congress members did not. Reimers, *Golden Door,* p. 75.

73. Briggs, p. 69.

74. Vialet, pp. 52–53.

75. Adopted from D. Reimers, "Recent Immigration Policy: An Analysis," in B. Chiswick (ed), *The Gateway: U.S. Immigration Issues and Policies*, Washington, DC.: American Enterprise Institute 1982, pp. 39–40.

76. Quoted in M. Teitelbaum, "Some Skeptical Noises on the Immigration Multiplier," *International Migration Review* 23 (1989): 895.

77. Reimers, "Recent Immigration Policy," p. 71.

78. Also, holding income constant between countries, more-skilled persons would emigrate from more-egalitarian countries, and less-skilled persons would emigrate from less-egalitarian countries.

79. LeMay, pp. 99–100.

80. Briggs, p. 190.

81. Hutchinson, p. 281.

82. Vialet, p. 47.

83. Senate Report, as quoted by Briggs, p. 195.

84. Briggs, p. 200.

85. This section relies on E. Galarza, *Merchants of Labor: The Mexican Bracero Story*, Charlotte: McNally and Loftin 1964; R. B. Craig, *The Bracero Program: Interest Groups and Foreign Policy*, Austin: University of Texas Press 1971; H. N. Miller, " 'The Right Thing to Do': A History of Simpson-Mazzoli," in N. Glazer (ed.), *Clamor at the Gates: The New American Immigration*, San Francisco: ICS Press 1985; A. Zolberg, "Reforming the Back Door: The Immigration Reform and Control Act of 1986 in Historical Perspective," in V. Yans-McLaughlin (ed.), *Immigration Reconsidered: History, Sociology and Politics*, New York: Oxford University Press 1990; 1983 CQ Almanac, pp. 287–292; 1984 CQ Almanac, pp. 229–238; 1985 CQ Almanac, pp. 223–228; 1986 CQ Almanac pp. 61–67; House Judiciary Committee Report No. 99-682, Part 1; and Senate Judiciary Committee Report No. 99-132.

86. Apprehension figures are generally from *Statistical Yearbook of the Immigration and Naturalization Service*, Washington, DC: U.S. Department of Justice, Immigration and Naturalization Service 1990.

87. *Washington Post*, 14 April 1952, p. 6. col. 4, cited in E. M. Hadley, "A Critical Analysis of the Wetback Problem," *Law and Contemporary Problems* 21 (1956): 339.

88. This section relies on 1988 CQ Almanac, pp. 83–84, 112–114; 1989 CQ Almanac, pp. 265–283; 1990 CQ Almanac, pp. 474–485; D. Kirschten, "Come in! Keep Out!" *National Journal* 22 (1990): 1206–1211; and D. Kirschten, "Opening the Door," *National Journal* 22 (1990): 2002–2005.

89. Teitelbaum, "Skeptical Noises," p. 894.

90. Congressional Record, 26 October 1990, p. S17106.

91. Calabresi and Bobbitt, p. 21.

92. See P. van Houten, "Immigration and Liberal Political Theory," manuscript, University of Chicago, 1994, for a categorization of philosophical approaches to immigration policy.

93. Cf. J. G. March and J. P. Olsen, *Ambiguity and Choice in Organizations*, Bergen: Universitetsforlaget 1979.

94. Higham, *Strangers in the Land*. See the Preface to the second edition, where Higham acknowledges that nativism is only part of the explanation.

95. Ibid., pp. 324–329.

# CHAPTER SIX

# Conclusion: Local Justice and American Values

## *Jon Elster*

I N THIS CONCLUSION I pull together some of the themes from the previous chapters—to suggest some generalizations about the structure of the American value system. I should state at the outset that what follows is very much a freehand sketch. Although I try to back up my claims with findings from the case studies, these do not offer anything like hard evidence. Many of my beliefs about what Americans think about fairness are little more than impressions. Although shaped by exposure to a large variety of local justice issues and their resolutions, my beliefs could also be distorted by incompleteness of the sample, and by my own biases and prejudices.

Some might question, therefore, the value and the point of the exercise. I hope, nevertheless, that by relying on studies of institutional behavior rather than on attitudinal surveys I can offer some novel perspectives on perceptions of allocative fairness. Responses to surveys are doubly removed from actual behavior: People may not always *do* in an actual situation what they *think* they would do when confronted with a similar hypothetical situation, and they may not always *say* what they think. By looking at what people actually do, one can overcome these difficulties. To be sure, behavior as an indicator has some flaws of its own. In allocative systems, perception of justice is only one of several determinants of behavior. Self-interest in various forms also counts for a great deal.[1] I cannot imagine a methodology that would enable one to eliminate all these sources of bias. Each approach has advantages and disadvantages. As emphasis in past research has been overwhelmingly on attitudes, I hope that the focus on behavior in the present volume will prove useful.

## Problems in Inferring Values from Choice Behavior

Choices—including the choice of choice mechanisms—reflect values. I shall draw on the analyses of allocative choices presented in the earlier chapters to make some inferences about values in American society. Because allocative mechanisms are under the constant scrutiny and influence of courts, political authorities, and public opinion, we can use them as a source of information about fundamental values in society. The procedure is remotely analogous to the principle of revealed preference in economic theory, although I would stress the remoteness rather than the analogy. Methodologically, the inference of social values from institutional behavior is subject to a number of problems that do not arise when we try to infer individual values from individual behavior.

*Problems of aggregation and misrepresentation.* We may first note that "society" does not have preferences that can be read off from "its" actions. Individuals have preferences and values that come together in complex ways to yield a specific allocative mechanism. As we know from bargaining theory and the theory of social choice, the outcome of preference aggregation may not in any reasonable sense represent the underlying individual values. For one thing, the process may yield cyclical social preferences: A is preferred to B, B is preferred to C, and C to A. The outcome that finally emerges may then depend on normatively irrelevant features of the process, e.g., on the order in which alternatives are held up against each other. For another thing, if the process creates an incentive for individuals to misrepresent their preferences, the final result may be worse for everybody than some other feasible outcome. In that case we could hardly say that the outcome reflects popular values, except in a very indirect sense.

*Problems of identification.* As I noted toward the end of the Introduction, allocative issues are often settled simultaneously with other matters. The outcomes of voting or bargaining over immigration or layoff principles reflect not only the values of the parties on a given issue, but also how much they care about that issue compared with other issues. In practice, we may not be able to disentangle these two components from each other.

*Problems of representativeness.* Allocative decisions often reflect the values of a small elite and not necessarily those of the population at large. In the long run, both politicians and courts are subject to forces that tend to bring them into line with popular values. The immigration chapter well illustrates how politicians have to look over their shoulders to make sure that they do not offend strong interest groups. The layoff chapter similarly illustrates how the attitudes of the courts grew more conservative toward the end of the 1970s, presaging the conservative trend that would put Reagan in office. But it is also clear that these correlations are both imperfect and subject to considerable time lags.

*Problems of value heterogeneity.* On many issues, there may be more than one "American public." It may not be very meaningful, for instance, to generalize about what "Americans" think about affirmative action. It is likely that the views of women and ethnic minorities on this matter differ systematically from those of white males, either because of self-interest on the part of the former or prejudice on the part of the latter (or both). Aggregate measures of bipolar distributions are not very informative. This being said, I believe that one can sometimes identify hegemonic values that are espoused to some degree even by those who do not benefit from them. I return to this issue below.

*Problems of overdetermination.* To identify the values that underlie an allocative mechanism we often have to look at the process by which it was adopted rather than consider the mechanism itself. Whereas the theory of revealed preference at the individual level

simply looks at the final choice and ignores any preceding deliberations, the latter come to the forefront when we move to the level
of collective decisions. This is so for the general reason that *procedures are overdetermined by principles.* As noted in the discussion of
coalition building in the Introduction, a given procedure, such as
layoffs by seniority or kin-based immigration, may owe its appeal
to its conformity with a number of different higher-level principles. With regard to layoffs, immigration, and transplantation, we
know a great deal both about the allocative mechanisms that are
employed and about the processes by which they came into being.
By contrast, it is often difficult to obtain specific details about the
admissions process at private colleges. For instance, even when
admission officers name the variables included in a point system,
they will not reveal the relative weights of the variables in producing the final decisions. I do not think it unreasonable to see a link
between this secrecy and the hypocrisy that has often surrounded
college admissions (see below).

**Problems of indeterminacy.** What I believe we can learn from
the case studies is, at most, which particular values Americans, or
many Americans, feel strongly about. It is much more difficult to
identify the overarching higher-order value that determines how
Americans trade these values off against each other. There may
not even be a fact of the matter: Perceptions may be indeterminate. I believe that people in general feel much more confident
about their *ceteris-paribus* judgments than about their all-things-
considered judgments. They may be able to assert firmly that they
care deeply about some values and less about others, but feel perplexed if asked how they would trade the strongly held values off
against each other. We might, to be sure, elicit an answer from
them, but it is likely to be very sensitive to the framing of the
question and other normatively irrelevant features of the eliciting
process. This reluctance to make tradeoffs may sometimes induce
a realignment of the values to be traded off against each other, so
as to enable people to make decisions they feel comfortable with.
The underlying hypothesis is that choices made about the tradeoffs between two or more strongly held values create cognitive
dissonance, an unpleasant state of tension caused by the worry that
perhaps one made the wrong decision. By some poorly understood

unconscious mechanism, the individual subject to this tension will then adjust his values so as to make one option appear unambiguously superior to the others.[2] In some of the layoff cases studies, for instance, we find that complex tradeoffs are avoided by the adoption of a lexicographic system. Often, employees are divided into three performance categories—definitely stay, definitely go, and maybe stay or go—and then seniority is used to decide within the "maybe" category.

With these caveats, I believe that it is possible to identify a number of salient values in American society. A brief preview may be useful. The single most important value cluster in the United States is, I believe, related to the ideas of *efficiency* and *desert*. The second most important cluster, potentially in conflict with the first, is related to status criteria such as *ethnicity* and, to a lesser extent, *gender*. Furthermore, I consider the salience of *need* in different contexts. Finally, I discuss two negative values, viz., the demands that allocative criteria be *nondiscretionary* and *nonmanipulable*. Before I go on to discuss these values, however, I shall raise a more general issue.

## Ethical Individualism and Presentism[3]

These are the views that for purposes of allocative justice, groups don't matter and the past doesn't matter. Justice is concerned with living individuals and with future individuals. The view that groups don't matter I call ethical individualism. The view that the past doesn't matter I call ethical presentism. (I apologize for the neologism. It is not only ugly, but inaccurate, given the reference to future individuals. A better but even uglier term, would be "ethical non-pastism.") The two principles are meta-ethical rather than substantive ethical theories. Whereas a substantive theory can be used to rule out policies, the two principles can at most be used to rule out theories. In general, a given policy can be justified on many different grounds because of the overdetermination of procedures by principles. Some of these grounds may be incompatible with ethical individualism or ethical presentism, but the policy itself is not affected by the fact that some of the reasons given for it are bad reasons. For instance, the fact that some arguments for affirmative action violate one or both of the doctrines is not itself an argument against affirmative action. Conversely, the fact that a theory passes these two hurdles does not mean that it is a good theory. For instance, "negative utilitarianism," that is, the view that society ought to be organized so as to maximize the sum of suffering, is compatible with both doctrines.

Among moral philosophers, there seems to be a consensus, albeit largely tacit, on these two doctrines. The attitudes of the American public, to the extent that they are reflected in our case studies, are more difficult to determine. It would appear that courts, when called upon to decide layoff cases, increasingly subscribe to ethical individualism. As Romm notes, "the primary question is the extent to which the costs of remedying a past wrong, viz., lack of women and blacks in the labor force due to discrimination, may be placed upon a group who had little or no role in perpetrating that wrong, viz., white male workers whose expectations concerning the extent to which their seniority protects them from layoff turns out to be wrong." In the late 1960s and early 1970s, some courts were willing to sacrifice the seniority expectations of white male employees in order to achieve the goals of Title VII. In an oft-cited early case, a Virginia district court in 1968 ruled, as Romm writes, "that the seniority rights of whites were not vested and indefeasible but subject to modification, and that a departmental system originally set up for the purpose of segregating blacks could never be bona fide even if currently administered neutrally." In another influential early case, the Fifth Circuit in 1969 articulated a "rightful place" theory of remediation which, according to Romm, "rejected the radical view that white incumbents should be displaced but also rejected the conservative view that fair application of a facially neutral system was necessarily sufficient to satisfy the purposes of the act." However, later Supreme Court decisions gave absolute priority to the seniority expectations of white males.

In the transplantation arena, issues of ethical individualism and presentism arise especially in the context of black transplant recipients. As Dennis explains, one of the obstacles to kidney transplantation for blacks is the reluctance of relatives of black donors to give their permission to recover an organ that could be used for transplantation. The reluctance has several causes, one of them being a belief that the organs are mainly going to white patients. Refusal to donate a kidney on the basis of this belief violates ethical individualism. The idea that a white recipient does not deserve a kidney because of the harm that whites inflict on blacks is flawed because it makes each white person responsible for the behavior of the whole group to which he or she belongs. (Refusal to donate a kidney because whites have harmed blacks in the past also violates ethical presentism.) The converse fallacy is also encountered. Among some groups in the transplantation community, there is a reluctance to change the allocation system so as to improve the prospects of black patients. Since blacks are not willing to donate kidneys, or so the argument goes, they cannot expect special treatment as recipients. This argument, too, unfairly treats each black patient as if he or she were responsible for the behavior of the whole group. In other words, the fallacy takes the form of making each black person responsible for the fact that some members of the black community commit the same fallacy. Although I do not believe that these fallacies reflect core values in black and white communities, they may not be entirely marginal either.

College admissions raises similar problems. Consider, for instance, admissions policies that favor children from high-income minority families at the expense of children from low-income nonminority families. This practice can hardly be justified on pragmatic grounds, because it would be quite easy to discriminate within the minority. Perhaps it might be defended on the ground that in the long run it will enhance the self-esteem, aspiration levels, or opportunities of low-income minority members. If that turned out not to be the case, however, the practice would seem inconsistent with ethical individualism or ethical presentism. The general point illustrated by this example is that equality among groups can occur at the expense of greater overall inequality among individuals, both within each group and within society as a whole. Assume, for instance, that initially both men and women are divided into two equal-sized groups of low-wage and high-wage individuals. Some men earn 10, others 8; some women earn 6, others 4. After redistribution, some men earn 9, others 5; some women earn 10, others 4. There is now complete between-group equality, but greater within-group inequality and greater overall inequality. Similarly, raising college admissions rates and, therefore, future earnings among minority applicants might violate ethical individualism if it leads to fewer low-income applicants being admitted.

Overall, the American value system is deeply torn and divided on this point. On the one hand, individualism—rely on your own efforts under conditions of fair competition, and don't blame others if you don't make it—is a deeply entrenched value. It is expressed in several recent books that decry the tendency of formerly oppressed groups to rely on their status as victims, rather than on their abilities, to get ahead. On the other hand, there is a widely held belief that the idea of fair competition must be taken in a broad sense, to take account of the handicaps that are the legacy of oppression and discrimination in the past. So far, however, it has proved very difficult to design schemes that take proper account of these handicaps without perpetuating stigma or self-victimization. I cannot see any easy, or imminent, resolution of this tension.

## Race and Ethnicity

The preceding section has already considered some issues related to the use of race and ethnicity in the allocation of scarce resources. But there is more to be said. First, I want to state that many years of immersion in matters of local justice have convinced me of the absolute centrality of race and ethnicity in virtually all allocative issues in this country. In addition to the case studies detailed in this volume, race matters deeply in issues such as induction into the army, allocation of public housing, or the selection of adoptive parents. Although some allocative systems may be facially neutral, they are rarely neutral ex post, as demonstrated by the kidney allocation system. As also illustrated by that system, detection of a disparate impact on racial groups regularly leads to adjustment in the primary criteria of allocation.

*Status-blind allocation.* As I mentioned in the Introduction, race and ethnicity can enter the picture in three different ways. (Much of the following also applies to gender.) First, there is the principle that allocation shall be *status-blind:* it ought to proceed as if the applicants' race or ethnic origin were unknown. Defended in the past as a progressive measure, this principle is now advocated by the right rather than the left end of the political spectrum. Those who defend the principle against the advocates of affirmative action also tend to label the latter policy "reverse discrimination." The tensions arising here are captured in Conley's analysis of *Bakke* and its sequel. On the one hand, the Supreme Court found in favor of Alan Bakke, who had been denied admission to the Medical School at the University of California at Davis, which had a special program for the disadvantaged with different standards of admission. On the other hand, the majority on the Court found that the Harvard practice of assigning points to race as one of many factors did not amount to discrimination in favor of minorities. The current admission practices detailed by Conley confirm the view of Justice White that this is a distinction without a difference. The majority decision in *Bakke* was little more than judicial hypocrisy. Affirmative action was acceptable if accomplished by indirect means. For an analogy, consider subsidies to ailing industries. Although neither workers nor the public find wage subsidies acceptable, they do not object to subsidized electricity for the purposes of maintaining jobs. Such hypocritical preference for indirect means over direct ones indicates more than simple value ambivalence. It shows that some ideals—equality of opportunity, merit, or efficiency—can have a dominant status that forces advocates of other ideals—need or equality of outcome—to avoid a direct confrontation. But it also indicates that the latter values are so strong that they cannot simply be suppressed, and so an uneasy accommodation has to be found.

Hypocrisy has, in fact, been a pervasive feature of admissions systems. Today, it is instantiated in the efforts to admit applicants who do not qualify according to academic criteria or nonacademic criteria of excellence. In earlier years, as Conley shows, it was found in efforts to deny applicants, notably Jewish ones, who did qualify. In current discussions it is sometimes claimed that the treatment of Jews is now replicated for Asian American applicants—overqualified but underadmitted. In one sense this has to be true: If underqualified minority applicants are admitted, then other groups must be underrepresented. To show discrimination beyond this statistical truism, one would have to show that Asian

Americans are less likely to be admitted than equally qualified white applicants. Because, to repeat, the process is largely shrouded in secrecy, such evidence is hard to come by.

*Status-representative allocation.* Next, there is the idea that allocation shall be *status-representative,* in the sense that the status composition of the recipients should match that of the population at large or, more frequently, of the applicants. This idea recurs in all the case studies. With regard to admissions, some state university systems are subject to requirements by the state legislature that the racial and ethnic composition of those admitted to college should mirror that of high-school students. The principle, although obviously on a collision course with the *Bakke* decision, is implemented by various forms of subterfuge. With regard to layoffs, Romm's case studies show that many firms look at the relative impact of layoffs on protected groups (minority members and women). In one firm, as he writes, "plus or minus 1 percent for any given protected group [was] seen as an acceptable impact for a workforce reduction." In the kidney-transplantation community, there is considerable concern about the low proportion of black recipients, compared to their high proportion in the ESRD population. With regard to immigration, Mackie details the various proposals that were made after 1920 to regulate immigration by proportionality to national origin. The proposal that was finally adopted pursuant to the National Origins Act of 1924 used the current composition of the population as the baseline on which the proportional quotas were calculated.

These proportionality criteria can be justified from several perspectives. First, as Mackie notes, they provide an obvious focal point to resolve controversy. Second, they may serve to implement affirmative action (see below). Third, they may be used to ensure representativeness in each and every case, or in each and every year, rather than on the average and in the long run.[4] Assume, namely, that the process is (1) status-blind and (2) has no disparate impact on status. An example might be the random selection of jurors, which is equally likely to yield men and women. If, however, one wants each jury to have an equal number of men and women, stratified random selection is necessary. One might consider proportional layoffs from this perspective. Even if there were, in fact, no systematic bias in the way in which status-blind criteria affect different status groups, employees at any given firm might not know whether a bias is the result of accidental, local variations or due to systematic causes. They might insist, therefore, on proportionality. Another possible reason for proportionality in layoffs is to avoid attracting the attention of government officials, e.g., the OFCCP, which oversees federal contractors. As is often the case in bureaucratic monitoring, it is not the acceptability or unacceptability of the original situation but rather sudden and unexpected departures from it that attract attention.

I believe that this demand for proportionality is another aspect of the idea of *local* justice. Instead of saying "Let the chips fall where they may" or "You win some, you lose some," people may call for closer supervision of each case if they suspect that the dice are loaded or that cases of bad luck are correlated rather than uncorrelated. There are two ideas at work here. On the one hand, black patients at one hospital may not know anything about the rate at which black patients are transplanted elsewhere, and women in one firm may not know anything about the proportion of women laid off in other firms. On the other hand, even if they knew that the system was fair in the aggregate, they might still not trust their local unit to be free of bias. If the selection, in fact, has no systematic bias, insisting on local proportionality is likely to create unfairness rather than remove it. Since the unfairness would not be systematic, however, it would be more acceptable than an identifiable bias.

**Status-offsetting allocation.** Third, there is the idea that allocation should be *status-offsetting:* The allocation of scarce goods shall take into account the need to improve the position of less-favored status groups in society. This idea can be taken in two ways. First, allocation might be seen as a way of compensating for general disadvantage; second, as a way of compensating for disadvantage with regard to the particular good being allocated. Suppose, contrary to fact, that black patients were transplanted at the same rate as white patients. In the spirit of the first kind of compensation, one would then offer blacks transplants at higher rates than others, as partial compensation for their generally disadvantaged status. I think I can say with confidence that this would never happen. It is part of the local-ness of local justice that compensation occurs only within a given arena, not across arenas. As mentioned in the Introduction, there are a few exceptions, but this would not be one. Nor do any of the other case studies offer evidence of this mode of compensation. For instance, Conley's survey indicates that college admissions pay relatively little attention to gender, presumably because female applicants do as well as male on gender-blind criteria. I believe that the idea of giving women an extra edge in college admissions to compensate for problems they will encounter later in other arenas would seem quaint. In the context of race and ethnicity, though, this remark is somewhat irrelevant. Because blacks, native Americans, and Hispanics, unlike women, are disadvantaged across the board, favoring them in one arena may be seen both as general and specific compensation.

I have already made some comments on affirmative action based on race and ethnicity. As I said, Americans are highly ambivalent about this practice because of its potential conflicts with other values, such as skill, merit, desert, efficiency, and need. The nature and intensity of the conflict differs across spheres. In the arena of kidney transplantation the issue does not give rise to strong value conflicts, because the poor matching of black patients with most kidneys is due to sheer bad luck, not to factors within their individual control. In the case of layoffs, the conflict is partly between race and ability, partly and more importantly between race and seniority. Although seniority may be seen as giving rise to desert, it does so more weakly, I believe, than skills acquired through the individual's own effort. Hence, the use of race as a layoff criterion is more likely to cause moral indignation when used to override skill than when used to override seniority.

An analogue of the latter statement applies with even more force to affirmative action in college admissions. In fact, race-based admission is often on a collision course with two other value clusters. On the one hand, there is a long-standing controversy over race versus merit, skill, efficiency, and desert. Many continue to believe it unfair if a college turns down an applicant who has worked hard in high school to get good grades and admits less-qualified minority applicants. If pressed, they might agree that the minority applicant with poorer grades may have worked just as hard and appeal instead to efficiency criteria to justify their opposition to affirmative action. Society, they would say, needs the best possible teachers, doctors, and engineers. Quite likely, for many individuals, both arguments amount to little more than racism that dare not speak its name. Children of alumni and athletes often are not the best qualified on academic criteria, and yet in their case the conflict between desert/efficiency and preferential treatment causes much less controversy.

On the other hand, there is a more recent tendency for race to be contrasted with disadvantage and need more generally. Many nonminority applicants to college come from a culturally and economically disadvantaged background and suffer from handicaps that are quite similar to those of many minority applicants. The role-model argument that is often used to justify affirmative action for minorities may apply to an applicant from a poor Irish section of a large city no less than to an applicant from a black section. And, of course, not all minority applicants come from disadvantaged backgrounds. Among the admissions officers we met, there was a clear, if cautiously expressed, desire to move from race to a more general concept of disadvantage, which was seen as more appropriate from a normative point of view. In some state colleges this tendency is reinforced, paradoxically, by a tendency to use disadvantage as a proxy for race. Caught between the *Bakke* decision that limits the explicit use of race and a state legislature that requires racial representativeness, these officers emphasize general disadvantage because they know that by using this criterion they will also admit a large number of minority applicants.

## Gender

Some of what I said about race and ethnicity applies also to gender. But I believe that, on reflection, the differences are more striking than the similarities. To begin with, it is obviously not the case that women systematically come from objectively more difficult circumstances than men. The backgrounds of men and women are, on average, identical. (This might change in the future, if the practice of choosing the sex of one's children becomes widespread and if the patterns of choice differ across social groups.) Two big (and related) differences remain. First, there are socially and culturally induced differences in motivations and expectations, reflected, for instance, in the low proportion of female college students who major in physics. Secondly, there is the massive fact that women bear children. With children, it is difficult—not impossible, but difficult—to have an uninterrupted labor-market career; also, many women want to stay at home when their children are small. As a result, women tend to do badly when seniority is used as a layoff criterion. Because ability, too, is built up over time, they may also suffer a handicap if this criterion is employed.

I believe that these differences between men and women are markedly unlike those between, say, blacks and whites. Although the rhetoric of a history of oppression of one group by the other is often employed in both cases, I believe that most people would say that it is much less relevant in the case of gender. This is armchair sociology, not based on the case studies, and I might be wrong. I do not think I am mistaken, though, because the differences are so striking that they can hardly be ignored. The past oppression and more recent discrimination of blacks by whites survives physically today in the form of segregated communities. The causal links are multiple and complex, but it is impossible to deny that they add up to an objectively disadvantaged situation for large parts of the black community. Although motivations, expectations, and self-esteem also form part of the explanation of why fewer blacks than whites end up in college or hold steady jobs, these subjective factors are very closely related to objective handicaps. Now, I am not saying that for women the sources of disadvantage are "all in the mind." This would be true, for instance, if we were discussing why less-handsome people do worse for themselves than handsome people. Because women bear and raise children, there exists a very tangible basis for differential motivations and expectations. But it is, in a very obvious sense, a very different kind of basis.

Given these truisms, we can understand why gender, by and large, is less salient than race and ethnicity in the allocation of scarce goods. In fact, I believe that the only arena where it assumes a major importance is in the labor market. When goods are allocated to families rather than to individuals, as is basically the case in kin-based immigration, gender is obviously irrelevant. Because young women who apply to college rarely have children, they have not met any obstacles that would prevent them from being admitted on an equal footing with men. Also, their success in being admitted to most programs shows that residues of past oppression must be minimal. Whereas some of the factors that cause blacks to be transplanted less frequently than whites are social rather than medical in nature, this is only to a small extent true of women, and then mainly as a matter of self-selection. In the labor market, by contrast, the irregular careers of women have an impact everywhere: in hiring, wages, promotions, and layoffs. Although firms, guided by the courts, have taken some steps to reduce this impact, it is my impression—again, I cannot be more affirmative—that these efforts are less vigorous than those made on behalf of ethnic minorities. (As Romm observes, the inclusion of women in the 1964 Civil Rights Act was the result of a strategic move that backfired and not of any kind of ground swell.) If I am right, the difference could reflect the obvious fact that having children is largely within the woman's own control, whereas nobody can choose whether to be born into a black ghetto. There may be an embryonic awareness of the fact that unless society takes steps to make childbearing and a satisfactory work career more compatible with each other, women might increasingly sacrifice the former rather than the latter, to everybody's detriment. I suspect, however, that as sources of subjective values, collective-action problems of this kind are less important than unfairness toward individuals.[5]

Reactions from several readers of a draft of this Conclusion show that I need to make it clear that the above comparison between ethnicity and gender is not intended to cover all parts of American life. If I had dealt with issues of domestic violence, pornography, prostitution, or abortion, I would certainly have given much more emphasis to gender-based conflicts. These are not, however, allocative questions.

## Desert

Over and over again, status criteria run up against the deeply held value that scarce goods ought to be given to those who *deserve* them. At the intuitive, pre-analytical level that concerns us here, desert can be generated on a number of successively overlapping grounds: bad luck, prior sacrifices, prior efforts, and prior achievements. When discussed by philosophers the concept is usually refined and narrowed down, sometimes to the point of losing all relevance as an ideal of distributive justice. But I am concerned here with the more amorphous idea of desert that underlies public debate and public values.

When people are selected for military service by a draft lottery, they suffer a piece of bad luck. (They are also called upon to make a sacrifice for the sake of the common good: see below.) As a consequence, draftee veterans are thought to deserve priority in university admissions and in hiring. Many arguments from desert rest on this idea: People ought to be compensated for bad luck, for the bad things that happen to them through no fault of their own. Whereas the concept of need is oriented strictly to the present (see Introduction and the following subsection), desert looks at the genesis of need. In the transplantation community, for instance, there is a small but growing minority who argue that in allocating organs one ought to take account of past life style (smoking, drug use, alcohol abuse) to the extent that it has contributed to the underlying medical problem. By contrast, having the wrong blood type or the wrong antigens is a piece of bad luck that does generate desert. There is, admittedly, some ambiguity here. The intuition is strongest on the negative side: Heavy smokers do not deserve a second heart transplant. It is less clear whether non-smokers, by virtue of their nonsmoking, can be said to deserve one. Not every nonsmoker has made a sacrifice by abstaining from smoking.

Those who are selected to serve in the military do not simply suffer bad luck: They also make a sacrifice for the common good. In their case, there is a positive ground for desert. The case would be perceived as even stronger if they had volunteered for service, but this element of free choice is not required. In the case of the professional volunteer army one might think that the risks of war are already incorporated in soldiers' wages, so that no ex post compensation is deserved. As recent events show, however, this does not correspond to popular perceptions. When American soldiers risk their lives in the Gulf War or Somalia, this is seen as a desert-generating sacrifice and not simply as fulfillment of their part of a contract. When sacrifice and free choice go together, as they do in the case of many political refugees, the case for desert can become overwhelmingly strong. As Mackie shows, American immigration policy has often been sensitive to such concerns, from Hungary in 1956 to the Vietnam War.

It is a central American value that hard work should be rewarded and shirking be penalized. This idea is almost inextricably mixed up with the ideas of freely chosen sacrifice and achievement. On the one hand, hard work often does entail a sacrifice, to the extent that "hard" means "painful" and not simply "sustained." Although some forms of sustained work are immensely rewarding in themselves, this fact is not generally perceived as detracting from desert. Claims by hard-working chief executive officers that they deserve their immense salaries are usually taken at face value, despite the fact that they also enjoy the rare privilege of having an intrinsically satisfying job. On the other hand, performance is often the best and sometimes the only measure of effort. Also, I am not sure whether hard work that does not produce anything of value would be widely perceived as a ground for desert. According to one philosophy of education, grades ought to measure how well students realize their potential, not how well they conform to intersubjectively applied standards. The relative lack of success of this idea suggests that some measure of objective achievement is needed for hard work to generate a perception of desert. It is possible, though, that the proposal simply had no chance to get off the ground because of obvious measurement and incentive problems.

Many—but not all—philosophers argue that achievements based on inborn skills do not create grounds for desert. I think this idea is at odds with popular values. Skills are perceived to be like property—their possessors deserve whatever they can get out of them. In theory, the two cases are not analogous. For the reward to property to be legitimate, the possession itself must be legitimate, with a clean pedigree. But nobody can be said to possess their skills either legitimately or illegitimately. In practice, this distinction has little impact. Because skills are so intimately bound up with the person, their exercise immediately creates an appearance of desert. Who else but the possessor of the skills would deserve the rewards for exercising them? (The thought that they might not be deserved by anybody does not seem to come so naturally.) Moreover, because skills are enhanced by effort and effort certainly is ground for desert, the element of brute luck in the possession of skills is blurred.[6] Also, I believe that many people insist on a reward for skills because they perceive, more-or-less clearly, that without such rewards the skills might not be exercised to a socially optimal extent. In logic, this argument from efficiency has nothing to do with desert. Also, in logic, the rewards needed to elicit the socially optimal exercise of skills might be much smaller than the rewards that effectively accrue to their possessors. But in the strongly emotional attachment that many people have for the ethics of desert, these distinctions are blurred.

In the arenas of local justice, *age* and *seniority* are often closely linked to desert. Older people are said to deserve access to medical goods, even if they can use them less efficiently, because of their past contributions to society. Senior workers are said to deserve protection from layoffs, even if they are less skilled than others, because they have given the firm the best years of their lives. I believe that these arguments are essentially vacuous, but there is no denying their rhetorical appeal. Desert is an immensely powerful and immensely confused value in American life. By its reliance on bad luck and good actions in the past as a guide to allocation in the present, it resonates directly with folk-tale morality. By its emphasis on the importance of free choice and control, it appeals to the individualist and voluntarist tradition in America. Denying the relevance of desert seems to imply a determinist conception of the world, in which nobody can claim credit or receive blame for anything. Finally, because of the close links between desert and many incentive systems, there is also a strong appeal on forward-looking, efficiency-oriented grounds.

## Need

The idea of need is defined in terms of the current level of welfare of the potential applicants. Those who are currently worst off are the most needy. The criterion disregards the past: We do not ask how they came to be the most needy or whether they or someone else were at fault. Nor do we consider the future, by asking how much they (or society) would benefit if they were selected to receive the scarce good. Allocation according to need is targeted to alleviate the misery of the most miserable. The idea is most clearly illustrated by medical practice. A doctor who treats a patient does not ask whether the illness was his own fault or whether the patient, if he recovers, will go on to lead a worthwhile life. Nor does the doctor ask whether the best use of medical resources might not dictate a somewhat cursory examination. Once a person has been admitted as a patient, nothing short of the "full treatment" is good enough.

Now, these statements are obviously false if taken literally. Doctors do, in fact, look to the past, to the future, and to alternative uses of scarce resources. I believe, however, that they represent extreme versions of a deeply held medical value, according to which the personal relation between doctor and client is the core of medical practice. The doctor is not a rational, impersonal dispenser of scarce goods and scarce expertise, but an individual who responds to the needs and sufferings of another individual. Most of us support this value because we know that if we ever need a doctor, this is how we would like him or her to treat us. What we do not perceive equally readily is that the pursuit of this value may prevent us or others from getting access to a doctor and to medical resources when they are needed.

Although alleviation of misery does not play an equally central role in arenas other than the medical one, several practices may usefully be considered from this perspective. Consider, for instance, the admission to college of applicants from culturally and economically disadvantaged families. Does it make sense to say that they "need" education more than others? Economic disadvantage obviously fits the need criterion as defined above. With regard to cultural disadvantage, however, the fact that neither parent went to college (the usual definition of such disadvantage) does not in itself qualify as "misery." Preferential admission on those grounds is more like compensating for undeserved bad luck. Or consider kin-based immigration: Relatives of immigrants are obviously not the worst off, in an absolute sense, among all applicants. When I said in the Introduction that kin-based immigration reflects need, I was not comparing the situations of the would-be immigrants. The more relevant comparison is between the immigrant whose family lives abroad and other Americans. In an obvious sense, and on the average, the former is worse off. To admit relatives is to alleviate misery.

There is no socialism in the United States. The values of social democracy, such as solidarity and need, are less central in the American labor movement than in its European counterparts. This difference is reflected in the layoff arena. Seniority and ability—both of which rest partly on desert, partly on efficiency—are vastly more central than the need criterion, as operationalized, for instance, by the number of dependents. Status, too, is much more important than need in this arena. Let me repeat, however, that in the arena of college admissions there is a trend away from status and toward need—away from ethnicity and toward disadvantage more generally.

## Toward Robustness

I use the term *robust* to characterize allocative procedures that are *nondiscretionary* and *nonmanipulable*. Criteria that require discretion on the part of allocators invite arbitrary and corrupt behavior. Criteria that can be manipulated by recipients invite strategic behavior and subterfuge. Even if such behavior is not observed, the suspicion that it might take place creates a strong pressure to adopt more robust procedures. And when it is actually observed, scandals may erupt that force drastic changes in the system.

Consider first discretion. Traditionally, many allocative decisions have been made by experts, who pride themselves on their highly specific skills. Doctors believe their clinical judgment is indispensable in assessing whether a given patient will benefit from a transplant. Admissions officers often say that they develop intuitions that allow them to make accurate assessments of the applicants on the basis of their files. In both cases, the claim is that these judgments are based on the sum total of many small observations and details, which could not possibly be incorporated in a mechanical formula.

There is strong evidence that these claims are not factually correct and that clinical judgment is often a poor guide to good decisions. This issue is not my concern here. Objections to the reliance on clinical judgment are usually not based on the poor quality of the ensuing decisions, but on the risks of bias, discrimination, and bribery. As Romm explains in his chapter, arbitrary layoff decisions by foremen were a major reason for the move to more formal systems such as seniority. Today, the potential for litigation created by discretion forces managers to establish a "paper trail" if they want to use bad job performance as the reason for laying off a person who belongs to a group protected by equal opportunity laws. Similarly, Dennis explains how the discretionary allocation of dialysis by the "Seattle God committee" caused a scandal that eventually made Congress decide to make the treatment available to everyone. More recently, concerns about discretionary selection of patients for transplantation led to the adoption of the mechanical UNOS point system.

In the American immigration system there is very little scope for discretion. In college admissions, by contrast, discretion is rampant. Although some colleges, such as the University of Texas at Austin, use a fully computerized procedure, most retain a strong element of discretion. We should distinguish, though, between secrecy and discretion. As Conley explains, some state colleges with large numbers of applicants use mechanical procedures (point systems), the details of which they refuse to divulge to the public. The reason for this secrecy is basically fear of litigation in the wake of the *Bakke* decision. In most private colleges, procedures are both discretionary and shrouded in secrecy. Discretionary admissions procedures allow for preferential admission of children of alumni, faculty, and staff—a big donor or an important professor can often pull a few strings for his children. It may even be desirable to bend the standards to admit children of city officials. Moreover, the particularistic nature of these practices induces an understandable desire for secrecy. This is not true of all colleges. At one Ivy League college, for instance, final decisions about admissions are made in a large committee (up to fifty people), with many different views and groups represented. It is essentially impossible to make choices that could not stand the light of day. In most private colleges, however, secrecy and discretion continue to reign without any public outcry or demand for more open or mechanical procedures.

The same is largely true of hiring in private firms. This fact suggests one explanation of the difference between the layoff arena and the admissions arena: Other things being roughly equal, discretion is perceived to be less acceptable in the allocation of bads than in the allocation of goods.[7] To explain the difference between the transplantation arena and the admissions arena we can invoke another variable: Other things being equal, discretion is perceived to be less acceptable in the allocation of life-saving resources than in the allocation of nonvital goods. When both factors are present, as with induction into the army in wartime, we should expect that discretion would be absolutely intolerable. If America ever went back to a draft army, one would not use the World War I system of delegating the selection to local boards with great discretionary powers. As this example suggests, this form of robustness is a relatively recent value. Many discretionary practices that seemed unobjectionable in a more hierarchical and status-ridden society would not be tolerated today.

Consider next nonmanipulability. I should first observe that adjustment by recipients to allocative criteria is not always a bad thing. If college admissions are regulated by high-school grades, layoffs by ability, and immigration by the possession of valuable skills, applicants have an incentive to work hard and to acquire skills. Other adjustments may be less desirable, a classical example being the young man who marries or enters college to get exemption from military service. One reason behind the introduction of the draft lottery in 1970 was probably the perception that such practices were unfair. The four case studies in the present volume show some evidence for such adjusting behavior. The most important examples are arranged marriages for immigration purposes, moving to another state to get into college, and coming to the United States to get a transplant. As Dennis explains, the last case created the "Pittsburgh scandal," which led to stricter regulation of the transplantation of foreign citizens. It is fair to say, though, that none of these examples indicates blatant and massive exploitation of the system, inducing widespread and strong protests. Although it is easy to show that Americans strongly disapprove of such sharp practices, the best evidence comes from other arenas.

Although robustness in itself is not an allocative principle, it is widely seen as a desirable feature of such principles. The hostility toward discretion is part of a secular trend toward administrative due process and procedural fairness. The suspicion that some individuals might engage in strategic manipulation of the system is much older—the exploitation of loopholes in the rules probably began as soon as there were rules to exploit. In fact, *the tendency for rules to create loopholes has often been cited as a main reason to have discretion rather than rules.* In earlier times, then, the second form of robustness—strategy-proofness, in technical language—was seen as more important than the first. In the value system of contemporary America, both are central. The result is a preference for selection mechanisms that are doubly robust: lotteries, queuing, and allocation based on nonmanipulable status properties.

## Conclusion

At the outset of this chapter I said that the most important value cluster is one associated with desert and efficiency. It is now time to address the latter value directly.

Implicitly, and at times explicitly, all the various values canvassed above have been held up against the ideal of efficiency. In discussing matters of justice in the abstract it is often said that equality is the baseline, deviations from which are in need of separate justification. In matters of local justice it is probably more correct to say that the baseline is efficiency, so that nonefficient allocations always require an explicit argument. Perhaps more importantly, advocates of other values take great pains to show that they are not really incompatible with efficiency. Thus need-efficiency coalitions are set up to show that scarce goods should be allocated to the worst off because the worst off recipients benefit most from getting them (assuming decreasing marginal value). Similarly, desert-efficiency coalitions are set up to show that by allocating goods to those who deserve them, one also creates a socially useful incentive to acquire grounds for desert. Status-efficiency coalitions are set up to show that by favoring groups that were formerly subject to oppression or discrimination, productive resources will be liberated that in the long run will benefit everybody.

The present case studies show several examples of these coalitions. In the layoff arena, efficiency most obviously points in the direction of the ability criterion. To maximize profits, the firm should retain the best workers. Against this, however, unions may point to the more subtle efficiency properties of seniority, which, by reducing turnover, allows the firm to economize on training costs. In transplantation, efficiency is usually spelled out as minimizing graft-rejection rates. Advocates of equity-based systems often argue, however, that after the introduction of cyclosporine there is no real conflict between equity and efficiency. In the college admissions arena, efficiency can be understood in a number of ways, perhaps the most important one being the idea of "value added" in education. This allows for the claim that although students from disadvantaged backgrounds may not do best in absolute terms, they do best in incremental terms. Also, by shifting the argument from the individual to the group level, one may claim that diversity as such has good efficiency properties because of interaction effects. To generate intellectual excellence on campus not all students should be selected on the basis of intellectual excellence. In the immigration arena, efficiency has traditionally been connected to the need of employers for cheap labor or skilled labor. In this case, however, the main alternative criteria—kin-based immigration or allocation of immigration slots in proportion to national origin—have not been defended on efficiency grounds.

Efficiency is a core American value. A system that is manifestly wasteful will not be tolerated for long. Waste may be acceptable, but not manifest waste. Once again, there is an incentive for hypocritical behavior and subterfuge. I believe that many value conflicts and tensions in American society are due to the need to accommodate two sets of deeply held values that often tend to undermine each other. On the one hand, there are the traditional American values of efficiency and desert. On the other hand, there are the more recent values associated with minorities, women, and the underclass: status and need. Our case studies of local justice in America demonstrate both the presence of these two value clusters, and the attempts—honest or disingenuous—to domesticate the conflict between them.

## NOTES

1. In addition, self-interest may contribute to the shaping of perceptions of fairness (D. M. Messick and K. Sentis, "Fairness, Preference, and

Fairness Biases," in D. M. Messick and K. Cook [eds.], *Equity Theory,* New York: Praeger 1983, pp. 61–94). Including this hypothesis yields something like the following structure:

$$\begin{array}{ccc} & \text{Behavior} & \\ & \nearrow \qquad \nwarrow & \\ \text{Self-interest} & \longrightarrow & \text{Perceptions of fairness} \\ & & \uparrow \\ & & \text{X} \end{array}$$

Ideally, perhaps, the psychological study of justice should aim at identifying X. That task would be hopelessly difficult, however, if only because one cannot infer from the fact that a perception of fairness coincides with self-interest that it is also caused by self-interest. Moreover, I suspect that X would contain a large component of sheer prejudice, so that even further laundering would be necessary to get at "pure perceptions of justice."

2. The adjustment may take place either before the decision or after the decision. For discussion see my *Solomonic Judgments,* Cambridge: Cambridge University Press 1989, p. 56 ff.

3. The following draws on my "Ethical Individualism and Presentism," *The Monist* 76 (1993), 333–348.

4. This paragraph and the following are somewhat speculative, and thin on the empirical side. I believe, however, that the issues they raise are real ones, and potentially important.

5. An interesting recent development in Norway indicates a potential for change in this area. As in many other European countries, fathers no less than mothers have the right to take leave from work after the birth of a child. Fathers, however, rarely use this right. As a result, the proposal to make paternal birth leave compulsory is now being discussed.

6. On the relation between skills, effort, and desert, see G. A. Cohen, "On the Currency of Egalitarian Justice," *Ethics* 99 (1989), 906–944, at pp. 914 ff., commenting on Rawls, *A Theory of Justice,* p. 312.

7. As Stuart Romm points out to me, an alternative or complementary explanation is that hiring requires discretion because it is usually made on the basis of much less information than layoffs, in part as a result of fear of litigation that makes previous employers reluctant to speak their minds.

# Index

ability, and job layoffs, 153, 155–171
ABO barrier, 91
Abraham, K. G., 167, 219n, 221n
Abrams, R. I., 156, 218n
academic merit, criteria of, 26, 37–38, 44–55, 65–67
accountability, and college admissions, 64–69
ACT tests, 45, 46, 48, 51
Act to Encourage Immigration (Contract Labor Act), 231, 236
Adams, P. L., 149n
Addison, J. T., 217n
ADEA (Age Discrimination in Employment Act), 161, 178–180, 182, 199–200, 204–205, 214
affirmative action, 296; and college admissions, 59; and job layoffs, 155, 181, 183–185, 189–193
AFL (American Federation of Labor), 32, 233–234, 245. See also AFL-CIO
AFL-CIO, 255, 268–269, 271
age, 13–14, 208; and job layoffs, 153, 161, 179–180, 214–217; and kidney transplantation, 118, 134–135
aggregation mechanisms, 21–22, 292–293
agricultural workers, 266–276
Alexander, S., 97, 98–99, 146n
Alien and Sedition Acts, 230, 232
Alien Contract Labor Law, 232–233
alumni, 26, 39, 66, 68, 303
Americanization, 237, 238

American Management Association, 154
American Medical Association, 135
American Party ("Know-Nothings"), 231
American Revolution, 228, 230
Americans with Disabilities Act, 160, 180
Amos, B., 90, 102
Anaise, D., 149n
antigen matching, 90, 101–102, 117–118, 119–121, 123
anti-Semitism, 237–238, 246
arbitration, 162–171, 170–171, 190–191. See also collective bargaining
Armata, R., 148n
Asian Americans, 66–68, 299
Asian immigration, 229, 239, 248, 256–257, 261–263, 278
Asiatic Barred Zone, 243

Bahnson, H. T., 148n
Bakke, A., 35–36, 60, 62, 299, 303, 311. See also Regents of the University of Califonia v. Bakke
bargaining theory, 292–293
Barnes, B. A., 145n, 147n
Becker, G. S., 218n, 226n
Belzer, F. O., 91, 145n
Bender, L., 78n
Bennett, M. T., 254, 286n, 287n, 288n
Billingham, R. E., 144n
Blackmun, H. A., 62

**317**